# e-Learning Skills

**Palgrave Study Skills**

Authoring a PhD
Business Degree Success
Career Skills
Critical Thinking Skills
e-Learning Skills (2nd edn)
Effective Communication for Arts and
   Humanities Students
Effective Communication for Science and
   Technology
The Exam Skills Handbook
The Foundations of Research
The Good Supervisor
How to Manage your Arts, Humanities and
   Social Science Degree
How to Manage your Distance and Open
   Learning Course
How to Manage your Postgraduate Course
How to Manage your Science and
   Technology Degree
How to Study Foreign Languages
How to Write Better Essays (2nd edn)
IT Skills for Successful Study
The International Student Handbook
Making Sense of Statistics
The Mature Student's Guide to Writing
   (2nd edn)
The Personal Tutor's Handbook
The Postgraduate Research Handbook
   (2nd edn)
Presentation Skills for Students

The Principles of Writing in Psychology
Professional Writing (2nd edn)
Researching Online
Research Using IT
Skills for Success
The Study Abroad Handbook
The Student's Guide to Writing (2nd edn)
The Student Life Handbook
The Study Skills Handbook (3rd edn)
Study Skills for International Postgraduates
Study Skills for Speakers of English as a
   Second Language
Studying the Built Environment
Studying Business at MBA and Masters
   Level
Studying Economics
Studying History (3rd edn)
Studying Law (2nd edn)
Studying Mathematics and its Applications
Studying Modern Drama (2nd edn)
Studying Physics
Studying Programming
Studying Psychology (2nd edn)
Teaching Study Skills and Supporting
   Learning
Work Placements – A Survival Guide for
   Students
Writing for Nursing and Midwifery Students
Write it Right
Writing for engineers (3rd edn)

**Palgrave Study Skills: Literature**
*General Editors: John Peck and Martin Coyle*

How to Begin Studying English Literature
   (3rd edn)
How to Study a Jane Austen Novel
   (2nd edn)
How to Study a Charles Dickens Novel
How to Study Chaucer (2nd edn)
How to Study an E. M. Forster Novel
How to Study James Joyce
How to Study Linguistics (2nd edn)

How to Study Modern Poetry
How to Study a Novel (2nd edn)
How to Study a Poet
How to Study a Renaissance Play
How to Study Romantic Poetry (2nd edn)
How to Study a Shakespeare Play
   (2nd edn)
How to Study Television
Practical Criticism

# e-Learning Skills

2nd edition

Alan Clarke

palgrave
macmillan

First published 2008 by
PALGRAVE MACMILLAN
Houndmills, Basingstoke, Hampshire RG21 6XS and
175 Fifth Avenue, New York, N.Y. 10010
Companies and representatives throughout the world

PALGRAVE MACMILLAN is the global academic imprint of the Palgrave Macmillan division of St. Martin's Press, LLC and of Palgrave Macmillan Ltd. Macmillan® is a registered trademark in the United States, United Kingdom and other countries. Palgrave is a registered trademark in the European Union and other countries.

ISBN-13: 978-0-230-57312-3
ISBN-10: 0-230-57312-6

This book is printed on paper suitable for recycling and made from fully managed and sustained forest sources. Logging, pulping and manufacturing processes are expected to conform to the environmental regulations of the country of origin.

A catalogue record for this book is available from the British Library.

A catalog record for this book is available from the Library of Congress.

10   9   8   7   6   5   4   3   2   1
17   16   15   14   13   12   11   10   09   08

Printed in China

# Contents

# List of Tables

# List of Figures

# Acknowledgements

I would like to thank my wife Christine for her help and support during an extremely busy period of our lives during which this book was written.

The author and publishers wish to acknowledge Google, Microsoft Corporation, NIACE, the Open University, the Quality Improvement Agency and PeanutButterWiki for the use of screen capture images.

Microsoft product screen shots reprinted with permission from Microsoft Corporation.

# Introduction

The term e-learning covers a wide range of techniques and methods. It includes the use of technology as part of a conventional or traditional course as well as an online course where learners and tutors will never meet face-to-face. This wide spectrum of applications makes the potential for confusion a real possibility. Throughout this book the term e-learning will be used to include the whole range but the emphasis will be on the use of technology to open up wider opportunities for learners, such as learning at a distance through using communication technologies. The book should be suitable for those who are learning at a distance or at a college which has integrated e-learning into its programmes. The term college has been used throughout this book but e-learning is provided by a variety of different organisations such as universities, private e-learning companies, employers and many other organisations. Please assume that college is a generic term covering all locations.

Within the book is a range of activities. To gain the most value you should attempt as many of them as possible. Many are followed by a section entitled 'Discussion' which provides some general feedback on the task. This should only be considered once you have undertaken the activity.

There are references to websites throughout the book. However, the world wide web is a dynamic environment with sites continuously developing, changing and in some cases disappearing. If you cannot locate the site directly through its address (URL), then use keywords from the text and search the world wide web to locate it or similar sites.

There are many ways to use the contents of the book to aid the development of your learning skills. You can simply work through the chapters in sequence or you can try to identify your needs and concentrate on developing particular skills and knowledge.

You need a variety of skills to be successful as an e-learner. Appendix A provides you with a checklist and a cross reference to the chapters which contain information and activities to address the relevant skill area. Some skills will be familiar to you from previous experiences but many will have been altered to meet the needs of the online environment. Before going any further, assess your current skills and then, as you progress through the book, you can return to the assessment and consider your progress. In a similar way it is useful to assess your ICT skills. Appendix C will help you assess your computer skills by providing you with a checklist. Chapter 3 is designed to help you develop some computer skills and knowledge which are appropriate to learning, such as presenting information, creating a podcast, copyright and plagiarism. If you already are a skilled computer user then you can probably skip this chapter.

Each chapter is designed to offer you a different insight into e-learning:

- Chapter 1 aims to offer you an introduction to e-learning, showing how it is different from traditional methods and what you can expect from it.
- Chapter 2 aims to refresh your awareness of traditional learning skills. e-Learning skills are built upon a foundation of traditional skills.
- Chapter 3 aims to provide you with an introduction to information and communication technology skills that are particularly relevant to e-learning (e.g. searching the world wide web for information).
- Chapter 4 aims to introduce you to the learning environments and approaches that you will encounter as an e-learner.
- Chapter 5 aims to explore with you the nature of e-learning skills.
- Chapter 6 provides you with additional practice to help you develop e-learning skills.
- Chapter 7 concentrates on the use of technology (e.g. e-portfolios) in assessing learning.
- Chapter 8 helps you consider the nature of communication technologies to take part in e-learning courses and programmes.
- Chapter 9 assists you to consider the nature of working and learning with others as part of an e-learning course (i.e. collaborative and co-operative learning).
- Chapter 10 provides you with a range of online resources.

The content list gives you the titles of each section and the index should help you locate particular topics.

Many of you will already be using information and communication tools as part of your work (e.g. developing spreadsheet models to analyse information and writing reports with word-processing) or social life (e.g. YouTube for loading videos, Flickr for photographs and Facebook for making friends). You should find that these activities are useful experience for becoming a successful e-learner.

# 1 What is e-Learning?

## Introduction

All parts of the education and training system are enthusiastically exploring and implementing e-learning in one form or another. In many ways a revolution is under way and some have made the comparison with the impact on learning of printing and the mass production of books. While this is an appropriate comparison, there are numerous differences, not least the time-scale of the developments. e-Learning has exploded on the awareness of education and training professionals and widespread use has been achieved in a few years whereas printing took centuries to reach large numbers of people. The pace of change is accelerating and new approaches are being tried almost every day. e-Learning is a major force for change. It is not merely confined to formal learning but is also having an impact on informal learning.

Learners are using social network technologies to create and store content and to network with other learners and their tutors. Blogs enable learners to produce online reflective learning diaries that they can share with their peers and tutors. They can then comment on the entries so that it becomes a tool for interaction, feedback and reflection and thus far more useful than a paper learning diary. Wikis are special-purpose websites that assist collaborative learning by allowing groups of learners to work on creating a joint document. e-Portfolios take many forms but they can assess learners' progress, showcase their achievements and help them reflect and share their work with others.

Podcasting and vodcasting provide learners with learning resources such as audio or video lectures and expert interviews. They can also be used as a focus for learners to create audio or video resources to provide a focus for interaction, reflection and collaboration.

These are all powerful tools that are rapidly being introduced into all forms of education and training. In addition to these developments, there has also been considerable development of mobile equipment such as smartphones and personal digital assistants (PDAs). These are now being increasing used in colleges and have been given the name m-learning (i.e. mobile learning).

e-Learning is a general term covering many different approaches that have in common the use of information and communication technologies. Terms and concepts are very new and often different language and jargon is used to describe similar approaches. This can make it difficult to understand what is involved in the learning programme. In this book we are concentrating on the use of e-learning to free learners from a rigid timetable of attendance at a college or other learning institution. It includes the delivery of learning at a distance from the tutor or institution but also adds a degree of freedom to more traditional programmes such as adding online discussion groups to a lecture programme, using text-messaging to keep students informed of administrative changes, delivering a programme based on interactive multimedia learning materials in the college learning centre and a distance-learning programme with learners based across a whole country.

Some common terms that you may encounter are:

- online learning;
- computer-based learning;
- blended learning;
- learning objects;
- learning resources;
- distributed learning;
- mobile or m-learning;
- interactive learning materials;
- computer mediated learning;
- computer mediated communication;
- web-based training;
- web 2.0.

Universal definitions of these widely used terms have not been agreed. It is good practice to ask users of the terms to explain what they mean by them. Online learning and e-learning, for example, are sometimes used interchangeably while on other occasions are seen as different. The glossary at the end of the book provides explanations of many terms with which you may come into contact.

e-Learning and online learning are general terms covering a wide range of approaches. They may combine a mixture of different elements such as:

- information and communication technology;
- interaction;
- learning resources;
- collaborative and individual learning;

- formal and informal learning;
- support.

There is considerable variation in the way the components are integrated together. e-Learning can simply consist of visiting websites to locate material that can help you complete an assignment. The websites may have been specially produced as part of the education or training programme or may have been designed for a wider purpose. In many ways this is similar to asking you to visit the library to locate books and other materials. The teacher may provide you with a booklist or a list of websites or simply a list of topics. In both cases you need the skills to locate the material searching either a library or the world wide web. There are both things in common and distinct differences within the search skills involved in traditional and e-learning.

e-Learning is not just confined to using the contents of websites but also includes creating content through websites that offer access to personal blogs or encourage collaborative working through wikis. There are sites that allow students to share sound and video recording in the form of podcasts or vodcasts.

Traditional learning methods are generally tutor-centred in that they determine what, when and how you study. e-Learning offers you more freedom to choose but in doing so you also have increased responsibility for your own learning. This means in practice that you need to plan your studies so that you achieve your goals. Managing your time becomes a major factor in maximising your choice of when to learn. You can no longer simply look a week or two ahead; you must consider the whole programme in order to plan and manage your work. You cannot rely on the tutor to remind you of the date that an essay is due or of the requirements of the course assessment. You need to become as self-reliant as possible.

## Comparison of traditional and e-learning skills

Table 1.1 shows a straightforward comparison of traditional and e-learning skills. Many of the individual skills can be broken down into a variety of sub- or related skills, for example:

- *Reading skills*: browsing/scanning skills (particularly important when using the world wide web to locate relevant websites);
- *Writing*: summarising the key points;
  referencing information;
  keeping records;
- *Research skills*: searching skills are essentially a part of research skills.

| Traditional skills | e-Learning skills | Difference |
|---|---|---|
| Time management | Time management | Time management is critical in e-learning since it provides greater opportunity to take control of your own learning. This is also true of other forms of open and distance learning. |
| Acceptance of responsibility | Acceptance of responsibility | e-Learning provides more opportunities for learners to take responsibility for their learning than does traditional learning. This is also true of other forms of open and distance learning. |
| Planning | Planning | The benefits of e-learning include giving learners more freedom to choose when and how they study so placing on them the emphasis for planning. Traditional courses are often determined by the tutor and are accompanied by timetables and study guides. This is also true of other forms of open and distance learning. |
| Searching skills – libraries | Searching skills – world wide web | Scale – the world wide web is enormous compared to any physical library. |
| Assessing quality – written and other physical content | Assessing quality – world wide web | The world wide web has few quality assurance mechanisms. Books and other printed educational content have established means of judging quality. Anyone can launch a website but producing a textbook requires the agreement of publishers, peers and reviewers. |
| Listening – to peers and teachers during presentations and discussions | Listening is required only occasionally e.g. when the programme is based on audio or video conferencing or involves listening to a podcast | Listening is a key skill in most forms of traditional learning while it frequently plays only a minor role or none at all in e-learning. |

| | | |
|---|---|---|
| Reading – mainly printed material | Reading is a key skill in e-learning. Most information is presented in text displayed on a screen. | Since the majority of the material is text, reading is a key skill in e-learning compared to the roles that reading and listening play in traditional learning. Browsing is the normal way that the content of websites is read in order to locate relevant content. |
| Writing – mostly in the form of note-taking or completing exercises (e.g. essays) | Writing (keyboard skills) – for communication, note-taking and exercises | Writing (keyboard skills) is essential for e-learning communication (e.g. e-mail) as well as for note-taking and exercises. Writing is the main online communication method. |
| Creating content – often associated with arts and crafts | Creating content – growing rapidly and covering many new areas | Creation of content is powerfully enhanced by the availability of sophisticated equipment (e.g. digital cameras and sound recorders) and applications that formerly were only used by professionals. |
| Self-assessment | Self-assessment | This is a key skill in all forms of learning. In traditional learning there are many opportunities to compare your performance with your peers (e.g. observing them in class, sharing results in the coffee lounge, etc.). In e-learning their performance is often not available to you. You need to find new ways of assessing your own performance. |
| Collaborating with others face-to-face | Collaborating with others through communication software (e.g. e-mail) | The key difference is time. A face-to-face group will often agree regular meetings so that tasks are achieved quickly. Members of an online group will each have their own time scales and may well live in different time zones so that collaboration is often spread over a long period. Motivation is sometimes difficult to maintain. |
| Problem solving – individually or small groups | Problem solving – individually or with a group at a distance | The significant difference when working with others is that in e-learning they are at a distance and it is therefore more difficult to judge their views. |

**Table 1.1**  Comparing learning skills

Table 1.1 is not intended to cover all the sub-skills but merely to provide an initial basis for comparison.

The two major differences between traditional and e-learning skills are the context and degree of importance of the skill. e-Learners may be learning at a distance from both their peers and tutors so they need to be far more self-sustained than the traditional learner. Traditional learning provides informal opportunities such as a brief chat in the corridor with other learners to discover their views, whereas e-learning requires you to send an e-mail, a more formal activity. Learners have had years of practice in face-to-face communicating while most will be relatively inexperienced at being dependent on short written messages (i.e. e-mail or chat). Nevertheless, this is changing as a generation of learners who have grown up with mobile phones, computers and the internet are entering post-compulsory education.

In face-to-face communications you can see the facial expression of people, hear the tone of voice and listen to the words used. In e-learning you only have the written words to communicate through and this notoriously leads to misunderstandings. It is more difficult to convey precise meaning. Various ways have been developed to help convey emotions such as the use of emoticons, a code based on punctuation or other symbols such as:

- using ☺ to mean happy;
- using ☹ to mean sad;
- using capitals or upper case to mean that you are shouting.

However, only a minority of e-mail users include emoticons and they are inevitably basic compared to the non-verbal communication that people grow up employing. They may confuse if the person receiving the message does not understand their purpose.

Traditional learners have the benefit of a tutor's judgement in observing their group and realising that individuals are confused by the topic or need to be reminded about the test. An e-learning tutor has far less information on which to base judgement, so the e-learner needs to be more self-reliant than other learners. Time-management skills become more important because you need to be in control of your learning. You cannot rely on the tutor or peers informally reminding you of deadlines. In later chapters you will be given the opportunity to develop your skills.

e-Learning assumes you are a competent and confident user of computers and communication technology. In Chapter 3 you will be provided with help to improve or revise your technological skills.

## Activity
## Assessment of skills

It is useful to start any learning process by assessing your starting point, so consider the lists of traditional and e-learning skills and judge your own competence in each one. In a later chapter you will consider your computer and communication technology skills.

| Traditional skills | Competence | | | e-Learning skills | Competence | | |
|---|---|---|---|---|---|---|---|
| | Poor | Acceptable | Excellent | | Poor | Acceptable | Excellent |
| Time management | | | | Time management | | | |
| Acceptance of responsibility | | | | Acceptance of responsibility | | | |
| Planning | | | | Planning | | | |
| Searching skills – libraries | | | | Searching skills – world wide web | | | |
| Assessing quality – written and other physical content | | | | Assessing quality – world wide web | | | |
| Listening | | | | Listening | | | |
| Reading | | | | Reading | | | |
| Writing | | | | Writing | | | |
| Creating content | | | | Creating content (e.g. photographs, video, sound and animation) | | | |
| Self-assessment | | | | Self-assessment | | | |
| Collaborating with others face-to-face | | | | Collaborating with others at a distance | | | |
| Problem solving | | | | Problem solving | | | |

### Discussion

If your experience of e-learning is limited, you may find that you have marked yourself low against the various characteristics. However, many traditional learning skills are very useful in online settings. You just need to be able to transfer and adjust them to the new context. This may seem a difficult process at the moment but with the help of the content and activities within this book you will achieve this.

Appendix A provides another checklist to consider your e-learning skills. It is cross referenced to the various parts of this book to enable you identify sections that will help you develop particular skills.

## ● e-Learning theories

There are a number of learning theories that apply to e-learning. This section is not intended to make you an expert on them but rather to help you understand the assumptions and expectations that designers may have made about you.

### Cognitive theory

The cognitive theory of learning is often the basis on which learning materials are developed. It covers how information gained through your senses (i.e. eyes and ears) is converted into knowledge and skills. Human memory has two information channels: visual and auditory. Information is initially held in working memory and needs to be integrated with other existing memories held in the long-term memory. Working memory has very limited capacity. To recall information from long-term memory it needs a relevant context.

Designers will aim to provide you with choices so that you can focus on those aspects that are most important for you to learn and avoid overloading your working memory. It is therefore important for you to select and concentrate on those aspects. Information needs to be integrated into long-term memory and this can be achieved through activities which are often provided. It is therefore important to take part in activities or exercises rather than simply seeing them as additional. They will help you to learn. The final step is to be able to retrieve information from long-term memory and that requires context. The context needs to be relevant to you so consider the new information in relation to your experience and make links. Some exercises ask you to select a context for an activity so choose one that is relevant to you.

### Constructivism

Constructivist learning theory tends to emphasise learning by doing. It therefore stresses the need for learners to discover, explore and try out new ideas. Learners are expected to make their own judgments of what they are experiencing. In e-learning programmes you will often be asked to carry out tasks, to read and consider evidence and to explore resources. The new experiences will need to be related to your existing knowledge and understanding. The tutor's role is often to facilitate your learning through questions or discussion. It is important that you participate so that the conclusions you have reached through your personal or group activities can be confirmed. However, the overall focus is on learning through your own efforts. You need to be self-actuated.

## Communities of practice

Historically communities are normally formed around a physical location so that the common factor that the members of the community share is a geographical place (e.g. everyone lives in the village or attends a particular college). There is a very different type of community in which the members have a common interest, profession or objective. This is called a community of practice.

Social networking, online communication, conferences and wikis are often related to the concept of a community of practice in that they bring groups of people together to allow them to form a group. A community of practice is more than a simple group of individuals. The members share common interests, experiences, aims and objectives. Participants in a community of practice will support each other to achieve the common goals. Communities of practice do not simply come into existence when people meet online; people need opportunities to work and collaborate together so that structures, methods, communication channels and commitment evolve.

e-Learning programmes will frequently expect student groups to become and behave as communities of practice. The expectation is that the group will be able to:

- solve problems;
- share information;
- discuss issues;
- pool knowledge and experience;
- work together.

It is important to be aware that your tutors may well expect you to contribute to your group in these ways. They will also often provide activities to help the group to form and develop as a community of practice. It is therefore important for you to realise that you need to participate.

## What makes a successful e-learner?

e-Learning is a new development so that good evidence of what makes for a successful e-learner is not readily available. However, some characteristics are:

- confidence as an independent successful learner, especially learning in non-formal settings (e.g. in your home, work or community);

- positive attitude to learning;
- self-motivated to succeed;
- effective communication skills;
- ability to collaborate and co-operate with other learners;
- competent and confident user of ICT.

(Nipper 1989; Clarke 1998; Palloff and Pratt 1999; Clarke 2002a)

## Activity
## Successful learner

Consider your own experience of learning and decide how successful a learner you are. You should consider all types of learning, especially your ability to learn independently (e.g. to teach yourself to use a video camera, to understand instructions and to plan a holiday), as well as more formal studies:

1. Are you confident that you can learn new ideas, concepts and skills in a variety of learning environments?
2. Do you enjoy learning new things and normally finish what you start?
3. Do you work well with other learners?

Write some brief notes

**Discussion**
If you have been a successful learner previously then it is likely that you will continue to be successful in online courses. This is not simply about success in formal education courses but in the wider sense of learning independently (e.g. teaching yourself skills and knowledge in any context).

Online courses are different from traditional forms of learning so if you have had little previous success in learning this is an opportunity to make a new start. If you have had problems in traditional courses with restrictive timetables, travelling arrangements or the pace of the course, then e-learning may help overcome them.

1. Are you confident that you can learn new ideas, concepts and skills?
   e-Learning tends to ask learners to take more responsibility for their own learning than traditional approaches. If you feel that you need a lot of support, guidance and direction from tutors then you should check if the course is right for you or work towards developing the skills that you will need. Many colleges offer support to develop study skills.
2. Do you enjoy learning new things and normally finish what you start?
   e-Learning uses many different methods and technologies so it favours learners who enjoy new challenges and ideas. Does taking on new challenges motivate you?

3. Do you work well with other learners?
   Although e-learning tends to be discussed as if it is about individualised learning, many methods include group, collaborative and co-
   operative learning. These require people who can build relationships
   with other learners.

   Appendix B contains a list of tips for the successful e-learner and you
   may want to consider it alongside this feedback.

## Benefits of e-learning

Your main benefits as an e-learner are that you have considerable freedom of:

- place;
- pace;
- time.

You are potentially free to study at any location that you want. So if you like
to work at home you can combine studying with family responsibilities or
avoid the frustrations of commuting. Many people are now able to learn as
they travel via the use of portable equipment.

In traditional learning the tutor and the other learners often set the pace
of studying. e-Learning gives you the choice of how fast or slow to learn. If
you want to work through the night you can or if you like to fit short bursts
of activity into your timetable for taking care of elderly parents or children,
you are free to do so.

All traditional courses have a fixed timetable of classes and activities
around which you must work. e-Learning provides you with a considerable
degree of choice. You can study in the middle of the night or during the day,
whatever is best for you.

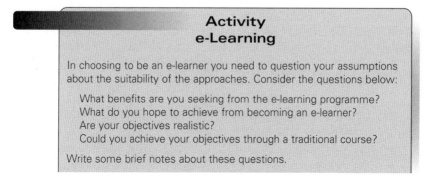

### Activity
### e-Learning

In choosing to be an e-learner you need to question your assumptions
about the suitability of the approaches. Consider the questions below:

What benefits are you seeking from the e-learning programme?
What do you hope to achieve from becoming an e-learner?
Are your objectives realistic?
Could you achieve your objectives through a traditional course?

Write some brief notes about these questions.

**Discussion**
There are various motives for selecting an e-learning course rather than a traditional one. You may want to combine your studies with a job or family responsibilities and an e-learning course will give you the flexibility you need. You may have been attracted by these new approaches to studying. Regardless of your reasons you will still need to work just as hard as in a traditional course. However, you have more choice of when, where and at what pace to learn. This places a lot of responsibility on you which in a traditional course is provided by its structure and the tutor.

The structure of e-learning courses varies considerably so you need to ensure that the selected course will meet your expectations.

## Learning styles

Everyone has preferred ways of learning and these are sometimes referred to as learning styles. When you have to learn in a manner that is different from your preferred learning style you will often feel uncomfortable and perhaps express doubts about the suitability of the approach. However, you have probably had experience of a wide range of learning styles during your education and successfully coped with them but this does not mean that you prefer them or seek them out. Some you will probably avoid because your own experience has shown you that do not like them and struggle to learn with them.

There are a variety of ways of expressing learning styles but one which is appropriate to e-learning considers preferences in terms of the seeing, hearing and doing. If you are a learner who prefers visual learning (i.e. seeing) then you will like:

- learning materials which include plenty of pictures, graphics, video and animation;
- images that support text.

If you are a learner who prefers auditory learning (i.e. listening) then you will favour:

- discussing ideas with other students (e.g. mailgroups, bulletin boards, chatrooms and e-mail);
- group working (e.g. groupware and collaborative/co-operative working);
- sound effects;
- video clips.

If you are a learner who prefers kinaesthetic learning (i.e. doing) then you will opt for:

- activities (e.g. lots of action – making choices);
- making notes;
- taking part in group work.

Some of these preferences translate straightforwardly into the e-learning environment. e-Learning is generally strong in providing many opportunities to make choices, to interact with content with a large visual element and to work with others through communication technologies.

There are other ways of considering preferences (Kolb, 1984; Honey and Munford, 1986) than in terms of visual, auditory and kinaesthetic. You could consider the following preferences:

- reflective – you may like to have time to reflect on experiences, learning content and discussion;
- analytical – you may prefer to analyse new content, ideas, etc. systematically;
- holistic – you may like to know the overall picture and are uncomfortable having the subject built up slowly, which is often the approach taken in lectures or presentations. You will appreciate overviews, abstracts and summaries.

Preferences are not mutually exclusive. Most people have a mix of them. If you consider your own experience of learning you will be able to identify what you like and dislike about the learning approaches you have experienced. It is important for you to be aware of your own preferences and the nature of e-learning. Consider the nature of the e-learning course you are intending to take part in and decide if it supports your learning preferences.

### Information and communication technology

e-Learning is learning through and being supported by the use of information technology. It therefore assumes that you are able to exploit technology. Most education and training providers will offer a technical helpline so that if you are studying at home or at a distance you can gain assistance. However, helplines do assume you have sufficient understanding of the technology to follow their instructions.

You are free to study at different locations including learning centres provided by colleges, companies, internet cafes and community sites. While they will often charge for the time spent online, they do provide assistance if you have technical problems, thus removing some of the stress. If you are studying using the college's own resources then many of the technical issues will be handled by them.

Computers are powerful aids to your learning and can help you by providing:

- ways to organise and store your notes, references and materials (e.g. folders, files and databases);
- tools to present your work (e.g. word-processing, presentation graphics, charts and graphs);
- tools to analyse your data (e.g. spreadsheets);
- tools to help you create content (e.g. blogs and wikis);
- equipment to capture evidence (e.g. digital cameras and scanners);
- access to the enormous library of information that the world wide web represents.

These aids are not confined to e-learning but are useful ways of assisting your studies in traditional, blended or e-learning courses. Many learners undertake traditional and e-learning modules at the same time.

## Interaction

When you speak to a tutor or another learner you expect them to respond to your words and in return you will react to them. The e-learning equivalent of this dialogue is called interactivity which is achieved, of course, through e-mail, chat, wikis and other forms of communication. Good learning materials and environments should respond to your actions in appropriate and helpful ways to engage you and hopefully assist you to learn.

Interactivity can be very simple. In some applications a helpful label will appear to help you understand an icon when you place your mouse pointer on top of that icon. The system is responding to your action.

It is useful to consider interaction as a dialogue between you and the learning system through what appears on the screen and the input devices (e.g. mouse and keyboard). This is called the interface. Figure 1.1 shows this model of interaction. Any learning system should offer you a considerable degree of support, opportunities for helpful dialogue and lots of choice. In a sense it is adapting to your needs in a way similar to that in which tutors will adjust their approach to meet your requirements. To take advantage of these possibilities you need to explore the interface. It is therefore good practice to investigate the interface systematically when you first encounter the system. You will frequently be offered an introduction to the system or a guided tour of the facilities. If this is not automatically suggested to you then seek it out. It is often included in the help system, the introduction or on the home page.

Many learning systems offer a virtual learning centre with what appears to be traditional equipment such as desks, computers, flipcharts, coffee bars and books. Often the intention is that these resources will behave in similar ways to the actual objects and facilities:

- the coffee bar (or common room, refectory, etc.) provides the means to communicate with other learners through an electronic chat room or similar facility;
- desks may provide the links to the administration;
- books and floppy disks are like handouts and other support;
- computers will lead to computer applications such as e-mail.

Virtual environments vary considerably in appearance and structure so you need to explore them to ensure you can take advantage of the resources. This is the equivalent of physically walking around the college campus on your first day to discover where everything is located. It is a vital step to prepare you for the course.

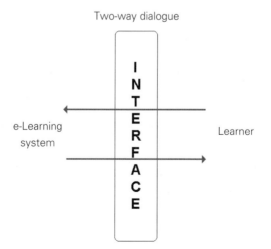

Two-way dialogue

e-Learning system

I
N
T
E
R
F
A
C
E

Learner

**Figure 1.1**   Simple communication between a learner and e-learning content

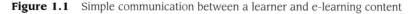

## ● Learning resources

Learning resources often play a significant role in e-learning. The materials may take a variety of forms and include:

- interactive materials that you access and interact with online (the materials can cover the whole subject or merely some aspects but are designed to enhance learning);
- stand-alone interactive materials such as multimedia CD-ROMs;
- traditional materials (e.g. workbooks, open learning texts and lecture notes) which are made available to you online, through the post or in the college library;
- content that you create (e.g. wikis, presentations or blogs) so that you have the opportunity to explore a topic from a different perspective;
- resources which are simply available on the world wide web (e.g. webpages, downloadable files, podcasts and online databases). (Chapter 10 provides an extensive list of resources on the world wide web that support e-learning skills development.)

Your e-learning course may have some or none of these forms of learning material depending on the subject and approach being taken. The key issue for you is that you need to be able to learn no matter how the course is designed. This requires that you are able to use and create interactive and other learning materials, analyse written content and locate and assess web-based content. These skills will be considered in later chapters.

### Activity
### Learning materials

You will have come into contact with many types of learning materials (e.g. text books, videos and handouts). Interactive materials are an important part of some e-learning programmes and it is important that you have some experience of them. In many college, company and community learning centres you can gain access to interactive learning materials. The learning centre staff will be able to help you with the materials. Work your way through a package then record your first impressions and compare them to your experience of other forms of learning materials.

**Discussion**
Interactive learning packages should engage you and provide you with a motivating and interesting experience of the subject being studied.

You should have considerable freedom to explore the materials, to retrace your steps and to have another go at exercises. You should be able to stop and mark your place so that you can return and start where you finished. The presentation of content should be to a high standard.

Unfortunately not all interactive packages meet this standard. The cost of developing professional interactive materials is very high so that some packages are little more than an electronic book. You should ask yourself whether a paper book or other forms of learning material would have served the same or a more effective purpose.

## Collaborative and individual learning

Face-to-face and e-learning can involve both group and individual activities. It is also perfectly possible to have a course involving both e-learning and traditional methods. It is widely accepted that online groups are often more effective if they are initially formed by some type of face-to-face meetings. However, it is not always possible to bring everyone together if they are living across a country or on several continents. A significant benefit of online learning is that it allows people to participate who cannot physically attend the educational institute. It allows learners from many different cultures to learn together and benefit from each other's experiences. Online learners are individuals who can collaborate with their peers through communication technology. This use of technology to allow people to communicate is sometimes termed computer mediated communication (CMC).

## Blogs, wikis and social networking

For many users of the world wide web the experience has focused on reading, viewing or listening to content that other people have created. Learning is not limited to this passive role and is often best served by a more active and creative approach. A new generation of online applications has been evolving over the last ten years and education has begun to exploit them to integrate more creative approaches into online and e-learning programmes. They are often called web 2.0 or social networking and include blogs, wikis, podcasting and e-portfolios.

Blogs have been used by learners to create diaries reflecting on their experiences of learning. However, their being online makes them available to the other members of the course to add their own comments and may thus become interactive. They are therefore a means of developing reflective skills. Many professions now require practitioners to be reflective, so the skill itself is valuable as well as being a route to enhanced learning.

Wikis are online applications that allow a group of people to share in the creation of a document. Each person is free to edit the content and make changes. It therefore offers a means of collaborative working in order to create a shared outcome. Employers value employees with the skills and experience of working with others to achieve a common purpose. In addition, collaborative learning will help you to improve your understanding of the topics being studied through the assistance and interaction with the other learners in your group.

Learning has always involved creativity and in all sectors of education and training the practical assignment to produce an agreed outcome has been shown to be very effective. e-Learning adds to this concept many tools, devices and applications to enhance the process. Podcasting is increasingly being used to provide learners with learning content. In addition, the creation of a podcast provides a focus for studying a topic, collaborating with others and also producing learning materials for other learners.

You will need to consider your own motivation and willingness to reflect, collaborate and create using these approaches. They provide interesting and exciting possibilities but will probably challenge many learners.

### Mobile learning (m-learning)

m-Learning is a natural outcome of the growth in small portable devices such as PDAs, mobile phones, MP3 players and sound recorders. The trend is to combine mobile phone technology with hand-held computer equipment to gain the functionality of both. You can now receive your e-mails almost anywhere through devices such as Blackberries and it is normal for phones to be combined with a camera.

Courses have been integrating these technologies into their programmes to gain additional benefits such as:

- providing administrative text messages (e.g. assignments are due on Friday);
- taking part in collaborative exercises while you are on the move;
- taking part in quizzes;
- checking your e-mail;
- providing e-learning materials to study as you travel;

- writing or recording notes while undertaking an assignment;
- using mobile office applications such as diaries, word processors and spreadsheets;
- offering recordings of lectures that you can listen to using your music player;
- listening to instructions for a particular task;
- using cameras to capture images during field trips – some phones now offer GPS so that the precise location of a picture can be mapped.

m-Learning increases the flexibility of learning so that you can study as you travel or in the short intervals between other activities (e.g. waiting for an appointment). It provides you with the means of fitting learning into your busy life. It is ideal if you are a commuter.

## Formal and informal learning

e-Learning courses involve both formal and informal learning. The world wide web is an enormous learning resource, available to any learner. However, in order to take advantage of it requires the skills of searching, identifying and evaluating the content. This is sometimes called information literacy. This indicates the balance of e-learning in that the potential is huge but the ability to take advantage of it requires significant skills. Informal learning is frequently incorporated into conventional and more formal e-learning courses.

Many organisations are developing formal e-learning courses but experience is relatively limited so that ideas and approaches are essentially being explored. However, in order to benefit from the flexibility of online approaches means that formal learning needs to include the freedom to learn when, where and at what pace the learner wants to work. More formal courses have:

- a start and finish date (i.e. complete freedom is reduced but is still substantial);
- assessment standards (e.g. a traditional examination on completion);
- intermediate deadlines (e.g. reports required by set dates).

Learners are more likely to drop out when too much responsibility is thrust on them too quickly. A degree of structure is often helpful and devices such as intermediate reports can help identify learners who need assistance.

Some courses provide trial assignments to allow learners to practise writing assignments. It is often difficult for tutors to judge when to offer help in a completely open ended course.


### Assessment

e-Assessment has been introduced across all sectors of education and training and is rapidly being extended. It can take a variety of forms such as on-screen tests, e-portfolios and simulation. Probably the largest use is made of on-screen tests using multi-choice questions. This enables assessment to be made available on demand from the learners when they feel ready to take the test. While this type of assessment is limited by the nature of multi-choice questions, many learners are motivated by being able to take the test when they want to and having results immediately available.

Technology allows tasks, events and processes to be simulated so that learners can be assessed on their competence before they are allowed to work in the real environment. This is very helpful in dangerous situations. Simulations have been used in many situations such as medicine, driving, chemical processing and engineering.

The use of e-portfolios is growing and not simply in replacing the use of paper-based portfolios but in many new areas. e-Portfolios allow the storage and sharing of multimedia evidence. They organise evidence of your accomplishments. This can be simply to show that you can pass the course assessment or for long-term use as a form of life-long curriculum vitae. In some cases, programmes will employ specifically designed e-portfolio systems that limit you to the objectives of the course. There are many commercial and institutionally designed e-portfolio products but all of them require you to select evidence for inclusion which demonstrates your competency, achievements and ability. The personal advantage of e-portfolio is that you gain an easily transportable source of evidence of your achievements that you can use for other purposes. In Chapter 7 we will discuss e-assessment and particularly the use of e-portfolios.


### Support

All forms of distance learning, including e-learning, suffer from higher levels of drop-out than conventional face-to-face courses. The key to successful distance learning is the degree of support that is available to you. Support is not limited to the formal support of your tutors but can include:

- other learners;
- study circles/groups;
- family;
- friends;
- learning centre staff;
- workplace instructors;
- mentors;
- tutors.

A supportive family can make the difference between success and failure. When you are choosing to take part in an e-learning course you should consider what support is available to you both formally (e.g. tutors, mentors and other learners) and informally (e.g. friends and family). Is the course structured to encourage mutual support between the learners? Is a mentor provided and is a personal tutor appointed for you? These are important questions to ask before starting the course.

## Activity
## Support

What sort of support do you need when you are studying? Do you want to be in control of your own learning or do you need someone to motivate, encourage and remind you directly of the course deadlines. Write some brief notes and reflect on the nature of e-learning, especially if you are learning at a distance.

### Discussion
Personally I like to feel in control of my own learning so I am content to plan my own studies and to take responsibility for meeting deadlines. However, I have always enjoyed the support of my family who have encouraged and motivated me to study. In terms of more formal support I have always found it useful to know that there is someone to telephone or e-mail to ask for advice. In several courses I have developed contacts with other learners so that we can swap ideas and answer each other's questions.

## Tutor's role

There are significant differences between a traditional and an e-learning tutor. Table 1.2 compares the traditional and e-learning roles. e-Learning is often presented as learner-centred while traditional education and training is

| Activity | Traditional | e-Learning |
|---|---|---|
| Lecture | The tutor is the presenter of information and decides what to communicate, the sequence of information and the speed of delivery. | Information is often presented as learning material so the tutor's role is to facilitate and assist the learner to understand. The learner chooses the pace, content and sequence of learning. Tutors will react to learners' requests although some will offer proactive help based on their experience. |
| Individual assignments | The norm in many forms of traditional teaching is for the tutor to set individual assignments. They are an important part of the assessment process. | Individual assignments are employed for similar purposes as in traditional methods. They are also used to assist learners to self-assess and are often designed centrally rather than by the individual tutor. |
| Group assignments | These are relatively rare in many forms of traditional learning. Group assignments are frequently used and devised by tutors within courses to explore ideas rather than as assessments. Tutors will facilitate the groups. | e-Learning also uses group assignments which serve a similar purpose to traditional courses. One of the main differences is that assignments are more often used for assessment in e-learning and are sometimes designed centrally rather than by the tutor. Co-operative and collaborative learning approaches are employed in e-learning. |
| Feedback | Feedback uses a mixture of methods but verbal face-to-face is frequently the dominant one. | Feedback again employs a range of methods but written feedback is often important where learning is taking place at a distance from the tutor. |

| | | |
|---|---|---|
| Assessment | The tutor is often also the examiner, sometimes devising the assessment and marking the answers. | e-Learning often contains many tests or assessments for the student to undertake and which the software marks. These are intended to help learners to self-assess. |
| Support | Formal support is often provided face-to-face by a variety of people including tutors, mentors and other support staff.<br><br>Peers, friends and family sometimes offer informal support. | Support is probably more important in that the risk of isolation is greater if you are studying at a distance. The tutor and other formal support workers may be less visible due to the distance and their role is more facilitation than direct delivery of learning.<br><br>Peer support is important in e-learning and often the course will be structured to encourage it. |
| Speed of response to individual and group questions | Normally this is determined by when the question is raised. In a lecture the answer can be given immediately but, in a large group, individuals may be discouraged from asking questions.<br><br>Individual issues may depend on a logistical arrangement to fix an appointment. There will often be a delay in meeting. | e-Mail culture tends to assume a quick response and even a short delay may be seen negatively by the sender.<br><br>Many courses have a standard for responding to messages (e.g. 48 hours).<br><br>Replies to group queries allow everyone to see the answer and this provides a permanent record. |

**Table 1.2**  Comparison of tutor roles

seen as tutor-centred. The e-learner is given control and allowed to make the significant choices of what, when and how to study. In traditional learning the tutor is essentially in command of the process. These are both stereotypes and the design of courses and approaches varies considerably. Just by presenting a course online will not in itself ensure it is learner-centred. Many traditional courses do offer a considerable degree of choice to the learner. The comparison does assume the stereotype to aid the discussion but it is important to realise that it depends on the design of the programme. You should ask about the design of your programme and the underpinning intentions before starting it to ensure it meets your needs.

In most traditional learning environments (e.g. colleges and training centres) the tutor is probably the most important component in the students' learning experience. They provide the critical elements of:

- support – providing help when things go wrong or to prevent errors;
- direction – explaining what the key issues are in understanding the subject;
- explanation – providing feedback on progression and advice on what is good practice;
- content – presenting content in a way that you can understand it;
- responsibility – accepting some of the responsibility for your learning (e.g. reminding you about deadlines);
- structure – designing and managing the structure of the course.

The tutors' role in e-learning courses is different. They are facilitators and moderators of your learning rather than having the more directive managerial approach of conventional learning situations. This places more responsibility for your learning on yourself but this does not mean that your tutor is not a critical resource. Tutors can provide you with a great deal of help. The nature of online learning is such that it is difficult for your tutors to identify immediately if you have a problem. They will be monitoring your behaviour by considering how often you send messages to the course conference as well as their content. However, e-mails tend to be short and focused so that diagnosing problems is more difficult than in face-to-face situations. If you are unsure or puzzled you need to ask your tutor for help directly.

The online tutor provides the key elements of:

- welcome/confidence – helping you to feel comfortable in the online environment (e.g. by encouraging you to take part in online conferences);

- support – answering questions, making suggestions and moderating discussion so that you do not exceed the agreed standards;
- feedback – (e.g. annotating assignments, posting messages, etc.);
- facilitation – encouraging discussion and participation so that a climate of mutual support is created;
- monitoring – considering the activities of each learner so that problems are identified as soon as possible.

There are some significant differences between the tutor's role in traditional and e-learning courses. One way of describing the difference is that traditional courses are tutor-centred while e-learning is more learner-centred. This is relative since a great deal depends on how the online course is designed.

## How to assess an e-learning course/programme

A key aspect of any form of learning is to choose the right course for yourself. This section aims to help you assess possible e-learning courses or programmes by providing you with a checklist. The list is in no particular order since e-learning courses can take many different forms and place the emphasis in variety of ways. Some of the items will require you to study later parts of this book so at the moment they will not be clear but it is useful to attempt to use the checklist to assess courses now and then to update it as you work through the book.

You should also check on other aspects of the course (e.g. qualifications, the standing of the college or provider and the value for money). To assess the e-learning aspects you should systematically ask about these topics. Some of the information should be available from the college or provider's website and their publications. However, you may need to ask additional questions.

The decision about the course is yours to make and e-learning is a mix of different features and services, so many combinations are likely to be effective. However, you may well have expectations that are best confirmed at the start. An overarching factor is that e-learning is normally associated with a student-centred approach to provide you with more choice of when, where and how you study. This comes with a transfer of responsibility for your learning from the tutor to you. e-Learning requires that you manage your own time and accept responsibility for your own learning. You may want to consider whether you want to take on these new challenges and assess your own attitudes and skills in relation to these new challenges.

1. Content (how is the content provided?):
   - specifically designed material for the course;
   - interactive content that meets a published standard;
   - traditional materials (e.g. books and other printed content) which is integrated with high quality support and communication technology.
2. Methods (what teaching and learning methods are employed?):
   - e-learning is blended/integrated with traditional methods;
   - distance learning;
   - any face-to-face contact with peers and tutors;
   - degree of freedom (i.e. choice of place, pace and time).
3. Feedback (how is feedback provided?):
   - annotation of assignments;
   - comments on blogs;
   - annotations on e-portfolio content;
   - personal tutor/mentor;
   - learners conference and/or chat room;
   - is there a standard for replying to your messages (e.g. 24 hours)?
4. Learning environment (what online environments are provided?):
   - Virtual Learning Environment (see later chapters for explanation of these systems);
   - Managed Learning Environment (see later chapters for explanation of these systems);
   - Intranet/Extranet;
   - website;
   - e-portfolios;
   - blogs and wikis.
5. Support (what support is provided?):
   - individual tutor/mentor;
   - links/communication with other learners.
6. Assessment (how is the course assessed?):
   - online assessment;
   - conventional assessment (e.g. written examination);
   - Continuous assessment;
   - peer assessment;
   - e-portfolios – are portfolios employed?
7. Flexibility (how much choice does the course provide?):
   - freedom to choose place, pace and time;
   - fixed timetable.
8. Standards – does the organisation provide a statement of its e-learning standards (e.g. minimum requirements for content)?

If you are considering a course then apply the checklist and it should help you make a more systematic assessment. You should also consider your own circumstances and preferences, such as:

- Do you want to learn via a computer screen?
- Are you content with making relationships at a distance?
- Are you planning to study at work? What support and time will your employer/manager provide?

## Summary

### 1.   What is e-learning?

e-Learning is a general term covering many different learning approaches that have in common the use of information and communication technologies.

### 2.   Comparison of traditional and e-learning skills

There are many things in common between the learning skills required for traditional and for e-learning courses but the main differences are:

- e-Learners are learning at a distance from both their peers and tutors.
- e-Learning is more formal with less opportunity for informal communication (e.g. chat in the corridor).
- e-Learners often have relatively little experience of e-mail and other communication technologies compared to face-to-face. Face-to-face is an immediate communication method while e-learning often involves a delay.
- e-Learning depends on written communication which makes it difficult to convey emotion.
- e-Learners need to be more independent and self-reliant than traditional learners.

### 3.   What makes a successful e-learner?

The characteristics of a successful e-learner are self-confidence, motivation, a positive attitude and being a good communicator and collaborator and a competent user of ICT.

### 4.    Benefits of e-learning

e-Learning gives you potentially more freedom to choose the place, pace and time of your learning. However, it does place more responsibility for your learning on you and the design of e-learning courses varies, so the degree of freedom will change from course to course.

### 5.    Learning styles

All learners have preferences about the way they like to learn. These preferences are called learning styles. There are several ways of describing learning styles but one which is appropriate to e-learning is in terms of the seeing, hearing and doing. e-Learning provides many opportunities to make choices, interact with content with a large visual element and to work with others through communication technologies.

### 6.    Information and communication technology

e-Learning is about learning through and being supported by the use of information technology. Learners need to be competent and confident users of ICT.

### 7.    Interaction

Interaction can be considered as a dialogue between yourself and the learning system through what appears on the screen and the input devices (e.g. the mouse and the keyboard). Interactive learning materials should engage and motivate you through their ability to adapt to your individual needs.

### 8.    Learning resources

In many forms of e-learning, learning materials play a significant role. Materials can take many different forms including online and stand-alone interactive materials, workbooks, open learning texts, lecture notes, webpages, downloadable files and online databases.

### 9.    Collaborative and individual learning

e-Learning allows participation in learning of people who would normally be unable to take part. It provides opportunities to collaborate with learners from many different cultures and backgrounds.

### 10.  Blogs, wikis and social networking

e-Learning provides many tools, devices and applications to aid the creativity of learners. Blogs assist the development of the skills of reflection, wikis aid collaborative working and podcasts allows learners to be creative. Creavity is a key element in all forms of education and training.

### 11.  Mobile learning (m-learning)

m-Learning is a natural outcome of the growth in small portable devices such as PDAs, mobile phones, MP3 players and sound recorders. Courses have been integrating these technologies into their programmes to gain the additional benefits of being able to study as you travel or in the short intervals between other activities.

### 12.  Formal and informal learning

The design of e-learning courses varies considerably, so the degree of freedom offered to learners will vary. The flexibility of the programme will depend on the objectives of the course and different courses will have a very different balance of methods and content.

### 13.  Assessment

e-Assessment takes many forms (e.g. on-screen multiple-choice questions, simulation and e-portfolios). They all offer the potential to enable assessment to be provided on demand. e-Portfolios can be narrowly focused on a specific course or for life-long use.

### 14.  Support

Successful e-learners need to be formally and informally supported by tutors, peers, other staff, friends and family

### 15.  Tutors' role

e-Learning should be more learner-centred than traditional education and training which is often described as tutor-centred.

Tutors act more as facilitators and supporters of learners rather than controllers or directors. The responsibility for your learning lies with yourself.

**16.   How to assess an e-learning course/programme**
You should systematically consider what you want from an e-learning course and, using the checklist, assess whether it is going to meet your needs.

# 2  Traditional Skills

To be a successful e-learner you need a foundation of traditional learning skills on which to build your e-learning skills. If you are returning to learning after a significant interval, this chapter will help you review and revise your skills. If you have well-developed learning skills, it aims to show how these can be employed in the e-learning environment (i.e. it will assist you to transfer your learning skills to the new situation). The chapter compares traditional and e-learning skills and considers:

- writing notes;
- reading;
- self-assessment;
- research skills;
- learning in face-to-face groups;
- stress;
- reflection;
- listening.

## Notes

There are four main reasons for making notes:

1. to record the contents of a lecture, seminar or other learning activity so that you can later use them to revise or aid your efforts in completing assignments;
2. to help you concentrate during a lecture, seminar or other learning activity – an activity such as taking notes during a presentation can assist you to focus on the contents whereas simply listening is often ineffective;
3. to assist you to understand the contents of the learning activity since note-taking encourages you to analyse what you are hearing;
4. to convert the contents of the learning activity into your own words.

e-Learning does not normally require you to take notes. All the content is presented in a form that you could save as an electronic file or print out. It would seem that you have the ultimate in note-taking in that you can capture everything. However, the danger is that because you can save everything there is no need to read the material or make any particular effort to understand the content. This can lead to the conviction that because you have a very comprehensive record, there is no need to do anything. What you need to do is read the content and then analyse it. Word processors allow you to annotate electronic text that you have saved or highlight the key phrases using the bold, italics or highlight function.

It may be that you do not immediately read your notes again. This is missing the opportunity of working from a guide to the content written in your own words. A common problem for many learners is that they are unable to understand their own notes when they come to read them some time later. Good practice is to review your notes soon after you make them to fill in gaps, correct errors and improve on their presentation.

**Writing notes**

There is a variety of ways of writing notes and a great deal depends on how you like to write. You could create:

- a comprehensive record of the content;
- an outline of the key points;
- a chart or spider diagram of the content;
- references to other documents, sources and websites.

These can all be effective. Some common points that should be included in all three methods are:

- details of the event – title, name of tutor and date;
- aims and objectives of the event;
- how the content relates to other material.

These common features will help you relate them to other material when you are reading them again months later. In order to record these features you do need to concentrate on the start and end of the event when the tutor or facilitator will often introduce and summarise the topics. This will often help you to gain a clear understanding of the content. This is also true of an e-learning experience. The initial e-mail or message will set the scene for the rest of the e-learning event.

Digital sound recorders are now widely available and are able to capture the contents of a lecture or other types of face-to-face learning experience. This will obviously provide a perfect record of the event but one that needs to be listened to again in order to turn it into a more useful form (i.e. a set of summary notes). It is probably best to reserve recordings to events where you need a perfect record, where you are being presented with a topic that you find especially difficult or when you are unable to attend and a friend can record it for you.

Another digital device that can help you make notes of a presentation is a camera. You can photograph visual displays (e.g. slides using PowerPoint® presentation graphics program) or demonstrations that would probably be difficult to record in other ways. Digital images can be printed so that you can add them to your normal notes.

You also need to take notes of written content from books, papers or other sources. This is similar to reading online content (e.g. a website) and it is often useful to have a highlighter pen or a notebook to record the key points. For online content, write down the main issues as this will help you reflect on the material as well as beginning the process of developing a set of notes. You can obviously print or save the webpage but this in itself will not assist your learning. You either need to read the printout, to highlight the critical topics, to annotate the document or indeed to do all of these things. It is useful to develop your own notes of the content. This can be done using a word processor or paper and pen, depending on your preferences. The key factor is to immerse yourself in the material in order to understand it and relate the content to your existing knowledge.

## Activity
## Note-taking

Read the content below, highlight the key points and annotate the document with your own reflections. Finally produce your own notes of the material.

*Information and communication technology has already changed many aspects of the way people work, relax and live their lives. Mobile computer equipment has enabled people to work in many different locations. It is now a familiar sight to see someone working on a train using a notebook computer. Many companies practise 'hot desking' where staff do not have a permanent desk but simply plug their notebook into the organisation's network and use mobile phones to communicate.*

*For many people the world wide web is the preferred way of arranging a holiday, booking theatre tickets, buying books and planning many aspects of their lives. You do not need to find reference books or send for leaflets. Searching the web to locate a relevant site has replaced these actions. There is no need to visit the supermarket since you can shop online and have the groceries delivered to your door.*

*Communication technology has assisted the development of a new type of community – a community of interest where members share a common need or interest. They may share a genetic illness and seek to discuss new medical developments or support each other. Other communities have an interest in collecting antiques, in military history, in tracing their family history, and so on.*

*Information and communication technology is still a new development so further change is likely to result. The difficulty lies in predicting what the changes or impact will be.*

### Discussion

My own efforts are shown below. Your own work will be different since notes are a personal record of the content so will depend on individual experience and understanding.

*Information and communication technology has already **changed** many aspects of **the way people work, relax and live their lives**. Mobile computer equipment has enabled people **to work in many different locations**. It is now a familiar sight to see someone working on a train using a notebook computer. Many companies practise **'hot desking'** where staff do not have a permanent desk but simply plug their notebook into the organisation's network and use mobile phones to communicate.*

*For many people the **world wide web is the preferred way** of arranging a holiday, booking theatre tickets, buying books and planning many aspects of their lives. You do not need to find reference books or send for leaflets. **Searching the web to locate a relevant site** has replaced these actions. There is no need to visit the supermarket since you can shop online and have the groceries delivered to your door.*

***Communication technology** has assisted the development of a **new type of community** – a community of **interest** where members share a common need or interest. They may share a genetic illness and seek to discuss new medical developments or support each other. Other communities have an interest in collecting antiques, in military history, in tracing their family history, and so on.*

*Information and communication technology is still a new development so further change is likely to result. The **difficulty lies in predicting** what the changes or impact will be.*

An alternative approach is a spider diagram as shown in Figure 2.1.

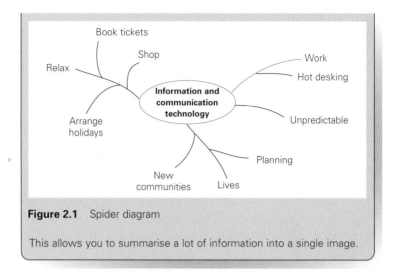

**Figure 2.1**  Spider diagram

This allows you to summarise a lot of information into a single image.

## Group working

Working in small groups is an important approach to learning and is often part of a course. The groups undertake a variety of different tasks (e.g. joint projects, topic discussion, role-playing and reviewing material). Note-taking is a part of this process but is often difficult since group working depends on participation. Combining writing with active involvement is not easy. Usually the notes have to be made later and only a few key points can be recorded during the actual meeting. This depends on your memory and useful parts of the experience may be lost. While group working is frequently a rich learning experience this can be an important weakness.

With online group working and discussion, the whole content of the dialogue can be captured. Many online conferences and mailgroups record every message so that you can review the communication. However, the danger is again simply too much information and so it is often useful to produce your own summary. Reading the contents of an online discussion can present you with scores of messages which is rather like reading a play script without the stage directions. Contributors can send messages whenever they choose so that the order of receipt frequently does not follow a simple logical process of discussion but rather involves back-tracking and in some cases several themes are intertwined with each other.

## Reading

Reading is a core part of learning. During a course you may be asked to read books, handouts, research papers, blogs, wikis, e-portfolios and other forms of written material including webpages. The key to effective reading is to understand why you are reading the material. What are you trying to achieve?

### Process

There are various reasons for reading (e.g. for pleasure). When you are studying, your aim is to understand the content and how it relates to your studies. The process described below encourages you to approach reading in a systematic and active way. Casual reading can often be ineffective as you may lose concentration, be easily distracted or fail to understand. Some useful tips to include in an active reading approach are:

1. The opening and closing paragraphs or pages in longer documents often give the objectives of the material and summarise its content so it is useful initially to read them both to gain a clear insight into the material as follows.
2. The abstract and conclusion of a paper will give you the main topics of the publication.
3. Written material is usually structured using headings so an initial review of them will provide you with an overview of the content.
4. Browse the material to develop your overview. It is useful to consider illustrations, tables of information or lists as these will often be associated with key issues.
5. Read the material identifying the main points (i.e. highlight key points, write comments in the margin or use a notebook to record the important issues).
6. Reflect on the content by comparing it against what you have already studied and understand. Are you convinced by the argument? Does the content support or oppose information you have already located? Try to form an overall image by linking the new material with the context and content from your existing understanding.
7. Review your highlights, comments and notes to produce your own summary of the content. This will help you reflect on the material as well as developing notes which will help your revision later.

Technology can assist reading. You can photocopy the material so that it is easier to write on or you can scan the content into a computer to turn your printed material into an electronic form which can be highlighted or cut and pasted to form your own set of notes. However, this does assume that you have the right to copy it. If you read the opening pages of the majority of books they severely limit the copying of the content (e.g. publication cannot be copied, saved on to a computer or reproduced in any form without the permission of the copyright owner). You should study the copyright conditions to check what you are able to do with the content and in many cases you can copy content for personal educational use. Many colleges will provide you with guidance.

## Reading online

Reading online content is similar to reading printed material, but online material is designed very differently from a book. It is based on the concept of hypertext – that is, linking ideas together rather than producing a simple linear presentation of the information. By following the links you can find out more about a particular topic but at the expense of moving away from the webpage at which you began. This can lead to confusion because it is sometimes difficult to know where you are. Links can be within a single website or to other websites so it is easy to become lost. Links can be text, pictures or any other object that appears on the screen. Any combination of link is possible (e.g. text to text, text to picture, picture to picture or picture to text). Figure 2.2 illustrates hypertext links.

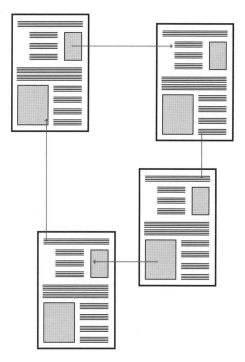

**Figure 2.2** Hypertext

| Printed publication | Website | Comments |
|---|---|---|
| Read opening and closing paragraphs or pages to gain objectives and summary of the content. | The home page provides an overview of the site and many designers provide summaries throughout the material. Some websites have site maps, introductions and help facilities that offer an overview of content and structure. In some cases an introductory tour is offered to new users. Hypertext links make identifying opening and closing sections difficult. | Content is hidden within websites compared to printed publications so it is critical to gain a clear overview about what the site contains before embarking on reading the content. Consider the home page, site maps, introductions and tours to gain an insight into the material. |
| Written material is usually structured using headings so an initial review of them will provide you with an overview of the content. | Websites are highly structured using headings to break presentation into distinct sections. Hypertext links are also part of the structure so need to be explored to gain an overview of the site. | Hypertext structure can be complex but good practice is to provide a consistent set of links following a distinct pattern. It is therefore useful to identify the approach taken. Site maps and early exploration can often help identify the approach. |
| Browse the material to develop your overview. | Browsing is a normal approach to considering a website. Rapidly jump around the site to explore the content. Illustrations are an important part of the information so make an effort to study them. Remember that pages are frequently longer than a book page and some content will require you to scroll down or up to locate it. | Websites are a visual medium so that illustrations, graphical devices and structured text (e.g. tables) are important elements. |

| | | |
|---|---|---|
| Read the material identifying the main points (i.e. highlight key points, write comments in the margin or use a notebook to record the important issues). | Read with a purpose. Links will help you follow a theme but can also lead to you missing the rest of the content on a page so do consider the whole content. Make notes and, if you find it helps, print the page and highlight and annotate it. Webpages can be saved as an electronic document so that you can electronically highlight content or produce word-processed notes. Small sections of webpages can be copied to form word-processed notes. You do not have to copy the whole page. | Remember that almost anyone can launch a website so that the quality of the content may not be assured. |
| Reflect on the content by comparing it against what you have already studied and understand. Are you convinced by the argument? Does the content support or oppose information you have already located? Try to form an overall image by linking the new material with the context and content from your existing understanding. | Reflection is vital to help you understand so critically consider the content, comparing it against other sources. | |

**Table 2.1**   Comparison – printed publication and web content – *continued overleaf*

| Printed publication | Website | Comments |
|---|---|---|
| Review your highlights, comments and notes to produce your own summary of the content. This will help you reflect on the material as well as developing notes which will help your revision later. | Review is again a key process in reading for learning. | It is important to record the URL (i.e. address) of the website so that you can find it again. Remember that websites are dynamic. Their content changes continuously so that if including a reference to a website it is useful to give the date when you accessed it. |

**Table 2.1**    *continued*

Hypertext links will often take you into the middle of a webpage and into the heart of a website, making it difficult to be aware of the context of the rest of the site or even of the page if you simply follow the links and take no other action. You are very reliant on the designers of the site and their analysis of the material rather than your own.

Many people find reading from a screen display more difficult than reading printed material. This is due to some extent to the lower quality of the text displayed compared to print. It is therefore good practice to avoid presenting large volumes of text on the screen but rather to use illustrations, bullet point lists of information and short sentences. If a large volume of text is needed, it should be in a form that can be printed out if the reader wishes to do so.

The reading process for a printed publication needs to be adapted for the different nature of the website and webpage. Table 2.1 compares a traditional printed document with a webpage.

Websites are often covered by copyright (i.e. they are owned) so it is important to check what the owner of the site will allow you to do with the content. Many sites have copyright statements at the foot of each webpage or offer links to the webmaster who manages the site so that you can ask questions or seek permission to copy the material. In many cases if you are simply copying the content for your personal study you will be given permission. Your college or training provider should be able to advise you.

Other types of online reading that you may need to undertake are reading your own or another student's blog, a group wiki or evidence of learning contained in an e-portfolio. The key issue here is to reflect on what you are reading. Consider the content by comparing it against what you understand about the topic. Does it provide a new insight into the area? Does it help you understand the content? Are you convinced by the argument? Does the content support or oppose information you have already located? Consider the different options and attempt to develop your understanding. When you are reading your peers' blogs or other work there is often an opportunity to help them with feedback. The key is to offer constructive comments. The process of adding comments can often help you formalise your own understanding of what you have read.

## Activity
## Reading online

Visit the British Library website at www.bl.uk/. Identify the information and resources that are provided for science and technology or your own subject and develop a short summary of the main elements of the resources. Explore the proposed reading process, perhaps comparing reading on the screen with printed webpages. Consider the British Library copyright statement.

Alternatively, visit a blog and consider the presentation of information. There are many different ones available and lots of newspapers and broadcasters offer blogs (e.g. the *Guardian* – http://blogs.guardian.co.uk/index.html) that you can read and add comments.

### Discussion

*Websites*
Websites are dynamic so it is likely that the British Library site which you have looked at has been developed since I studied its contents. However, you should have noticed that:

1. The home page, site map and introductions provide good overviews of the site.
2. Many different groups of resources are provided by the British Library in relation to science and technology. These include:
   a)   electronic sources;
   b)   electronic databases;
   c)   electronic journals;
   d)   collections;
   e)   publications.
3. Some resources are not available online but only from the library itself.

The copyright statement provides clear guidance to learners on the use of the material.

*Blogs*
You might like to consider:

   a)   if the presentation of information in date order is helpful;
   b)   how you felt when adding a comment;
   c)   whether other peoples' comments were helpful.

It is useful to consider several blogs and compare their approaches.

## Writing

Writing as part of a course of study is quite different from other forms of writing. You are seeking to show that you understand the subject through your writing. This requires that you:

- demonstrate a systematic and logical approach to the question you are answering;
- use evidence from your studies to support your case effectively;
- show a clear understanding of the topic (e.g. use technical terms correctly);
- present the argument objectively (i.e. sometimes in the third person);
- analyse the evidence and do not simply present everything that you have read or heard.

This approach to writing is the same whether you are using a pen or a word-processed application on a computer. That said, word-processing provides you with distinct benefits. Writing with a pen then redrafting your assignment or essay is a significant task whereas with a word processor it is a straightforward part of writing with a computer.

If you are writing an essay with a pen you may well follow the approach below:

- notes;
- rough draft;
- final draft.

Each step requires a significant amount of time and is liable to error because it involves copying previous work. Word-processing involves the same steps but they are all part of a continuous process that does not require you to copy, thereby reducing mistakes. You can also now add a fourth or even fifth stage, which is revising your essay. Revisions can be undertaken quickly to improve your work.

There are also extra advantages to word-processing such as spell and grammar checking, electronic thesaurus and adding extra ideas late in the writing process which can be difficult to include in a handwritten document. Illustrations, tables and figures can be added to the text with little effort and blended accurately into the text. A handwritten document would require you to draw the illustration or to paste a photograph or other item into the document. You can produce a high quality document which, unless you have excellent handwriting, is difficult to match.

The development of web 2.0 approaches offers new challenges. Blogs, wikis and e-portfolios require a different approach to writing than does an essay or other form of academic assignment. The foundation of web 2.0 technologies is to provide the means of creating content and changing the web from a resource where you read to one in which you write as well.

## Blogs

A blog is a website that you create which shows its contents in date order. It is normally open to other learners and to your tutors and offers you the opportunity to write about your reflections, ideas and conclusions in relation to the subjects you are studying. As part of the course you may be asked to maintain a learning diary in the form of a blog to aid your reflections on the content of the course. You may be asked to provide entries on specific issues (e.g. How does the definition of a professional engineer provided in the course materials compare with your own experience?). The key aspect to consider when writing your own blog is that it concerns your own reflections and is not simply providing a summary of what you have read.

Another type of writing linked to blogs is that of adding comments to another learner's blog. In this case you are reflecting on their reflections. It can be useful when your peers offer you feedback so you need to be able to reciprocate. The approach should be positive and constructive, with comments aimed at helping your colleague.

Blogs can serve many different purposes and the writing style required will depend on the blog's role. These roles include:

- personal learning diary;
- showcase of work produced as part of the course;
- resources that you have located on the world wide web which have helped you and may help your colleagues;
- your response to topical items relevant to the course;
- reflections on course materials and textbooks.

In the wider world blogs are increasingly being used in areas such as politics, news, society and health. Writing in a blog is different from more traditional forms in that it is more concise and personal but there is little objective guidance on what format to follow. Your style is likely to take time to develop and you should perhaps encourage feedback which will advise you.

## Wikis

Wikis enable you to create content in collaboration with others. You can edit each other's entries, add new material and delete content. The aim is to gain the benefits of a group collaborating to produce a joint outcome. It requires practice to get the best results and at the start you may be reluctant to change other people's contributions. Inexperienced users will simply add new content so that you can end with a series of statements rather than a single integrated document. The main aims are to:

- build on the contributions of others, so read each one carefully;
- don't react to other members of the group changing your words – it is important to consider whether the outcome is improved;
- collaborate, don't compete;
- change other contributions if you can add value to them.

The most important first step is to join in and have a go at collaborative writing.

## Activity
## Writing for a blog

Writing a blog entry is different from other forms of writing and it is likely to take time for your style to emerge. It is therefore useful to practise as much as you can.

1. Identify some public blogs, read their entries and assess the approach they have taken to writing
2. Start your own blog (https://www.blogger.com/start?hl=en) and begin to publish your thoughts online.

**Discussion**
Writing a blog is a challenging task in that you are trying to combine a number of components into a single short entry. You need to write clear and concise messages about your subject combined with your personal and professional reflections. This is not easy especially when you are publishing them to the world and encouraging anyone to comment on your ideas. Many people are daunted by the prospect of the openness of blogging.

*Additional activity*
Try to find an opportunity to join in a wiki collaboration to experience the writing of a wiki document.

1. **Select, interact with and use ICT systems independently to meet the needs of a variety of users**
   The attached documents illustrate how I undertook a project to develop a financial model of a new product in order to determine an appropriate selling price:
       project brief;
       financial model;
       feedback from Product Manager.

2. **Follow and understand the need for safety and security practices**
   I have included a certificate showing that I attended and passed the Data Security course. In addition, the company health and safety officer has provided a witness statement supporting my safety awareness and practice:
       certification from data security course;
       witness statement safety awareness and practice.

3. **Manage information storage efficiently**
   I have provided screen captures showing the file structure that I have created in order to store my files:
       File structure.

**Figure 2.3**    Example overview of an e-portfolio aligned with the ICT functional skill standard

### e-Portfolios

e-Portfolios can serve a variety of purposes such as a showcase of achievements, evidence for assessment and reflection on work undertaken. In many cases you will be presenting your work to the world or at least to your peers and tutors. It is therefore important that your contents are organised and structured so that other people can understand their purpose. This is often assisted by short introductions to groups and individual items of evidence explaining their context and relevance. This is important because it provides guidance for readers and helps them to understand why it demonstrates your abilities. Another simple but important task is to provide evidence with meaningful names. An example overview of an e-portfolio is shown in Figure 2.3.

### Self-assessment

In all forms of learning it is important to be able to assess your own performance. This allows you to seek help when you need it or to make an extra effort when required. In conventional courses you have many opportunities to judge your progress. These include:

- feedback from your assignment marker;
- comparing the outcomes of different assignments as this will assist you to evaluate what is required;
- sharing results with other learners;
- tutor feedback to you individually and to the whole group;
- listening to answers to other learners' questions;
- discussions with other learners both formally and informally (in the corridor);
- deadlines provide a means of assessing your ability to keep pace with the course;
- reflecting on your own efforts – are you making sufficient effort? Be honest with yourself. You are often provided with information about what the course designers expect from you (e.g. number of hours that you should study each week) so you can check your own workrate.

There are a variety of sources of information to help you assess your performance. Many involve face-to-face contact with tutors or other learners. This is absent from online courses. Other sources are available but do require more individual action and acceptance of responsibility. In both cases it is vital that you take advantage of your tutors by asking them questions, keeping them informed of your problems and requesting feedback. It is rarely enough to speak to your tutor only when you want an extension to a deadline.

e-Learning courses require a more proactive approach to self-assessment than equivalent conventional ones, although many features are still available to you. Your work will be marked and feedback provided. You need to consider this feedback and ask for explanation if you need it. It is more difficult to ask other learners informally how they have done but e-mail groups do allow you to share information. If you share your results and thoughts then you will find that others will reveal theirs since they also need to judge their own progress. The use of blogs and e-portfolios to share your work provides additional opportunities to gain feedback from your peers and tutors.

### Research skills

In all courses there is a need for learners to be able to find, interpret, compare and analyse information. This is essentially research. An e-learning course is no different from a conventional one in this respect except that the learners can access a huge library of information through the world wide web without leaving their desks. The scale of this resource makes research skills more important because, with far more to consider and to judge, you can be overwhelmed with information.

## Locating information

Regardless of what you are learning, you need the skills of finding information and assessing if it is suitable for your purpose. This may simply involving understanding how the college or public library works so that you can locate books and journals. However, even this task has more depth than initially appears. You need to judge the contents of the publication. Is it suitable for your needs? Is it up to date? Does it cover your subject at the correct level?

To answer these types of questions you must be able to:

- analyse information;
- assess content;
- compare alternative sources.

An approach to assessing the suitability of a book quickly in a library or bookshop is to:

- review the contents page – to decide whether it covers areas that you are interested in;
- look up key words in the index and consider how the book covers one area you know about – this will help you assess the approach and quality of the book;
- check the publication date – some subjects are fairly dynamic so a book more than a few years old will be unsuitable;
- check the author – is he or she on your course reading list?

Locating a book within a library is often dependent on your skill in using the library catalogue. These are often available on the college network or website and enable you to search for the books or paper without leaving your home. This can save you time in travelling to the library to search for a book which is already out on loan to another learner. Many libraries offer training programmes, awareness sessions or printed guides to help you to use the library effectively and you should take advantage of them to become a competent user.

## Library catalogues and literature CD-ROMs

Many library catalogues or literature databases are provided on the library network or on CD-ROMs. Searching these resources is not dissimilar to searching an online database. They are all slightly different but many follow a similar pattern. Often the catalogue or literature database will offer several ways of searching it. A well-used approach is to allow you to search by:

- author;
- title;
- ISBN – this is a unique number at the front of most books;
- subject;
- keyword.

For example, if you search for a particular author then you will be presented with a list of the books or other items written by authors with that name. You then review the list to identify the one you are seeking.

## Online bookshops

If you are buying a book from an online bookshop you will sometimes be able to review the contents pages and selected chapters in a similar way to a physical book. In addition many books have readers', reviewers' and author's comments. Virtual bookshops often have enormous stocks, making searching for a book the equivalent of visiting a large library.

## Research evidence

It is not sufficient to locate information and evidence. You need to be able to assess its appropriateness and suitability to your work, sometimes termed critical reviewing. All information, regardless of its source (e.g. book, research paper, blog or website), needs to be considered. If a document has been published, then the content has been through some form of checking and assessment process. Many journals only publish papers after they have been assessed by other researchers working in the same field. This is known as peer reviewing and is a quality assurance process to ensure that the paper is suitable for publication. Websites, however, can be developed by anyone so it is essential to check their quality. Blogs offer personal views but often present links to other sources of information. Podcasts offer an alternative to reading information. Later we will consider searching for information on the world wide web in more detail and assessing its quality.

Critically reviewing information involves a variety of steps including consideration of:

- the source of the publication (e.g. government survey, peer-reviewed research paper, university research centre, recognised expert, personal blog, Wikipedia, thesis, etc.);
- the basis of the information (e.g. research findings, personal opinions, collaborate writing in a wiki, etc.);
- how well the information relates to other sources you have located – whether it is radically different from other evidence or supported by it;
- when the evidence was published – many subjects are continuously developing so only recent information is likely to be appropriate.

It is essential that you do not accept everything you read as accurate. You must actively challenge the information and make a decision about its suitability.

**Numerical data**

Table 2.2 shows some data about climate (i.e. average rainfall, hours of sunshine per day, percentage of cloud cover and wind speed in the four quarters of the year). A useful skill is the ability to interpret this type of numerical information. The table assists your understanding by presenting the data in a systematic way but it is still quite difficult to identify trends or to compare the different quarters. A more effective way is to present the data in a visual way (e.g. histogram or pie chart). Figure 2.4 illustrates the table rainfall information as a pie chart comparing the four quarters. Figure 2.5 shows the data presented as a line graph so you can see and compare all the information.

Charts and graphs are quickly and effectively produced from tables produced in Microsoft Excel®. These allow you to investigate and present information effectively. Although you could draw the charts and graphs using paper and pen, Microsoft Excel® allows you to consider quickly a wide

| | 1st quarter | 2nd quarter | 3rd quarter | 4th quarter |
|---|---|---|---|---|
| Rainfall (inches) | 12 | 34 | 17 | 11 |
| Sunshine (hours per day) | 6 | 3 | 4 | 7 |
| Cloud (% of sky) | 25 | 45 | 18 | 12 |
| Wind speed (m.p.h.) | 4 | 11 | 15 | 6 |

**Table 2.2**   Weather data by quarter

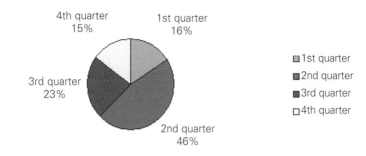

**Figure 2.4** Rainfall

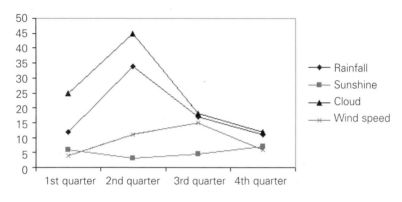

**Figure 2.5** Climate data

range of charts and graphs, thus letting you explore the best way of presenting and analysing the data.

## Synthesis

A critical part of any learning process is synthesis, combining and integrating information from several sources with your own analysis. When you write an essay, undertake an assignment or simply make notes from a series of sources you are synthesising the data. Word processing and other applications are helpful when you are trying to integrate several sources together. If you are handwriting an essay you may work through several drafts to produce a finished product and each draft requires that you rewrite the whole document. A word-processed document, on the other hand, can be edited many times without your having the burden of rewriting. You are not limited to the number of drafts and are able to focus your effort on integration and analysis and not simply rewriting.

## Learning in face-to-face groups

When you are learning in a group there are several different approaches in which you may be participating. These include:

- listening to a lecture, presentation or tutorial;
- observing a demonstration;
- working with other learners to achieve a common goal;
- undertaking a practical activity (e.g. laboratory experiment).

This involves the use of a range of skills such as listening, observing, co-operating, questioning and note-taking. In face-to-face learning you have the opportunity to ask questions either to clarify your understanding or to establish links with other areas or simply because you are confused. A parallel benefit is that you can hear other learners' questions and the associated answers. It is obviously better to ask your own since this will directly benefit your own needs but on many occasions you have probably thought 'I wish I had asked that'.

e-Learning enables you to ask questions of your tutor using e-mail and if these are shared through an electronic mailgroup or other form of online conferencing you can also benefit from your peers' questions. Many participants in mailgroups have found that they gain a great deal from reading the other messages. This is called vicarious learning (Cox et al., 1999).

Face-to-face approaches can provide you with numerous opportunities for informal conversations – in the corridor, over refreshments and before and after the formal session. These are usually with fellow learners but occasionally involve the tutor or lecturer, allowing you to check your understanding against your peers, seek help or share ideas. This is often very useful. In e-learning courses there are will be opportunities to discuss the course informally with your peers using chat rooms or mailgroups. These may be moderated by tutors who will offer advice or answer questions if they feel they need to intervene but in some cases tutors are not permitted entry, letting you debate issues in private. Chat rooms and other forms of online discussion require you to take the initiative by sending a message and this can be a little strange at first but participation will help you.

## Activity
## Face-to-face learning

When you are next in a face-to-face group-learning situation, note each question and answer and reflect on how much you have gained from hearing the dialogue.

**Discussion**
You should be able to identify clearer benefits than simply being able to hear the discussion. Asking your own questions adds considerable value to the process since participation is not simply about passive listening. Your tutors gain from your questions in that they are able to adjust their presentation to ensure your understanding is more likely. Without feedback, tutors will naturally assume that you understand. This applies to both face-to-face and e-learning courses.

Face-to-face learning enables you to see what is happening with your tutor or peers. When you communicate by e-mail you have no way of knowing what is going on at the other end. Your tutor or colleague may be ill, away on a trip or simply busy. We all expect an immediate response to an e-mail message and it is often frustrating when you ask a question or request a change and nothing seems to happen. In face-to-face learning you can at least go along and find out what is wrong. Some e-mail systems allow you to ask for a receipt when your message is opened but some computer systems block receipts, so this is not a guarantee. Nevertheless, when they are available they can at least reassure you that your message has arrived. Some courses have published standards for replying to messages (e.g. within 24 hours) and this is a useful feature to check when you are considering a course.

Communication in face-to-face situations is a mixture of speaking and listening while in online learning it is about reading and writing. In face-to-face situations you need to take notes in order to record the discussion whereas online learning provides you with a full written record. It is always wise to keep your own copy since access to online system sometimes changes and faults sometimes delete records.

### Stress

Learning can be a stressful process. You have deadlines to meet and assessments to pass, placing considerable pressure on you. How you deal with stress in learning situations can depend on the support that you have available – not just the formal support of your tutor, although this is very important, but also the relatively informal help of other learners, your friends and family. This is true of all forms of learning whether conventional or e-learnjng.

In face-to-face situations sometimes your fellow learners and tutors will realise that you need assistance when your behaviour or demeanour is unusual. In the online environment it is more difficult to identify, so you need to take more responsibility to ensure that stress produced by learning pressures does not cause you too many problems. If you can identify the causes, you are better equipped to deal with stress.

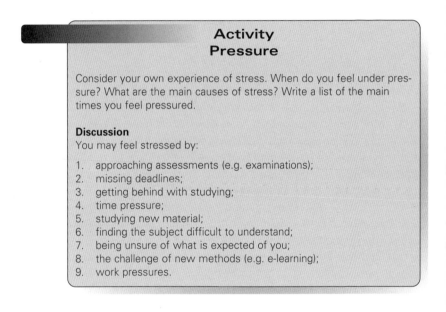

### Activity
### Pressure

Consider your own experience of stress. When do you feel under pressure? What are the main causes of stress? Write a list of the main times you feel pressured.

**Discussion**
You may feel stressed by:

1.  approaching assessments (e.g. examinations);
2.  missing deadlines;
3.  getting behind with studying;
4.  time pressure;
5.  studying new material;
6.  finding the subject difficult to understand;
7.  being unsure of what is expected of you;
8.  the challenge of new methods (e.g. e-learning);
9.  work pressures.

If you know what your main causes of stress are, you need to take action to reduce or eliminate· them. Insufficient time to complete work is often a source of stress and is frequently caused by poor time management. In face-to-face learning the responsibility for time management is divided between you and your tutor. He or she will often remind you of deadlines and encourage you to start work at the appropriate moment. e-Learning courses are likely to place more responsibility on you for managing your time. In later chapters you will consider the time-management skills you need as an e-learner. However, some general points to consider are:

- be systematic in your approach to learning;
- little and often is a better approach than trying to do too much with long intervals between studying;
- plan your time by considering what is required and when you need to do it.

## Reflection

It is good learning practice to reflect on your learning and studying. Many professional bodies require reflective practitioners inasmuch as they encourage members to consider their experience in order to learn from it. Kolb (1984) developed a model of experiential learning based on four stages that form a cycle of learning activity. The four stages are:

- concrete experience;
- observation and reflection;
- abstract conceptualisation;
- active experimentation.

For a meaningful learning experience, learners must complete a full cycle (Figure 2.6) although they can start at any point. The four steps are undertaking an action, reflecting on the experience, considering the principles underpinning the experience and transferring the understanding to a new situation. Reflection is a key stage and the cycle provides a means of identifying the benefits of reflection. It can lead to identifying the principles behind

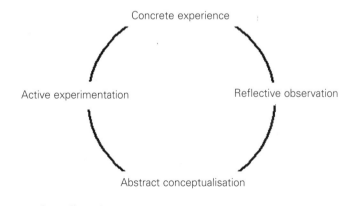

**Figure 2.6**   Kolb Cycle

an experience and it allows you to transfer the understanding to a new context and then experiment with it.

Dewey (1933) defined reflection as 'active, persistent and careful consideration'. It is important in all forms of learning, including e-learning. In traditional education you can discuss learning experiences immediately with your peers who may well have had an identical experience. This provides a useful way of motivating the sharing of the experience through discussion and debate. An e-learning experience can be unique to you or at least experienced on your own. Sharing the experience and discussing what you have learnt can rarely be spontaneous and for this reason may be more difficult to achieve. Individual reflection is therefore likely to be more important in e-learning since discussion is more challenging.

Asynchronous communication is structured to allow you the opportunity to reflect on each message that is sent to you because there is a natural interval before you need to respond and also after you send a message. The natural space between messages offers the possibility to reflect on them. e-Mails are often associated with misunderstanding as a result of the informality and the ease and speed with which you can send them. If you take the opportunity to reflect briefly, then you should reduce the possibilities of misunderstanding and improve your contribution to discussions.

Reflection can play a variety of roles but is essentially concerned with considering some experience or understanding in more depth. It is useful to give yourself an objective for reflecting but in some cases it provides spontaneity where a new idea results from the reflection. It can help you to develop a deeper understanding of your own skills, knowledge and attitudes.

## Activity
## Reflecting

How do you react to feedback?

Feedback in e-learning is a critical feature. You receive formal and informal comments from your tutors and peers through various sources such as e-mail conferencing, blogs and e-portfolios. It is important to develop your ability to get the best from all forms of feedback. Equally it is useful to know how to give feedback to your own peers.

Refection allows you to develop your own understanding of your ability to accept and provide feedback. Reflect on the feedback that you have had and how your own feedback to others has been received. Remember that reflection involves active, persistent and careful consideration (Dewey, 1933).

**Discussion**

Personally, I find it difficult to accept critical feedback. I have learnt not to react too quickly but to reflect on what has been said. I normally find that on reflection I can see the fairness of the comments and I am able to address the criticism.

Perhaps owing to my own sensitivity to critical comments, I am very careful to balance any feedback I give and I am quite reluctant to provide comments unless asked for them.

How do you react to feedback?

## Listening

Traditional learning is based around listening. You listen to lectures and various other forms of presentation so it is likely that you are an experienced educational listener. e-Learning is based on the written word so listening may not seem to be important but there is considerable interest in providing multimedia resources and, in particular, podcasts. These require that you listen to audio resources of a diverse nature.

Listening to a podcast is different in several aspects compared to attending a lecture. You have control of the podcast in that you can:

- choose when to listen to the resource;
- choose where you listen (e.g. as you walk, using an iPod);
- stop the recording and take a break;
- listen to the same recording several times.

You have lots of choices when listening in e-learning which should enhance the learning but they do require that you manage the process. You should ask yourself when, how and where to listen if you want to retain as much of the content as possible. A lecture room is designed to aid listening in that it is quiet and aims to help you concentrate. Sitting on a train listening to a podcast is quite different. It is important to be an active listener and take advantage of its flexibility. Many learners find writing a summary a useful aid to helping them to understand the information presented and an aid to later revision. It can be very time-consuming listening to several podcasts as part of a revision process. However, listening to key ones can introduce some important variation into revision, which may help your concentration.

## Summary

### 1. Notes

e-Learning courses provide most of the content as text and you can save or print it. This appears to do away with the need to take notes but there is the risk that you will record everything but study very little of it. It is vital to read and analyse the material. You can annotate and highlight electronic documents which will assist you during revision months later by identifying the key points.

### 2. Reading

Online reading material is structured differently to a printed publication. Online text is based on the concept of hypertext, whereby concepts are linked together rather than presented as a linear flow of information. To read more about an idea you need to follow the links.

It is important when reading hypertext documents that you initially gain an appreciation of the content and structure. The home page of a website will often provide an overview and some websites have site maps, introductions and help facilities which will also aid you.

### 3. Writing

Writing in any form of study is concerned with showing your understanding of the subject. This is the same whether you are using a pen or a word-processing application, although word-processing does give some additional benefits (i.e. redrafting assignments, spell and grammar checking and thesaurus).

Writing is the main communication method of e-learning. Blogs, wikis and e-portfolios and other web 2.0 approaches now actively encourage you to create new material. You can add comments to your peers' work but focus on offering constructive helpful feedback that you would welcome yourself.

### 4. Self-assessment

It is important to be able to assess your performance in all forms of learning. This is especially true of e-learning in that you are often working at a distance from your tutor or peers so there is less opportunity for informal assessment.

You need to be proactive in self-assessment, using assignment marks and feedback but also asking for explanations from your tutor or enquiring how your peers are doing. Systematically read the comments added to your blog or e-portfolio.

## 5.  Research skills

All forms of learning require you to be able to find, interpret, compare and analyse information. This requires you to be able to find information (e.g. use a library and search the world wide web) and judge its appropriateness. A key skill is use of the library catalogue. This is often available on the computer network or on CD-ROM. Libraries will often help you to understand how to use them effectively.

Judging the suitability of information requires consideration of the source and basis of the publication, how well the information relates to other sources and when the evidence was published.

An important way of considering numerical information is to use charts and graphs.

Learning requires you to synthesise information by combining and integrating information from several sources. Word processing is very helpful when you are trying to integrate several sources together.

## 6.  Learning in face-to-face groups

When you are learning in a group you use a range of skills such as listening, observing, co-operating, questioning and note-taking. A benefit of face-to-face learning is the opportunity to ask questions and hear the answers to other people's questions. A similar opportunity exists in e-learning through the use of e-mail or other forms of computer mediated communication.

Face-to-face approaches give you the opportunity for informal conversations to check your understanding or judge your own performance. e-Learning requires more formality in that you need to send an e-mail, add a comment to a blog or use a chat room.

### 7.  Stress
All forms of learning can be stressful. e-Learning is potentially more demanding because you are responsible for your own learning. If you can identify the causes of stress you are better equipped to deal with it.

### 8.  Reflection
Reflecting on your learning experience is a key part of the learning process. In e-learning it is perhaps even more important, since opportunities for discussing experiences are more limited than in traditional education. e-Learning does offer many opportunities to reflect (e.g. blogs and e-portfolios).

### 9.  Listening
Traditional learning is based around listening (e.g. listening to lectures) so that you will probably be an experienced educational listener. e-Learning is based on the written word but multimedia resources including podcasts are often provided. e-Learning offers you control over your listening (e.g. listening several times to the same material).

# 3  Computer Skills

In order to be a successful e-learner you need to have a good range of basic computer skills. Computers are good at keeping records, presenting information and manipulating data – all fundamental requirements of any form of education. Communication technology provides additional advantages by allowing you to locate sources of information on the world wide web or within the college's online resources as well as being able to communicate quickly with tutors and other learners. A range of new web applications are becoming part of e-learning and these offer you the opportunity to create content as well as to find it (e.g. blogs, wikis, podcasts and e-portfolios). This chapter assumes that you have used a computer for doing tasks such as word-processing and using a spreadsheet. It aims to help you develop skills that you will need as a learner. It covers:

- assessing your skills;
- accessibility;
- file management;
- compressing files;
- tracking changes;
- saving and backing up your information;
- applications;
- searching the world wide web;
- assessing the quality of online information;
- presenting information (i.e. tables, charts and graphs);
- transferring information;
- saving and backing up your information;
- digital images;
- e-portfolios;
- podcasting;
- blogging;
- plagiarism;
- copyright;
- utilities.

## Assessment of skills

A useful place to start is to consider your existing skills. The activity below provides you with a straightforward table to assess your competency.

### Activity
### Assessment of information and communication skills

Assess your skills and understanding against this simple structure. Forming the basis of this chapter, they are a mixture of practical skills and technical knowledge, which is what you need for e-learning. If you would like to undertake a more detailed assessment of your ICT skills, you will find a more comprehensive checklist in Appendix B.

| Skills | Competence | | |
|---|---|---|---|
| | Poor | Acceptable | Excellent |
| Adjusting the operating system to meet your personal preferences and needs | | | |
| Filing systems | | | |
| File formats | | | |
| Applications | | | |
| Computer memory | | | |
| Compressing files | | | |
| Searching the world wide web | | | |
| Judging the quality of online content | | | |
| Presenting information (charts and graphs) | | | |
| Working with numbers | | | |
| CD-RW | | | |
| USB storage | | | |
| Digital images | | | |
| e-Portfolio | | | |
| Recording and editing sound | | | |
| Accessing audio/visual materials | | | |
| Wikis | | | |
| Blogging | | | |
| Copyright | | | |

### Discussion
A wide range of ICT courses and books are available to you to help develop your skills and knowledge. Your college and employer may offer opportunities to improve your ICT skills.

## ⬭ Accessibility options

Windows® operating system provides users with a range of options to help make the system more accessible. These include:

- changing the contrast of the display to making reading easier;
- StickyKeys letting you press one key at a time rather than having to press multiple keys to enact a function;
- FilterKeys allowing you to instruct the system to overlook repeated key presses;
- ToggleKeys instructing the system to play a tone when pressing the capital, number or scroll lock keys;
- SoundSentry telling the system to display a warning when it makes a noise;

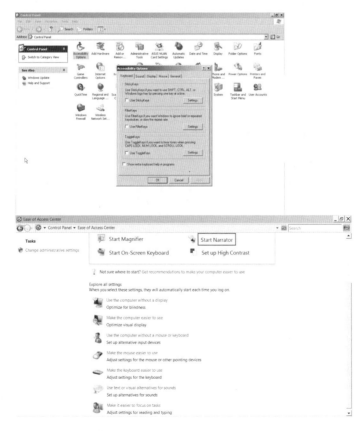

**Figure 3.1**  Accessibility options

- ShowSounds instructing the system to display a message when it uses speech or sounds;
- controlling the cursor blink rates and width so that the pointer is more visible;
- controlling the mouse pointer with the keyboard number pad for users who find controlling a mouse difficult.

These features can be accessed by selecting the Control Panel Option in the Start menu. This will open the Control Panel window in which you can see the Accessibility options icon or file name. If you click the Accessibility option then a window opens, providing you with access to the range of choices. Figure 3.1 shows the options in Windows XP® and also in Windows Vista®. Different operating systems will provide different presentations of the various options. You will need to explore them. In this chapter we have focused on Windows XP® but you should be able to locate similar functions in the operating system that you are using.

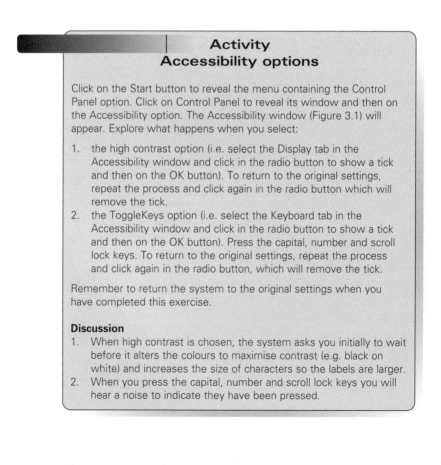

### Activity
### Accessibility options

Click on the Start button to reveal the menu containing the Control Panel option. Click on Control Panel to reveal its window and then on the Accessibility option. The Accessibility window (Figure 3.1) will appear. Explore what happens when you select:

1. the high contrast option (i.e. select the Display tab in the Accessibility window and click in the radio button to show a tick and then on the OK button). To return to the original settings, repeat the process and click again in the radio button which will remove the tick.
2. the ToggleKeys option (i.e. select the Keyboard tab in the Accessibility window and click in the radio button to show a tick and then on the OK button). Press the capital, number and scroll lock keys. To return to the original settings, repeat the process and click again in the radio button, which will remove the tick.

Remember to return the system to the original settings when you have completed this exercise.

**Discussion**
1. When high contrast is chosen, the system asks you initially to wait before it alters the colours to maximise contrast (e.g. black on white) and increases the size of characters so the labels are larger.
2. When you press the capital, number and scroll lock keys you will hear a noise to indicate they have been pressed.

## Mouse

One useful accessibility option is to make the mouse suitable for a left-handed person. If you click on the Start button and select the Control Panel option, it will reveal the Control Panel window. If you select the mouse icon, it will open the Mouse Properties window. Under the button tab is the radio button to switch the mouse buttons around, making it suitable for a left-handed user.

The Mouse Properties window also provides options for you to adjust:

- the double-clicking speed;
- the pointer;
- the mouse wheel.

## File management

Computers provide the means of storing vast amounts of information. The world wide web adds to this ability by offering enormous volumes of data that you can save electronically. You should not have any problem with a shortage of information. Often the dilemma is that you have too much. Information is not useful unless you can quickly locate it, so it is important to have an efficient and effective filing system that is, one which is:

- meaningful – the names of files and folders should be easy to recognise so that information can be located in a straightforward way;
- clearly structured – simple, consistent and clear. Too many files and folders can make location more difficult.

It is also important to back up your information so that it is safe should you have a problem with the computer. There are various ways of storing your information. Most computers now offer a CD or DVD burner (i.e. you can make your own disks). Alternatively, external hard drives are cheap and simple to use (you plug them into your computer). These options enable you to make a copy of your files.

To create a filing system in Windows® operating system, you need to employ Windows Explorer®. This can be opened by selecting the Start button, highlighting the Programs option to reveal the list of applications and then highlighting the Accessories item to show a sub-menu that includes Windows Explorer®. The location of applications does depend on the operating system and how the system is configured so this may be different on your computer. Click on Windows Explorer© and the application will open (Figure 3.2). Figure 3.2 shows my own folders. The display is divided into two areas. The left shows a list of folders while the right shows the detailed contents of the selected folder (My Documents – highlighted on the left). A plus sign indicates that the folder contains other folders.

When you use a computer regularly you will rapidly produce a large number of folders, so it is important to understand how to use the Explorer® functions to maintain your files and folders. The main functions are:

- creating a new folder;
- deleting a file or folder;
- renaming a file or folder;
- cutting, copying and pasting (copying or moving files and folders);
- dragging and dropping (moving files and folders – an alternative to copying and pasting).

Figures 3.3 and 3.4 show the main maintenance functions available in the File and Edit menus.

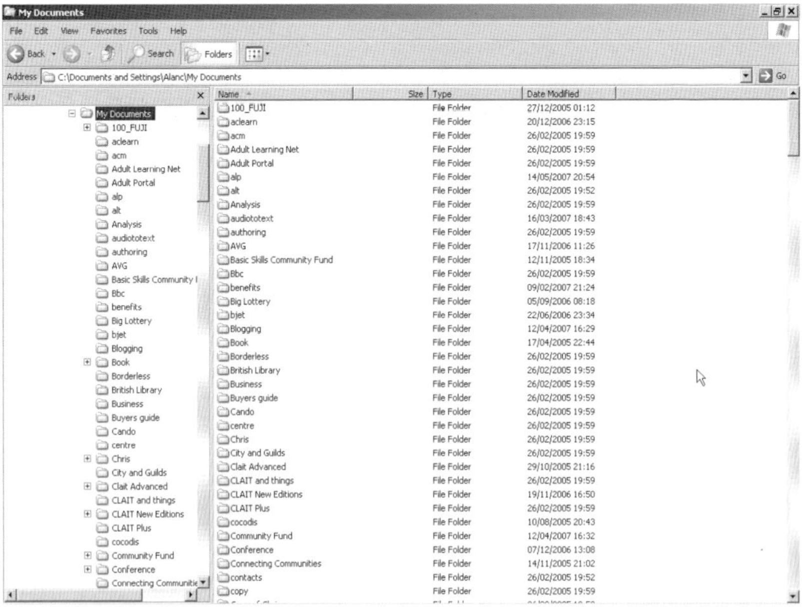

**Figure 3.2** Windows Explorer®

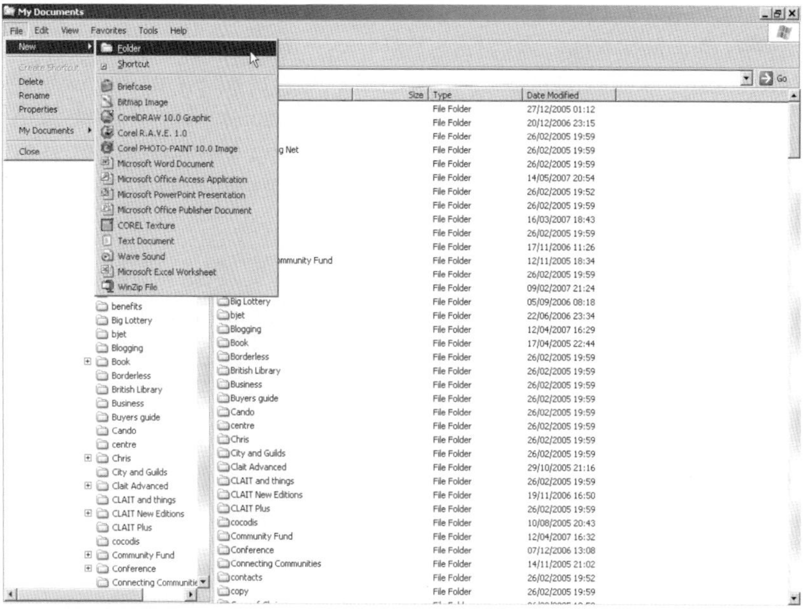

**Figure 3.3**   Maintenance functions – file menu

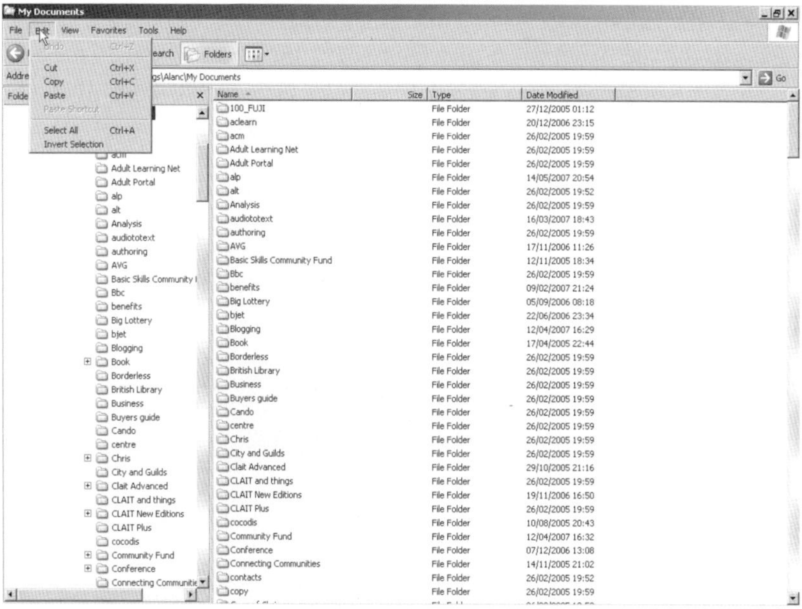

**Figure 3.4**   Maintenance functions – edit menu

## Creating a new folder

To create a new folder, select the File menu, highlight the New option to reveal a sub-menu and click on the Folder option (Figure 3.3). A new folder will appear in the right-hand area of the Explorer application with the name New Folder highlighted. You need to enter a name for the folder from the keyboard. If you want to create a folder within an existing folder then initially you highlight the existing folder by clicking on it.

## Deleting a file or folder

Highlight the folder or file and then select the File menu and click on the Delete option. A message will appear which asks you to confirm that you want to remove the folder you have deleted. This ensures that you avoid errors.

## Renaming a file or folder

Highlight the folder or file and then select the File menu and click on the Rename option. The folder or file's existing name will be highlighted and you can enter a new name.

## Cutting, copying and pasting

Highlight the folder or file and then select the Edit menu and click on the Copy or Cut options. Move your cursor to the folder where you want to copy or move the file or folder to and then select the Paste option in the Edit menu. The Cut option moves the file or folder permanently while the copy leaves the original file or folder in place.

## Dragging and dropping

Highlight the folder or file. By holding down the left mouse button you can drag the file or folder to a new position. If you place a dragged file or folder over an existing folder you can insert it into the folder. This is an alternative to cutting and pasting.

## Activity
## File management

Consider e-learning skills – what folders and structure would you need to cover this subject? Use Windows Explorer® to develop a filing system that is meaningful and clear.

**Discussion**

It is likely that this filing system will only be part of an overall system so a master folder called Electronic Learning Skills is appropriate.

Within this folder a range of sub-folders can be created to cover such issues as:

1.  traditional skills;
2.  computer skills;
3.  communication skills;
4.  group and co-operative learning;
5.  Other resources.

My effort is shown in Figure 3.5.

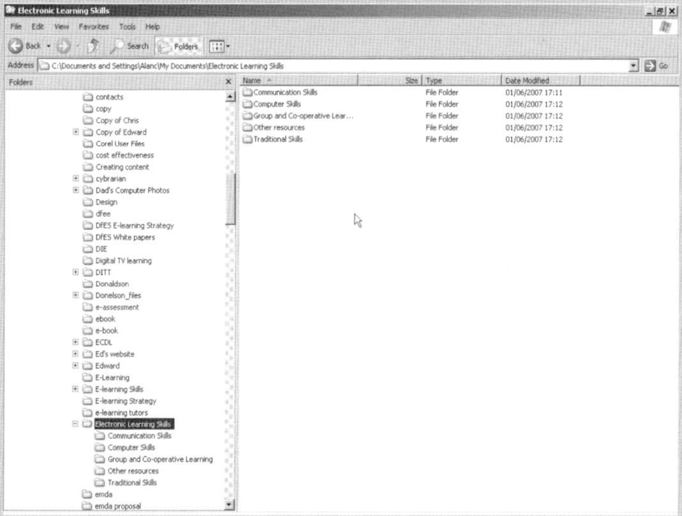

**Figure 3.5**    File structure

## File formats

All computer information is provided in the form of files – that is, a collection of similar information (e.g. text, pictures, etc.). It is important that you are able to distinguish between different files since this will allow you to select what is suitable for particular applications and uses. In Windows® operating system, files are given extensions (e.g. word.doc, spreadsheet.xls, etc.) to their names depending on the type of data they contain. This lets you locate them quickly. In addition, an icon is added to assist with identification (see Figure 3.6).

Windows® operating system lets you change the layout and display of files. One of the most useful options is Details which provides you with information about the nature of the file. Within Windows Explorer®, select the Views menu and click on the Details option. Figure 3.7 shows the options.

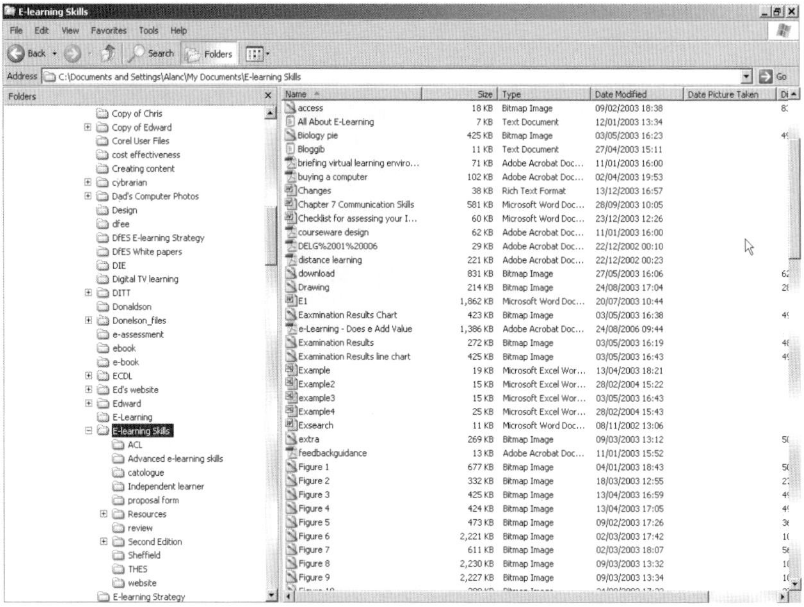

**Figure 3.6**  Example – file formats extensions and icons

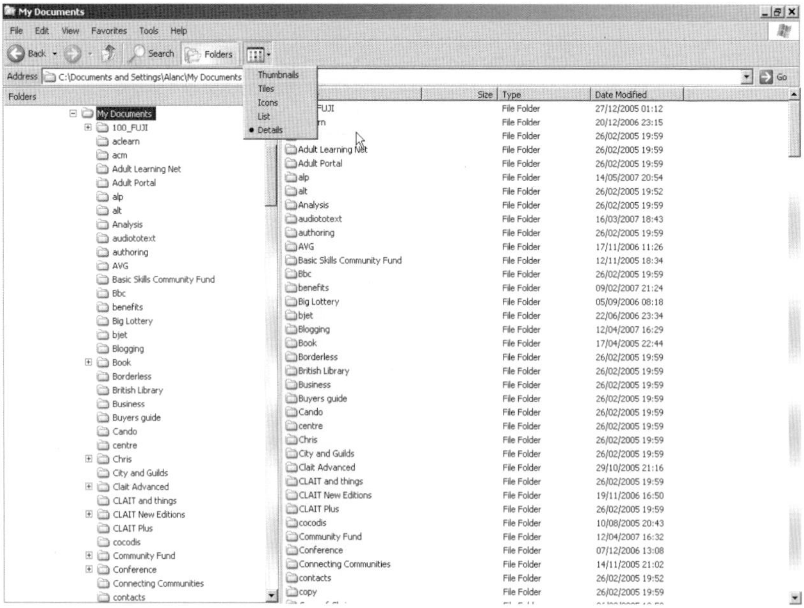

**Figure 3.7**  Details option

Figures 3.6 and 3.7 show the Detail display. It offers you information on:

- the name of the file;
- the size of the file;
- the type of the file;
- the date the file was last modified.

This is important information to help you identify and use the files.

**Adobe Acrobat**

Adobe Acrobat is a document file format that is widely used on the internet for disseminating publications. The file can be identified by its extension .pdf – portable document format. In order to read these files you need to use the Adobe Reader application which is a free application widely distributed on world wide websites. You can obtain a copy from www.adobe.com. If you need to create Adobe Acrobat files you must purchase the full system.

● **Applications**

Buying an application does not give you complete rights to use the product in any way you like. When you install an application you are agreeing to the seller's conditions which are often referred to as the licence. This limits your use of the application. One of the key conditions is a restriction on the number of copies of the software that you can install, often limited to a single computer. Each licence is different so it is important for you to read them. They are included in the packaging or displayed during the installation process on the computer. You are infringing the copyright of the application owner if you break the licence conditions.

As well as commercial software products, there are other types of products:

- Shareware products allow you to evaluate them before you purchase them. They are sometimes limited in their functionality but once you agree to buy the application you are supplied with a full version and sometimes a manual. Their use is controlled by a licence.
- Freeware or open source applications are free and frequently do not limit your use of them. The only small condition is often that you acknowledge their source. Normally no formal support is available.

Some developers offer people the opportunity to use their work under a Creative Commons licence (http://creativecommons.org/) which frequently allows a high degree of user freedom but you must read the specific licence. Before you use or buy any product it is important to check the following:

- What conditions govern its use? Read the licence and ask the seller or supplier for information.
- What system requirements does the product need (e.g. type of processor, random access memory and storage)? Many suppliers will provide this in two forms:
  - the minimum requirements to operate the applications (e.g. it may run slowly);
  - the recommended requirements (e.g. the optimum to run the application).

Many e-learning providers offer advice on what hardware and software you will need to undertake their courses.

There are a variety of open source and free applications available. These are alternatives to commercial products and often can be downloaded from the world wide web. Some free and open source applications are (website addresses are given in Chapter 10):

- Openoffice;
- Google Calendar;
- Google Docs and spreadsheets;
- Google Mail;
- Picasa – a picture organisation application;
- Gantt Project – an application to manage project;
- Firefox – a web browser;
- GIMP – an image manipulation application;
- Google pack – a selection of free applications.

More open source applications are becoming available so a search on the world wide web is likely to locate what you need.

### Compressing files

Sending or moving a file between computer systems appears to be a straight-forward task and in many cases it is. However, if the file is large it will take a lot of time to send over the internet and then it can be more difficult. Some e-mail systems limit the size of attachments and large files are not accepted. If you send e-mails with a large attachment to people in their own homes it may take them a long time to download it, effectively blocking their e-mail system and this will not make you popular with them.

To overcome the problem, compress your file (i.e. squeeze it down into a smaller size). The process of compressing files is now often called zipping. One of the best known of several products is WinZip, a tool to compress files for Windows® operating system. Currently, you can download an evaluation version of WinZip from their website at www.zinwip.com/ to assess whether it is suitable for you. There are also a variety of compression tools available on the world wide web that can be downloaded, some of which are open source or public domain products.

Image files are often very large and computer users are frequently surprised by the size of a single picture. A bitmapped file can occupy many megabytes of space. A file compression application and some paint or image-editing applications offer ways substantially to reduce image files. Another way is to change the image file format using an image application but this will sometimes reduce the quality.

## Saving and backing up your information

A common problem that almost every computer user has experienced is that of losing work but this does not have to happen. You need to develop your own good procedures to safeguard your work. The first basic step is to: save your work regularly (i.e. every few minutes, so that if the computer has a problem you only lose a few minutes' work). Many applications can be set so that they will automatically save your work.

*Example:*
Microsoft Word lets you set the automatic save for a period of your own choice by selecting the Tools menu and clicking on the Options item to reveal the Options window. Within the Save tab are the options.

Saving your work will give you protection against temporary computer problems like a power failure but will not entirely protect you if there is a major problem such as a virus infection or permanent system failure. It is good practice to copy your entire set of files to a medium that you can move to another computer should your own computer fail.

There are several ways of saving or backing up all your files. These include copying files to:

- a CD-RW disc;
- a USB memory stick;
- a DVD-RAM disc;
- an external hard drive.

Select the one that suits you best; but the key is to establish a system for regularly backing up your information. If you have a disaster, you will lose the information from when you last made a back-up to the point of the problem. Thus a weekly back-up means that you are risking a week's worth of information. A daily back-up risks, at most a day's worth. You need to decide what you are prepared to lose.

## Transferring files

You will often need to transfer files between systems. This raises the issue of viruses. Many college and training organisation computers have restrictions on transferring files to them because of the risk of infection. You should always check the files with your virus protection software before transferring

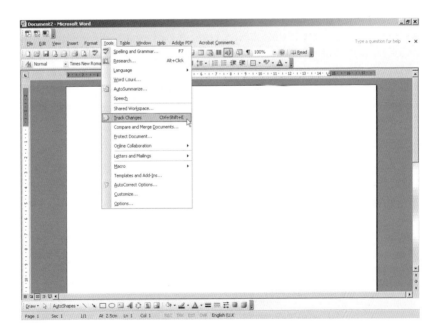

**Figure 3.8**  Track changes

them. It is possible to set up your protection system to check both incoming and outgoing files attached to e-mails and regularly to check your whole system and those files stored on external drives and USB memory sticks. This is essential to prevent virus infection.

## Tracking changes

Group work is often a part of e-learning so that frequently you may be working on a document with other learners. To help you with this process Microsoft Word has a function within the Tools menu called Track Changes (Figure 3.8). This highlights the changes that a writer makes to the document so that partners can see what has been added. If the changes are accepted then you can add them to the document either one at a time or all at once.

## Searching and quality

The world wide web is an enormous information resource covering almost every subject that you are likely to be interested in. However, finding the information you require in the millions of websites that make up the web can be difficult. You have to be able to decide if the web's content is accurate, reliable and suitable for your purpose.

You need to develop two separate sets of skills:

1.   searching for information;
2.   judging the quality of information.

To help you locate information on the world wide web there are search engines, which are essentially large databases of webpages that have been created by the engine. The search engine indexes the webpages based on the words they contain. To find information you ask the engine to search the database for pages containing the keywords you have entered. The database rather than the web is searched so it is very quick.

### Types of search engine

There are a wide variety of search engines. All of them will locate information for you but the way they operate does vary. There are three different types:

- individual;
- meta;
- directory.

An individual search engine is essentially that which we have described above, while a meta engine does not develop its own database but searches the databases of several individual search engines. Both these types of engine will often provide a directory of websites linked to particular subjects (e.g. shopping, property, computers, health, etc.), normally based on the most popular types of searches made. A directory of websites is compiled and edited by the staff of the search engine and so will sometimes save you time searching since they have listed the main sites. Some search engines are specialist directory services (e.g. Yahoo).

Search engines enable you to search for a variety of resources including:

- webpages;
- images;
- discussion groups;
- news;
- individual and business e-mail addresses (i.e. White Pages and Yellow Pages, respectively);
- blogs.

There are many different search engines. Some of the larger ones are listed below:

| | |
|---|---|
| AllThe Web.com | www.alltheweb.com |
| AltaVista | http://altavista.com/ |
| | http://uk.altavista.com/ |
| Excite | www.excite.com/ |
| Google | www.google.co.uk |
| HotBot | www.hotbot.com/ |
| Looksmart | www.looksmart.com/ |
| Lycos | www.lycos.co.uk/ |
| Metacrawler | www.metacrawler.com |
| MSN Search | www.msn.com |
| Northern Lights | www.nlsearch.com/ |
| Webcrawler | www.webcrawler.com/ |
| Yahoo | www.yahoo.co.uk |

Most people find it easy to search the web but difficult to locate exactly what they are seeking. Almost all search engines will provide help to users. You should always investigate the different options since they can save you time and effort. Search engines will locate information in different ways, so you will achieve different results if you use several engines.

*Example – comparing different search engines*
Locate webpages about climate warming using the Google, Webcrawler, Metacrawler and Yahoo search engines.

Enter Climate Warming as key words into the engines:

- Google – located 97,800,000 pages;
- Webcrawler – located 112 pages;
- Metacrawler – located 87 pages;
- Yahoo – located 24,000,000 pages.

The world wide web is very volatile and dynamic so it is likely that if you repeat this search you will get different detail results but the overall emphasis should be similar. Explore the engines and discover why they produce different results (e.g. Metacrawler searches the top results from a range of other search engines, so providing a way of identifying the main links).

## Activity
## Comparing search engines

Explore a range of search engines in order to compare what services they offer.

**Discussion**
My own experience is likely to be different from your own since the world wide web is dynamic and in a state of continuous change. I considered Google and MSN.
Both the search engines are sophisticated tools and I will only describe some features to illustrate their services.

*Google*
This search engine offers a number of different ways of searching including:

1. webpages;
2. images;
3. news;
4. maps;
5. products;
6. groups;
7. scholar;
8. more (e.g. blogs and books).

In addition Google provides help with advanced searching techniques, languages and a wide range of specialist services.

> *MSN*
> This search engine allows you to search for:
>
> 1. webpages;
> 2. images;
> 3. news;
> 4. maps.
>
> In addition, MSN also provides access to e-mail accounts (i.e. hotmail)
> and specialist directories.

## Keywords

How you enter your keywords will influence your search. Some search engines will assume you are searching for any of the words your have entered while others will match pages that contain all the words in any order. Some will match the exact phrase. You need to explore the engine to understand how it works. Even small changes in keywords can dramatically change the search results.

Some straightforward tips to improve your searching are:

- Explore – it is often useful just to try some word(s) to see what result you get. This provides useful information to help you concentrate your search.
- Be direct – if you want to find out about rainfall in Lancashire then do not enter rainfall but rather Lancashire rainfall.
- Feedback – sometimes search engines will give you feedback when a search has failed (e.g. that you are too specific). Take notice of the feedback and alter your keywords accordingly.
- Use the plus sign to ensure that all the words you enter are present on the matched pages (e.g. +Lancashire +rainfall). Some search engines automatically match all the words you enter.
- Use inverted commas to match the exact phrase (e.g. 'Lancashire rainfall'). This is very specific and can sometimes result in obtaining very few or no matches.
- Use the minus symbol to eliminate pages containing information you do not need (e.g. +Lancashire +Rainfall –Snow will not match any page with snow).
- You can combine symbols (e.g. 'Lancashire rainfall' – Burnley will match pages with the exact phrase Lancashire rainfall that do not contain the word Burnley which is a town in Lancashire).

## Boolean searching

An alternative to using symbols in keyword searches is to employ Boolean logic. This is essentially the way you search databases. The world wide web is rather like a huge database. There are three Boolean logic operators:

1. OR;
2. AND;
3. NOT.

If you were searching for information about Kings you might search for:

Kings OR Princes

This would match with pages that had at least one of the keywords (i.e. Kings or Princes).
    Alternatively you might use:

Kings AND Princes

This would match with pages that had both keywords. You might use also:

Kings NOT Princes

This would match only with pages that contained the keyword Kings but which did not have the keyword Princes

---

### Activity
### Boolean logic operators

Using a search engine of your choice undertake the following Boolean searches:

1. Kings OR Princes
2. Kings AND Princes
3. Kings NOT Princes

Also combine the Boolean operators with symbols:

4. Kings NOT Princes – Queens

**Discussion**
When the three keyword searches using the logic operators were entered into AltaVista search engine the following results were obtained:

1.  Kings OR Princes – produced 1,723,679 matches;
2.  Kings AND Princes – produced 14,770 matches;
3.  Kings NOT Princes – produced 132,606 matches.

You can also combine Boolean with symbols so that:

4.  Kings NOT Princes – Queens – produced 128,603 matches since it does not match with pages that contain the word Queens.

Your searches will probably have produced different results due to the dynamic nature of the world wide web and your choice of search engine.

## Other tips

Some other tips for searching are:

- Each search engine has its own set of conditions so it is useful to explore the help function to find out how the engine operates.
- Some engines allow you to choose to search only UK sites and thus narrow down the search immediately. This is useful if you want to find specific UK information such as train times.
- Some engines let you search the results of an earlier search. This can be helpful when you are seeking to focus on a particular topic by refining the keywords.

## Favorites

Having invested time in locating a useful site, the next step is to ensure that you can locate it again. Internet Explorer® and other browsers provide a function to save your sites so that you can rapidly visit them again. Figure 3.9 shows the Favorite menu in Internet Explorer® 7.0. While you are visiting the site you want to save, select the Add to Favorites icon to reveal a short menu and select the Add to Favorites option to reveal the Add a Favorite window (see Figure 3.10). You need to give the site an appropriate name. The system will suggest one based on the webpage and you can accept or change this name. You can also group your favourite sites into folders to help you organise them. Having used the world wide web for a few months you will be surprised at the large number of favorites you will have accumulated. It is therefore good practice to organise your favorites into folders and to give them names you will remember. To visit a favorite you simply open the

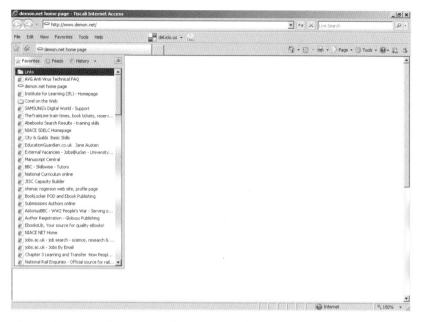

**Figure 3.9** Favorites function in Internet Explorer

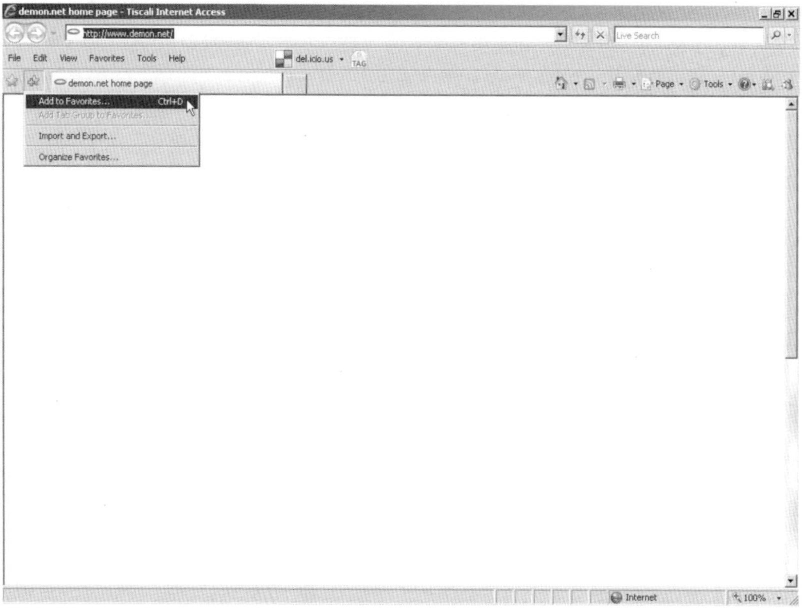

**Figure 3.10** Add Favorites to Internet Explorer

Favorite menu and click on it. The browser will then take you to the webpage.

Good practice with using favorites is to:

- use memorable names so that you can find the site again;
- organise your favorites into folders;
- edit your lists regularly to avoid confusion;
- remember you are saving links to individual pages rather than the site.

If you are using Firefox as your browser you will find that the favorite function is called Bookmark and it operates in a similar way.

## Sharing bookmarks

Del.icio.us (http://del.icio.us/) is a web-based service that allows members to share their bookmarks with each other. It provides a way of keeping a list of favorites or bookmarks online so that you can access it from anywhere. It can be a very useful way of locating interesting and useful websites.

## Judging the quality of websites

Having located a website, you need to be able to assess the quality of the information that it offers you. A search engine will present you with a list of webpages from which you can choose. You need to determine the quality and suitability of the information present on the pages.

Anyone can develop a website and put personal views on the pages. Your first step is to determine the quality of information by considering who produced the content. Is it a personal website – that is, one produced by an individual for presenting his or her interests/opinions? This is often shown by the website address or URL having an individual's name included in it (e.g. /Jbrown/) or being hosted by an internet service provider that specialises in websites. You can determine this by jumping firstly to the home site (e.g. www.homesite.co.uk/staff/sss99/Jbrown/ – reduce this to www.homesite.co.uk). Some major hosting services include:

- www.geocities.com
- www.doteasy.com
- www.freeservers.com

Information that is solely the opinion of one individual is limited in value and can be very misleading. Nevertheless, individual sites can be useful and, in order to judge their value, you need to know something about them. Does the site provide any information about the site author? For example, many academic researchers have individual sites that provide papers and information about their research. Often these sites give biographical information about the author that can give you a valuable insight into the quality of the content of the site.

The address of a website shows you the domain of the website owner (e.g. government, non-profit, commercial, education, etc.). These include:

- gov – government;
- mil – military;
- org – non-profit;
- edu – education;
- ac – academic;
- co or com – commercial company.

Is the domain appropriate for the information presented and is there any vested interest involved (e.g. manufacturers of equipment providing information about their own products)? In some cases this is valuable – when you are seeking the technical specification of a product, for example, the manufacturer's website is an excellent place to look. However, marketing information is often presented on many commercial sites.

There is a great deal on the webpage that you can use to assess quality. Who owns or is responsible for the page? You might find links called 'About' or 'home page'. These should take you to descriptions about the organisation or individual who published the site which will let you make judgements about the content. Some sites will allow you to contact the organisation or individual by using a link called 'Contact', enabling you to e-mail the person responsible for the site.

If you cannot locate a link then you can reduce the URL (website address) by deleting parts of the address as shown earlier (e.g. www.examplesite.co.uk/index/lld34/lord/ – reduce this to www.examplesite.co.uk/). This lets you to return to the home page of the site and should help you determine who the author of the material is. The key is to consider whether the organisation or individual is appropriate for the page contents.

## Activity
## Appropriate sites

Which of these sites is appropriate for the presented information?
How would you judge the quality of the content?

- university site – content about scientific research;
- individual site (John Smith) – opinions about a motor car;
- sports club – data on the team's performance;
- government site – statistical information about the population of the country;
- non-profit site – comments on particular law cases;
- commercial company – the benefits of their products.

**Discussion**
In order to judge the quality of a site it is important to consider who is responsible for it, but on its own this is not sufficient to form an objective judgement.

Although it is important to know the author or organisation controlling the page, you will often need more information to judge quality. Several other factors can help with this, including:

- When was the material updated? Many subjects are very dynamic and rapidly become out of date. Websites often state when the page was last updated.
- Any statistical information needs to be accompanied by an explanation of how it was collected (e.g. nature of sample, methods used and date collected).
- You should expect the same from a webpage author as a conventional author of printed material (e.g. references, justification of conclusions, etc.).
- Material should be supported with references or links to other sites that contain quality information – explore the links.
- Is the same information available on a range of different sites? You can search for the same data on other sites and one positive indication is whether it features in directories (i.e. the editors have chosen it).
- The presentation of information can provide valuable clues to its quality (e.g. spelling and grammatical errors)
- Is the site well designed (e.g. does it provide assistance for using the site – site map, indexes, summaries and a help system)?

## Activity
## Judging quality

Using a search engine of your choice, try to locate information about one or more of the following topics:

1.  First World War;
2.  First computer;
3.  Australia.

Use the checklist below to assess the quality of the information presented in one or more pages.

*Quality checklist*
Who is the author? Is biographical information provided?
Who owns the site (e.g. consider the domain)? Are they appropriate for the information provided?
Is it a personal site? Is it simply an individual's opinion?
What references are incorporated within the information?
What links are provided from the page? Are they good quality pages?
When was the page last updated?
Compare and contrast the different results.

**Discussion**
I located a quality site for information about Australia. It was the National Library of Australia (www.nla.gov.au). The indicators of quality are:

1.  It is a national government site.
2.  The site provides visitors with a detailed explanation of the site.
3.  The pages are reviewed regularly, indicated by statements about when pages were last updated.
4.  The site is governed by a service charter which is explained for users.
5.  Users' privacy is protected by the site and this is explained by a privacy statement.
6.  Feedback is encouraged in several forms including e-mail, telephone, fax and postal address.
7.  The site is linked to many other appropriate sites.
8.  A search engine is provided to locate information.
9.  Help with using the site is provided.

The world wide web is dynamic so if you locate this site it is likely to have changed since my visit.

## Other resources

The internet is increasingly becoming the major way that students are locating information to help their studies. Many universities, colleges and other educational organisations are seeking to assist their learners by providing lists of useful websites. These are quality assured by the teaching staff and are therefore very useful. They are normally available within the organisation's intranet or Virtual Learning Environment but in some cases on the organisation's website, so even if you are not a student of that institution, you can access them.

Many professional bodies also offer similar services to their members. These are often directly related to the interest area of the institution. The Association of Computer Machinery (ACM), for example, offers its members the opportunity to access a digital library of papers relating to the use of computers. Many educational institutions offer access to their library catalogues so that you can identify books and other documents that might be useful. In most cases, however, these are not available in digital form and you would need to visit the library to use them. Some educational libraries allow students of recognised organisations to use their facilities though usually you cannot borrow materials.

In recent years there has been a growth in online journals, sometimes linked to academic bodies and frequently having similar quality assurance procedures to the traditional print-based journals. These are sources of good quality information.

Wikipedia is a source that is used extensively for definitions, background information and other content. It is easy to locate and use. However, it is a source reliant on individuals to edit content, update entries and correct mistakes. There are likely to be some errors and an individual bias that for academic writing might make it unsuitable in some cases. However, it can be a useful starting point. If you visit Wikipedia and read the section About (http://en.wikipedia.org/wiki/Wikipedia:About) then you will gain a clear insight into the content of the encyclopaedia.

In some cases you can locate the e-mail addresses of researchers working in your field to ask for advice. However, the growth of communication technologies has lead to a large increase in the use of e-mail and many researchers receive hundreds of requests for information making it difficult for help to be provided. If you need help from researchers, e-mail them with a short, modest, polite request explaining what you are seeking but you should have first explored the topic extensively to ensure that you cannot answer your question in any other way. A simple request is more likely to get a reply than a complex one. Some researchers have established websites to present information about their work and will simply direct you to consider their site so seek it out before you e-mail.

### Presenting information

ICT applications provide a number of useful ways of presenting information. For example:

- Microsoft Word® is a modern word-processor which, in addition to helping you to write and present documents, will assist you in creating tables of information and inserting images within documents.
- Microsoft Excel® is a modern spreadsheet which lets you explore and model numerical data. In addition it will allow you present your numerical information in the form of charts and graphs.
- Digital cameras and scanners enable you to capture images and import them into your documents.

## Tables

Using Microsoft Word®, you can create tables of information. If you select the Table menu, by highlighting the Insert option, a pop up menu will be revealed. Click on the Table option to reveal the Insert Table window (Figure 3.11). This allows you to select the number of rows and columns that your table will contain.

Microsoft Word® also provides numerous other functions to manipulate the table presentation of information, including:

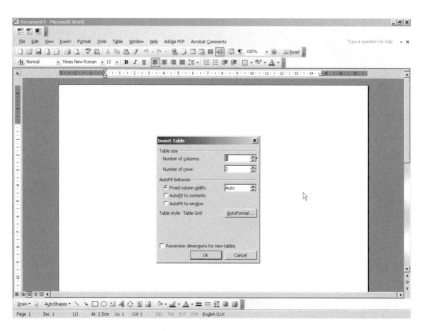

**Figure 3.11**   Inserting tables

- inserting extra rows and columns;
- inserting extra cells;
- deleting rows and columns;
- deleting the whole table;
- fitting content of the table to its size;
- converting text into a table and a table into text;
- changing the thickness of the table lines using the Borders and Shading option within the Format menu;
- selecting table, row, column or cell;
- merging or splitting cells.

## Activity
## Manipulating a table

Use Microsoft Word® to create a table with three columns and ten rows. Using the functions within Word® merge some cells, split some cells, delete two rows and make lines thicker.

**Discussion**

*Merging cells*
Highlight two adjacent cells, select the Table menu and click on Merge Cells. The chosen cells will now be merged into a single cell.

*Splitting cells*
Place your cursor in the chosen cell, select the Table menu and click on the Split Cells. The chosen cell will now be split into two cells.

*Deleting rows*
Select the Table menu, highlight the Delete option and click on the Rows item. The row in which the cursor is placed will be removed.

*Thickening lines*
With the cursor within the table, select the Table menu, highlight the Select option and click on the Table item. The whole table will be highlighted. Now select the Format menu and click on the Borders and Shading option to reveal the Borders and Shading window. Change the width of the line and click on the OK button.

The changes are shown below:

| | | |
|---|---|---|
| | | |
| | | |
| | | |
| | | |
| | | |
| | | |

## Charts and graphs

Using Microsoft Excel®, you can present your numerical information as charts and graphs. Figure 3.12 illustrates a straightforward spreadsheet. Figures 3.13, 3.14, 3.15 and 3.16 illustrate different ways of presenting the data. There are several other ways to present information using Excel®.

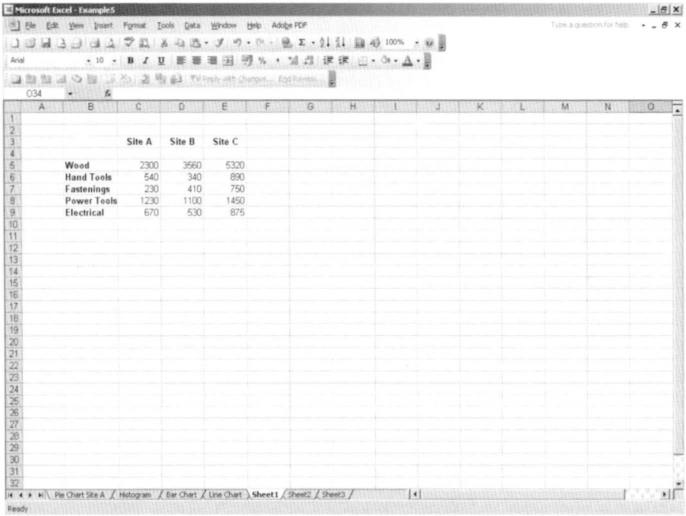

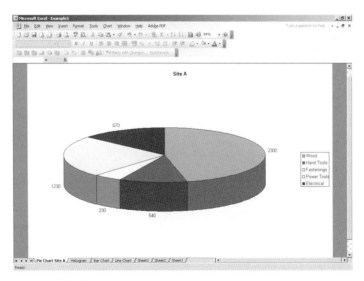

**Figure 3.12**    Spreadsheet

**Figure 3.13**    Pie chart

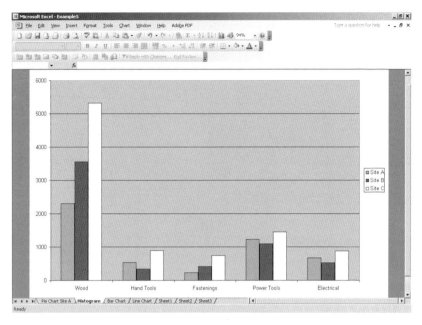

**Figure 3.14**   Histogram

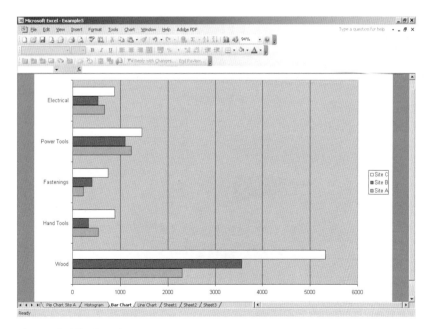

**Figure 3.15**   Bar chart

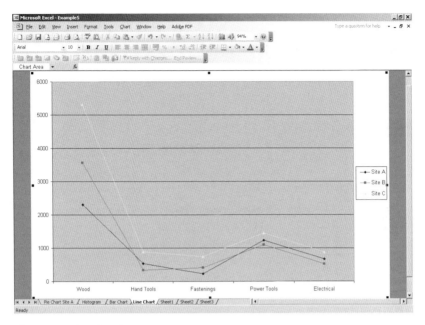

**Figure 3.16**    Line chart

**Figure 3.17**    Chart Wizard

To use the chart features of Microsoft Excel®, input a spreadsheet into Excel. Highlight the parts of the sheet that you want to include in the chart or graph and then select the Insert menu and the Chart option to reveal the Chart Wizard – Step 1 to 4 – Chart Type window (Figure 3.17). You can select the type of chart and then adjust labels, axes and scales.

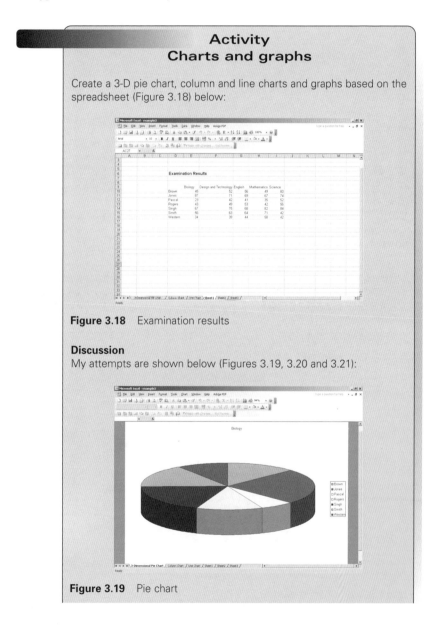

## Activity
## Charts and graphs

Create a 3-D pie chart, column and line charts and graphs based on the spreadsheet (Figure 3.18) below:

**Figure 3.18** Examination results

**Discussion**
My attempts are shown below (Figures 3.19, 3.20 and 3.21):

**Figure 3.19** Pie chart

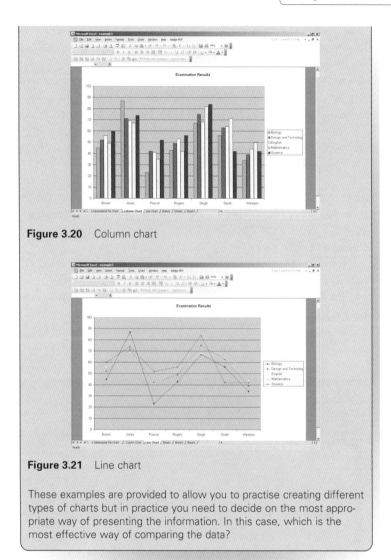

**Figure 3.20**   Column chart

**Figure 3.21**   Line chart

These examples are provided to allow you to practise creating different types of charts but in practice you need to decide on the most appropriate way of presenting the information. In this case, which is the most effective way of comparing the data?

## Digital images

There are a variety of ways to insert images into a document including:

- digital cameras – used to create a digital photograph which can be saved on to the computer and then inserted into your document;
- scanners – used to scan an image into the computer and in some cases into the application directly;

- clip art – these are collections of images supplied with applications or provided separately.

Microsoft Word provides functions to insert images from a camera or scanners as well as clip art and other pictures stored in a folder. You can also create a chart or insert one created in Excel®. The functions are accessed by selecting the Insert menu then highlighting the Picture option to reveal a sub-menu (Figure 3.22) which contains options for inserting pictures stored in a folder, clip art and from a camera or scanner.

If you select the Clip Art option then the Insert Clip Art window will appear to allow you to select an image. In some cases you will see a message asking you to install the clip art option. This requires the use of the Microsoft Office CD-ROMs which will provide a step-by-step explanation of what you need to do.

If you select the From Scanner or Camera option then the Insert Picture from Scanner or Camera window appears to allow you to identify the device you will be using and to decide if you want the image suitable for printing or website.

An alternative to importing an image into Word® is to employ Windows Paint® with which you scan or import pictures from a digital camera. It allows you to crop the image using the Paint functions.

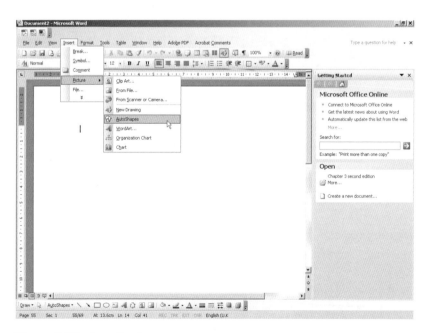

**Figure 3.22**   Inserting images

## Activity
## Picture

Using a scanner or digital camera, import a picture into a document using either Microsoft Word® or Windows Paint® applications.

**Discussion**
The image below (Figure 3.23) was imported into the document.

**Figure 3.23**   Imported digital image

## Creating an image

You can create images yourself using a variety of tools, but Windows® operating system includes an application called Paint within the Accessories (see Figure 3.24).

## e-Portfolio

Many of the technical skills that you need to develop an e-portfolio are also required for other activities. There is an emphasis within a portfolio on the presentation of evidence in a variety of media. An online portfolio provides the opportunity to link to evidence on websites such as blog entries, conference discussions, podcasts and wikis. It is therefore important to understand the nature of hyperlinks and also to have the practical skills to establish them.

e-Portfolios are also about presenting evidence in a way that assessors,

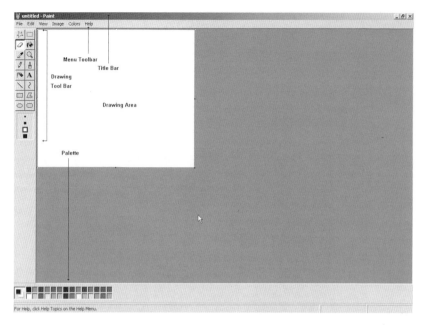

**Figure 3.24**   Windows Paint®

peers and tutors can easily locate what they seek. One rule of thumb is never to have data more than three clicks away (i.e. keep your folder structure to a maximum of three layers deep). It is important to provide a straightforward folder and file structure using meaningful names that your visitors can understand. For example, a series of files named XJ1 to XJ3 is meaningless except to suggest they are related. It would be better to name them to indicate their content – Presentationslides1 to Presentationslides3. It can be quite difficult to describe content only using the file name but many portfolio systems allow you to add notes and you should use them to explain your evidence and why it is appropriate.

e-Portfolio content offers you the opportunity to present proof of your abilities, competences and experience so there is an emphasis on using a range of applications such as audio and picture editors to capture and display your evidence.

Many students invest enormous amounts of effort in developing evidence but fail to present it to its maximum potential. If you offer your assessors the equivalent of a pile of files to sort through then you can only blame yourself if they miss items or fail to understand the significance of some of the evidence. It is important to invest time in providing:

- an overview of the content (i.e. the equivalent of a contents page);
- an explanation of why you have selected the particular items;
- a clear structure with meaningful names;
- the evidence required for the assessment (you will often be given detailed guidance on what to demonstrate).

The skills required for successfully using a portfolio will include:

- creating hyperlinks;
- file and folder management;
- effective use of word-processing, spreadsheets and databases;
- effective use of presentation applications (e.g. PowerPoint® presentation graphics program);
- effective use of multimedia equipment (e.g. digital cameras and sound recorders) and editing applications;
- effective use of graphics application.

## Podcasting

Podcasts provide you with online audio and video learning materials and are available on educational and other websites. You can locate them by searching the world wide web. Once you have found a suitable source of podcasts, you can be kept informed about new materials through RSS (Real Simple Syndication) feeds.

An RSS feed is a technological means of subscribing to content produced by a website so that you don't have to visit the site to view it. The content is sent to you. If you employ an aggregator you can take feeds from a range of sites that you are interested in, which can save you considerable time.

You need to subscribe to an RSS feed on your chosen sites so that you will receive notification of a new podcast being available. Additionally, podcasts are also available simply as downloads from some websites. You can listen to podcasts on an MP3 player or your desktop computer or laptop. You therefore have the choice of where and when you study them.

The first step in using an aggregator is to download a newsreader, which will involve you in registering with the site. The site will often have feeds from scores or even hundreds of locations from which you can choose. However, you can often add your own choices. When you are visiting sites you need to identify if they offer a feed. This is frequently shown with the symbol RSS. There are many variations so you will need to explore and try out the different approaches. Aggregators are offered in a variety of ways such as websites (i.e.

**Figure 3.25**    RSS feeds

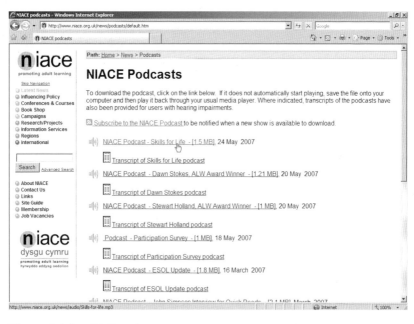

**Figure 3.26**    NIACE podcasts

you visit the site to gain access to the newsfeeds), a software application that is installed on your computer or plug-ins that work with your browser or e-mail system. The key to using software aggregators is to add the website address or URL to the list of podcast sites. It is then able to access the feed.

Internet Explorer® 7.0 allows you to subscribe to RSS feeds through its built-in functions. If you select the Favorites Centre icon, a window will open offering you access to a list of feeds. To add a new feed, visit the site and select the RSS feedback by choosing the subscription options. Figure 3.25 illustrates a list of feeds in Internet Explorer® 7.0 while Figure 3.26 shows a podcast webpage with subscription option.

### Creating a podcast

You may well be asked to create a podcast as part of an individual or group assignment. It may serve as a means of reflecting on an experience such as a field trip.

1. Basic equipment
   In order to create a podcast you will need some basic computer equipment to edit and process the audio files. A computer that is able to use the Microsoft Windows XP® or Vista® operating system is adequate for the task. In addition to the computer you must have:

   - 512kb or more of random access memory (RAM);
   - 5 gigabytes or more of free storage space;
   - a sound card with connections for a microphone and headphones (i.e. sound in and out);
   - broadband connection to the internet;
   - microphone;
   - headphones;
   - MP3 player.

2. Software/applications
   In addition to the hardware you will need an audio application such as Audacity that will allow you to record and edit sound. This can be downloaded from the world wide web (http://audacity.sourceforge. net/) and is an open source application. The Audacity site also provides tutorials to help you use the application.

   Most podcasts are provided in MP3 format so that they can be played as people move around. It is therefore important to convert your audio files into MP3 format. LAME is an application that is compatible with Audacity and will convert audio files into MP3 format. It can be downloaded from the world wide web (http://lame.sourceforge.net/index.php).

It is probably sensible to install Audacity and LAME into the same folder since when you first want to convert an audio file into MP3, the Audacity software will require you to identify where LAME is installed.

3.  Creating a podcast

    It is natural to focus on making sure you have the hardware and software to produce a podcast. However, it is vital to consider what you are going to say and how you are going to present the information. Only a small number of people are able to speak naturally and coherently on a topic for more than a few minutes without a pause or hesitation. When you record, even a tiny hesitation can adversely affect the quality of your podcast. For most people it is vital to have a script and to have practised the delivery before recording.

    Most listeners will have a limited attention span, meaning that a long continuous podcast is unlikely to be welcomed. It is perhaps best to present the information as a series of short pieces with pauses between them to allow the listener the option of stopping and listening later. It is difficult to judge the length of each section but probably no more than three or four minutes.

    A podcast of a single voice will not exploit the media to its full potential so consider using more than one or introducing music at the start and finish or as background. If your podcast has several sections, then start with a short overview of the contents and structure of the presentation (e.g. there are four sections covering . . .). At the end, provide a short summary to remind the listener of the contents.

    To summarise:

    1.  Prepare a script.
    2.  Practise the delivery.
    3.  Break up the presentation into a series of chunks (i.e. three or four minutes maximum) focusing on one topic at a time.
    4.  Start the podcast with an overview and explanation of the structure.
    5.  Finish with a short summary (i.e. one minute).
    6.  Use music at the start and finish to provide a professional presentation

4.  Checking your podcast

    Once you have recorded your podcast, it is important to check it. It is far better to identify your own error than to wait until it is available to the world to discover a mistake.

5.  Uploading

    After you have created your audio podcast, you need to upload it to a website. If you are completing the podcast as part of your course then this is likely to be linked to your college and they will provide you with guidance on how to upload. However, there are several websites that will allow you to store your podcasts and make them available to subscribers (e.g. www.switchpod.com/).

## Blogging

A blog (short for weblog) is a website in which entries are presented in date order (i.e. latest first). There are two main ways that blogs can form part of your course. You can be asked to create a blog and that could well be in the form of a learning diary in which you reflect on activities and tasks that you have undertaken (e.g. your views on reading a research paper). Blogs can be private, in that only designated individuals (e.g. your peers on the course) can access them, or they can be open to the public. Often you can add comments to a person's blog so that you can give and receive feedback on your reflections. The second main use is as a source of information, since many public blogs offer information across a wide spectrum of academic subjects. Search engines (e.g. Google) frequently provide facilities to search for blogs as well as access to blog applications. Figure 3.27 shows Blogger. This allows you to create your own blog and is available through Google.

**Figure 3.27**   Blogger

Your college or educational provider will almost certainly provide you with a blog if one is required and in general they are straightforward to use. You can add text, digital images and links to other websites. The main features of a blog are:

- dated entries and comments;
- archives of past entries and comments;
- links.

Many public blogs allow you to subscribe to them through an RSS feed in the same way as podcasts so you can keep up to date with a range that you find useful.

### Copyright

It is important to realise that information published on the world wide web is covered by copyright in the same way as traditional forms of publications. It is therefore critical to check the conditions placed on the online content, usually available on the home page. You will sometimes need to look at the bottom of the page where in small text you will see statements about copyright terms and conditions. In other cases, sites will clearly indicate if you can copy the material.

In all cases you must assume that the material is copyrighted. This does not mean that in all circumstances you cannot copy the material. You can do so under the Fair Dealings Provision which allows individuals to copy content for personal research, study, criticism and review. However, you must only copy those parts which are essential for the purpose and you must acknowledge the source and copyright holder. This does not apply to music, video and sheet music.

Many colleges, training centres and other educational institutions provide their students with guidance about copyright and you should seek the advice of your tutor and institution.

### Plagiarism

The world wide web provides you with access to a huge resource of information. It is very easy to copy this work. However, to represent as your own work the efforts of other people (plagiarism) is a serious offence which, if discovered, may lead to you failing your course. Many colleges will be able to provide you with guidance on how to quote the work of writers without plagiarising them. It is a part of academic writing to quote from the work of other people but it is essential to identify it clearly by enclosing it in quotation marks, identifying the source in the text (e.g. Clarke, 2001a) or by some other acceptable means. Your college will provide specific guidance.

There now exist a number of electronic methods to identify plagiarism so be aware that it has never been easier to detect cheating.

## Utilities

Often when you are accessing online resources you will need utility programmes called plug-ins which extend the capabilities of the browser, allowing you to hear audio files, see videos, experience animation, etc. Plug-ins are normally freely available and when you access a resource that requires one, they will offer you the opportunity to download the utility. Some examples of plug-ins are:

- Apple QuickTime;
- RealPlayer;
- Macromedia Flash.

Some employer and college networks will not allow you to download files in order to prevent virus infection. However, if they are providing e-learning opportunities then they will also provide all the plug-ins and utilities you need.

## Summary

### 1.   Assessing your skills
You need a range of information and communication technology skills in order to be an effective e-learner. It is important to assess the level and range of your skills and to develop a personal programme continuously to improve them.

### 2.   Accessibility options
Within the Windows® operating system is a range of options to help you make the system more accessible. These include changing the contrast of the display, removing the need to

press multiple keys, allowing you to make errors with key presses, adding sound effects, displaying messages when the system uses sound, making the mouse suitable for left-handed users and using the keyboard as an alternative to the mouse.

### 3.  File management
It is important to establish an efficient and effective filing system. The key is to make file and folder names meaningful and to create a clear structure.

Windows® operating system provides many functions within Windows Explorer®. These include:

- creating a new folder;
- deleting a file or folder;
- renaming a file or folder;
- cutting, copying and pasting files and folders;
- dragging and dropping files and folders.

### 4.  File formats
Computer information is stored as a file. Files are given extensions (e.g. word.doc) to their names depending on the type of data they contain and an icon is added to assist with identification.

### 5.  Applications
When you buy an application it is governed by a licence. This controls your use of the application (e.g. limiting the number of copies of the software that you can use simultaneously). It is important to read the licence which is included in the packaging or displayed during the installation process.

In addition to commercial software products, there are:

- shareware products which allow you to test them before purchase;
- freeware applications which are free.

The degree of technical support varies considerably between commercial, shareware and freeware products. Before you buy any product it is important to check the system requirements of the product (e.g. processor).

### 6.    Compressing files

There are several ways of transferring files between computer systems. These include:

- saving the files to a floppy disc;
- sending the file as an e-mail attachment – some e-mail systems limit the size of attachments they will accept;
- saving large files to a CD-RW disc;
- saving large files to a USB memory stick.

There are several ways of reducing the size of files. These include:

- compressing the file using a specialist application (e.g. WinZip);
- changing the format of the picture file; but this may reduce the quality of image files.

It is good and essential practice to virus-check all files that you receive from any source and also those files that you transfer to other systems.

### 7.    Tracking changes

Microsoft Word® provides you with the Track Changes function which lets you see all the changes that have been made to a document. You can then accept or reject each change.

### 8.    Saving and backing up your information

It is essential to:

- save your work regularly (i.e. every few minutes);
- back up all your files regularly;
- assess how often you need to copy all your information to a transferable medium.

### 9.    Searching the world wide web

Two vital skills for using the world wide web are locating information and judging its quality. To help you find information there are specialist sites called search engines. There are three main types:

- individual – searches a database it has created of webpages;

- meta – searches several databases created by other search engines;
- directory – searches a list of sites compiled by the staff of the search engine.

You can search for a variety of resources including:

- webpages;
- images;
- discussion groups;
- news;
- individual e-mail addresses.

*Keywords*: All search engines require you to locate information by entering keywords. Each one operates differently so you need to learn how your chosen one works. Some tips are:

- Explore what happens with different words.
- Be direct.
- Read search engine feedback and act on it.
- Signs will change how your words are matched with webpages (e.g. a plus sign ensures that all the words you enter are present on the matched pages; inverted commas match the exact phrase; the minus symbol eliminates pages containing the information, and you can also combine symbols). However, each search engine will treat symbols in a different way.

*Boolean*: Another way of searching is to use Boolean logic. There are three operators:

- OR (i.e. Napoleon OR Wellington – locate pages with the words Napoleon or Wellington);
- AND (i.e. Napoleon AND Wellington – locate pages with both the words Napoleon and Wellington);
- NOT (i.e. Napoleon NOT Wellington – locate pages with the words Napoleon but not Wellington).

*Favorites*: A browser provides you with the means of recording the addresses of important webpages so that you can easily locate them again. In Internet Explorer you use the Favorites function and in Firefox it is called Bookmarking.

## 10.  Assessing the quality of online information

It is essential to be able to assess the quality of information presented on the world wide web, not least because anyone can develop a site. Some ways of assessing quality include:

- Who produced the site – are they appropriate to the information it displays?
- Does it display personal views?
- Can you contact the site to ask about the content?
- When was the site material last updated?
- Does the site explain how the information was collected (e.g. samples)?
- Is the information shown justified (e.g. references to other published sources)?
- What links to other sites are presented?
- Is the information presented available on a range of other sites?
- How well presented is the information?
- How well designed is the site?

## 11.  Presenting information (i.e. tables, charts and graphs)

You will often need to present information effectively as part of your studies. Computer applications provide various ways of displaying information, for example:

- Microsoft Word® helps you to create and manipulate tables of information;
- Microsoft Excel® allows you to change numerical information into a wide range of forms.

## 12.  Digital images

There are numerous ways of importing images into a document such as:

- digital camera;
- scanners;
- clip art.

You can also create your own images using painting and drawing applications (e.g. Windows Paint®).

### 13. e-Portfolio

An e-portfolio in simple terms is an electronic equivalent of a portfolio of evidence demonstrating your skills, knowledge and experience. It provides you with the opportunity to include a multimedia range of evidence and links to other online sources.

Many of the technical skills that you need to develop an e-portfolio are also required for other activities. The skills required for successfully using a portfolio will include:

- creating hyperlinks;
- file and folder management;
- effective use of word-processing, spreadsheets and databases;
- effective use of presentation applications (e.g. PowerPoin® presentation graphics program);
- effective use of multimedia equipment (e.g. digital cameras and sound recorders) and editing applications;
- effective use of graphics application.

### 14. Podcasting

Podcasts provide you with online audio and video learning materials. They can be downloaded from websites. To enable you to access them without the need to visit each site individually, you can subscribe to RSS feeds.

An RSS feed is a technological means of subscribing to content produced by a website so that you don't have to visit the site to view it. The content is sent to you. If you employ an aggregator you can take feeds from a range of sites that you are interested in. This can save you considerable time.

### 15. Blogging

A blog (short for weblog) is a website in which entries are presented in date order (i.e. latest first). There are two main ways that blogs can form part of your course. You can be asked to create a blog so that you can reflect on your learning or you can simply use public blogs as a source of information. RSS feeds can be used to subscribe to blogs.

### 16. Copyright

All content published on the world wide web is covered by copyright in the same way as a printed document. You must check the conditions for its use before you copy any information. Conditions are often displayed on the home page.

### 17. Plagiarism

It is easy to copy information using a computer but representing the work of others as your own (plagiarism) is a serious offence. You may fail your course if you are discovered plagarising other people's work

### 18. Utilities

Plug-ins are utility programmes that extend the capability of your browser to access audio, video, animation or other resources.

# 4  Learning Environments

e-Learning can take many forms and is often linked to the environment in which the course or programme is based. This chapter will concentrate on developing an understanding of the nature of the e-learning environments and approaches including:

- synchronous learning (e.g. text, audio or video conferencing);
- Managed Learning Environments (Course Management Systems);
- Virtual Learning Environments (Learning Management Systems);
- the world wide web;
- Intranets/Extranets;
- groupware;
- WebQuests;
- blended learning.

It will discuss how these different environments provide support for learners and what they expect from them. It will cover peer support/communication, tutor support/communication, moderation of online communication and assessment. There is also a physical component of e-learning in that you need to access the computer and communication systems. There are several choices of location such as learning centres, cybercafés, mobiles, your home and your workplace, and you may well use more than one.

## Places to learn

### Learning centres

Although not an online environment, a learning centre is often the physical location where you can access the e-learning resources. Many colleges, training facilities and community sites have developed learning or ICT centres to provide individuals with access to computer and communication technology. In colleges they are often in or closely associated with the library while private companies may link them to a collection of learning resources. There can be appreciable differences in size, facilities and environment between different centres. College centres, for example, can be large with hundreds of computers whereas community sites may contain only two or three.

Using a public facility is different from studying in your own room and requires different preparation. A college learning centre may well encourage the establishment of a quiet structured climate in which to study and most will provide you with technical and learning support. In large centres, people's comings and goings can be distracting. If you feel you need a more disciplined environment, then a college centre may be a good choice. You also frequently gain the benefit of a high speed link to the internet.

The limitations are that you probably need to book a terminal and your use will be limited by the centre's policy on how long, for example, you can use the terminal. However, many colleges are now opening centres 24 hours a day for 365 days a year so if you want to study in the middle of the night you can. Although college centres are often free for registered students they will often charge for extra services such as colour printing and photocopying. You may also not be allowed to bring information from home on a floppy disk or CD-ROM (to prevent the transmission of viruses).

## Cybercafés

Many cybercafés have been opened across the world so when away from home or college you can carry on with your studies. Cybercafés and associated public access take a variety of forms. Internet kiosks are often found at airports, railway stations and other public transport sites. Cybercafés are found in many holiday resorts including on some cruise ships. The cost and nature of using this type of service will vary but often the price limits the length of time you can spend online. You may also need to pay extra for printing or downloading information.

## Mobiles

Portable computer equipment (e.g. laptop computers and PDAs) combined with mobile phone or wireless technologies enable you to connect to the internet almost anywhere. The convergence of computer and mobile technology has already provided hand-held devices that can access the internet. Wireless links are now widely available on trains and in hotels, cafés, libraries and a variety of other public spaces. This provides the possibility of learning while you are travelling or away from home or work. For those who travel as part of their work, learning on a train or in an airport is now feasible.

Although portable equipment has become lighter and easier to transport, it still needs to be carried and although portable printers are available, their use is probably limited to hotel rooms rather than on trains. Nevertheless, you require more than access to online resources to learn. You also need an environment that helps you learn. A busy and noisy waiting room or a crowded train is not ideal. Learning as you travel requires self-discipline and an organised approach. Many courses are seeking to exploit these possibilities and m-learning (mobile learning) is now widely discussed and implemented.

## Home

In your own room you have ready access to your materials, books and other resources, whereas when you visit a public resource you need to take everything you will require with you. You are free to employ your personal computer in any way you want but a public/college resource will require you to comply with its conditions. Your freedom is therefore maximised at home but in order to benefit from it you will need self-discipline. Learning normally requires a quiet and distraction-free environment. If you share your home with other students or your family then it is likely that at times it is noisy and full of people.

To be a successful home-based online learner requires that you create a suitable learning environment. The environment is not simply a physical space, although you do need to be organised with your books, papers and other learning tools. It is also about agreeing with the people who share your home that they will help you learn by providing you with the peace and the space to learn in. Family and friends may be important learning supporters who can help when things are difficult.

## Workplace

For many people, a computer linked to the internet is now a normal tool of their employment, making the workplace a suitable place to take part in e-learning. It is a familiar place and you have some freedom to customise the environment to meet your needs. You will probably have access to a fast connection to the internet as well as printers and technical support. However, with many workplaces being open plan, telephones and colleagues are likely to interrupt your studies and it is not easy to achieve privacy, quiet and freedom from interruptions.

Many employers provide learning centres since they feel that the workplace is unsuitable for long periods of studying. However, the concept of learning in small chunks (e.g. 15 to 30 minutes) is well established and this is probably suitable for workplace learning even in a noisy environment. Another alternative is to divert your telephone, put on earphones and put up a sign asking not to be disturbed. This may give you a relatively quiet and distraction-free area to study in.

| Environment | Strengths | Weaknesses |
|---|---|---|
| Learning Centre | 1. Fast broadband connection<br>2. Technical support<br>3. Learning support<br>4. Structured learning environment<br>5. Access to peripherals (e.g. colour printers, scanners, etc.) | 1. Need to book time<br>2. May be visually distracting due to size<br>3. Charge for colour printing and other services<br>4. Restrict or prevent the use of your own disks and data from home |
| Cybercafe | 1. Many locations throughout the world<br>2. Informal and easy to use<br>3. Sometimes will have a fast connection to the internet | 1. Are sometimes expensive<br>2. Restrict or prevent the use of your own disks and data from home<br>3. Charge extra for colour printing and other services |
| Mobile | 1. Learn wherever you want and need to<br>2. Maximise the time you have available<br>3. Keep up to date with administrative and other changes to the course<br>4. Continue to participate in online discussions | 1. Need to own or have access to portable computer, smartphone and mobile phone or similar technology<br>2. Equipment has to be carried<br>3. Limited peripherals available when travelling<br>4. Some limits on access to the internet<br>5. Unstructured and distracting learning environment |
| Home | 1. Freedom to learn in the way you prefer (e.g. during the night)<br>2. Personal learning resources readily available | 1. Limited range of equipment available at home<br>2. Speed of access to the internet may be limited<br>3. Unstructured learning environment<br>4. Potentially noisy and distracting at times |
| Workplace | 1. Fast broadband connection<br>2. Technical support<br>3. Familiar place<br>4. Integrate learning with your work<br>5. Access to printers and other peripherals | 1. Possibly a noisy and distracting environment (e.g. telephones)<br>2. In some cases a stressful environment<br>3. Needs a desk-based job with some freedom<br>4. Need to agree study time with manager and colleagues<br>5. Work always likely to take priority over learning |

**Table 4.1** Comparison of learning environments

Obviously, if you do not work at a desk or have the freedom to ask for uninterrupted time, then the workplace is unsuitable. Managers are familiar with staff being given time off to attend a class but may find it difficult to adjust when you do not leave but are studying and therefore unavailable. It is sensible when you are seeking agreement to undertake an e-learning course to explain to your manager that there will be times when you cannot be disturbed. Try to agree a pattern so that your manager and colleagues know when you are studying. However, even if everything is agreed and you have a supportive manager, you are still likely to be disturbed since in the workplace the work is always likely to be given priority over your studies. Table 4.1 compares and contrasts the five locations we have discusssed for e-learning access.

## Activity
## Learning location

Consider your own needs and approach to learning and which learning environments would be best for you.

**Discussion**
It is likely that all the options will have both attractive features and also negative aspects. None of them is likely to be perfect for everyone. People have their own preferences. Some like complete quiet while others prefer some background music. Some people are able to concentrate in noisy environments and some even find noise an aid to concentration. There is no one ideal place for e-learning for everyone and often learners use several locations such as home, college, on the move and work.

## Synchronous learning (e.g. text, audio or video conferencing)

A great deal of emphasis is placed in e-learning on asynchronous methods (e.g. e-mail) but text, video and audio conferencing are also part of e-learning and they are all synchronous – that is, you need to use them at the same time as the other students and the tutor. The technology for text, audio and video conferencing varies. It can mean interacting with other learners through a large screen with high quality images and sound or through a computer display where a small image of your peers and tutor can be seen. In other cases, you can only see a still image of the students combined with their voices or even simply sound only. Internet telephony (e.g. Skype) is developing rapidly since it offers a low-cost way of making telephone calls and this is being used to support voice-only conferences.

The concept behind text conferencing is simple and perhaps because of this it is probably the most used form of synchronous conferencing. You can send a message which everyone else logged on to the system can see and respond to. However, text-conferencing systems can vary considerably so that what appears on the screen can, to a large extent, be different from application to application. The original systems simply presented the messages one after another in the sequence in which they arrived at the computer. Later in this chapter we will consider threaded discussions in an asynchronous e-mail group. Threads are a way of presenting separate elements of a discussion so that you can more easily follow the flow of the discussion. Synchronous text conferencing can also be presented as threads (i.e. each part of the debate identified). Messages to text conferences are stored, enabling you to trace ideas and discuss them later.

There are several ways of organising conferencing including:

- students being placed together in a classroom with the tutor linked to them through text, video or audio conferencing;
- several groups of students in different locations interacting with a remote tutor;
- individual students at many different locations interacting with a tutor at the educational institute or in some cases a student undertaking the facilitator's or moderator's role.

In some of these scenarios the experience is broadly similar to listening to a lecture and, in fact, video conferencing has frequently been used to provide a lecture from an expert to thousands of people simultaneously. This is highly efficient in that many can see and hear the lecture, but the opportunity to question the speaker is poor. It is similar to listening to a lecture in a large hall and so, in this situation, you need to consider it as a lecture and take notes.

In some cases the lecture will be recorded and you can review the material later on your own or with other learners. It is often more effective to watch video material with others so that you can discuss it, thus gaining a better insight into the content than if simply working on your own.

Let us consider the e-learning skills required when taking part individually with other students in different locations. This is likely to mean that the technology will be via the computer screen, with relatively low quality images but probably reasonable sound. The closest traditional method to this scenario is a tutorial or seminar where you can interact directly with your

| Structure | Text conferencing | Video conferencing | Audio conferencing |
|---|---|---|---|
| Learners are together but separated from the tutor | 1. This is not a common model for text conferencing and you will rarely encounter it | 1. Note-taking is important<br>2. Discuss and organise with your colleagues to gain the maximum benefit<br>3. View the recording later to complete notes or clarify any confusion<br>4. Regard the event as a lecture or seminar | 1. Note-taking is important<br>2. Discuss and organise with your colleagues to gain the maximum benefit<br>3. Opportunity to discuss with peers during the conference away from the communication technology |
| Learners and tutor all at different locations | 1. Text conferencing tends to be more spontaneous than other synchronous methods but it is useful to have identified questions, concerns and ideas in advance<br>2. Record of the discussion is normally stored by the system<br>3. Concentration is less important since all messages appear on the screen and you can catch up if interrupted but it is best practice is to focus on the communications without interruptions. | 1. Prepare your contribution and questions in advance<br>2. Note-taking is important, including recording other learners' comments<br>3. Concentration is critical so ensure you are not interrupted | 1. Prepare your contribution and questions in advance<br>2. Note-taking is important, including recording other learners' comments<br>3. Concentration is critical so ensure you are not interrupted |

**Table 4.2** Text, video and audio conferencing

peers. The difference is that in a face-to-face situation you can easily judge when to make a contribution. It is quite difficult during video conferencing since you are likely to see only one person at a time or if there are many people displayed, then the size is so small that details are unclear. The tutor's role is to ensure that everyone has an opportunity to contribute. This can make the method a little mechanical and slow since you have to wait for your turn to speak. If the conference is not carefully managed by a tutor or a participant, it can be quite chaotic.

Audio conferencing is similar to a telephone conference call, with a group of people seated around a conference telephone. It is possible to have a pure audio conference or audio with still images. The tutor can send you images or documents as part of the system or as e-mail attachments. Internet telephony enables you to meet with everyone at different locations but, as with video conferences, careful organisation and chairing is required.

Synchronous learning is broadly similar to a traditional classroom approach. If you are taking part as a group of students, then both video and audio require you to take notes fully to benefit from the experience. Working together maximises the opportunities for asking questions. With audio conferencing you may be able to confer with the other learners during the conference away from the microphones. Table 4.2 gives an overview of the learning skills and strategies that may be beneficial.

Synchronous text conferencing can be used for a wide range of purposes, such as expert discussion and tutorial. A tutor may publish a paper on a course topic to all the students and invite questions, views and ideas arising from reading it. The messages can be archived to form a type of annotation to the paper. Some institutions employ text conferencing to provide additional student help in that a tutor is available between set times to answer any questions arising from the course. Students can ask their questions and the tutor will answer immediately. Other students can join in if they wish but there is normally no compulsion to take part. This is similar to a tutor being physically available on a Wednesday afternoon in classroom three to provide extra help to anyone who chooses to attend. The text conferencing allows the limitations of a set location to be eliminated.

### Groupware

'Groupware' is the term for applications that allow people linked through a network (e.g. the internet) to share information and work co-operatively and collaboratively. It is possible with groupware to work with others in sharing an application (e.g. a whiteboard) as part of a synchronous group project.

The application-sharing is usually combined with an audio conference or real-time text communication. The group may be seeking, for example, to design a product or investigate a concept. Group working is only suitable for small groups of learners (i.e. four to six) and requires that everyone is a competent user of the shared application and communication system. A successful group activity requires that:

- the objectives of the exercise are agreed and limited;
- a time limit has been agreed (i.e. more time is normally needed online than for a similar face-to-face task);
- a structure has been agreed so that everyone has an equal opportunity to contribute;
- each learner has a role within the team (e.g. note-taker, spokesperson, etc.) although in some cases the initial task is to agree roles for each participant;
- there has been good preparation so that the effectiveness of online time is maximised.

### Managed Learning Environment (MLE) or Course Management System (CMS)

A Managed Learning Environment (MLE) or Course Management System (CMS) is the integration of a variety of software systems that form the overall online administration and learning environment for the institution. There is a variety of commercial MLE products available and many educational organisations have developed their own structures and processes. There is no single definition of all the elements contained within an MLE. However, an MLE is likely to provide:

- an administration system that tracks learners' achievement and maintains records of their progress;
- financial, attendance and registration records;
- course information about all the learning opportunities available;
- learning resources:
  - interactive learning materials;
  - learning resources (e.g. guides, examples and self-assessment tests);
  - links to off-line resources;
- library catalogues and loan system;
- quality assurance systems;

- communication systems;
  - e-mail;
  - conferencing;
  - chat rooms;
  - bulletin boards.
- an assessment system (e.g. records of test results and in some cases the actual online assessments (in many cases testing involves both online and off-line methods);
- support systems (e.g. tutors, mentors and peers);
- advice (e.g. finance, childcare, health and careers);
- information (e.g. health and safety, equal opportunities and policies);
- online courses.

## Virtual Learning Environment (VLE) or Learning Management System (LMS)

A Virtual Learning Environment (VLE) or Learning Management System (LMS) is essentially those elements of the MLE that are intended to support and deliver the online learning (e.g. course information, learning resources, communication systems, e-portfolio and online courses). The systems can be called by either name or neither. In some cases a VLE stands alone. There is no universal definition of what a VLE contains, so each institution may offer a different environment. Some have developed their own system and called themselves Virtual College or other locally derived name. Figure 4.1 shows a simple example of the home page of a Virtual Learning Environment. The list of links down the left-hand side of the page shows a range of facilities and functions that you might expect to find in an MLE/VLE. Figure 4.2 shows an online library with a search facility to help you locate books or other resources to help your studies. Often a list of popular facilities is included to provide rapid access to them. News items are sometimes displayed in various parts of the environment to draw your attention to new developments.

Many institutions provide similar facilities and functions to those co-ordinated and managed within an MLE/VLE. In some cases these are signposted within the institution's website or intranet. Figure 4.3 shows a webpage from the Quality Improvement Agency's Excellence Gateway website, showing the community's forums that allow discussion of learning and teaching issues.

For many institutions the introduction of an MLE/VLE requires significant organisational change because it represents a major difference in the way the organisation operates.

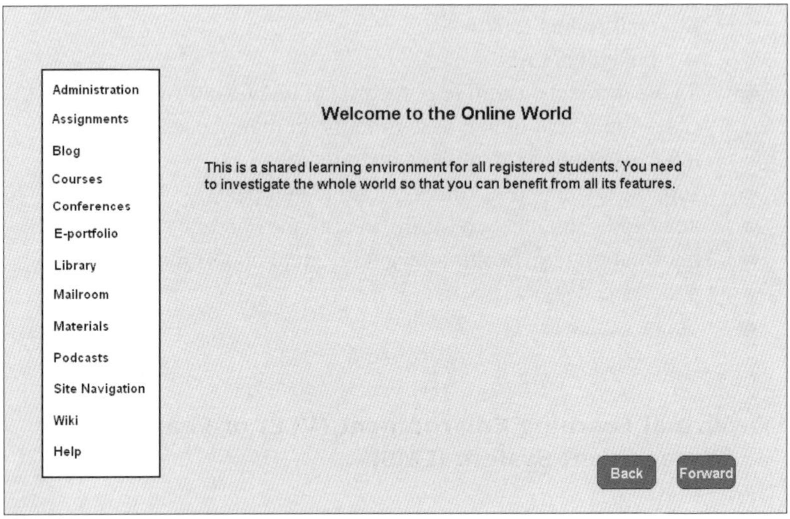

**Figure 4.1**   Example Virtual Learning Environment

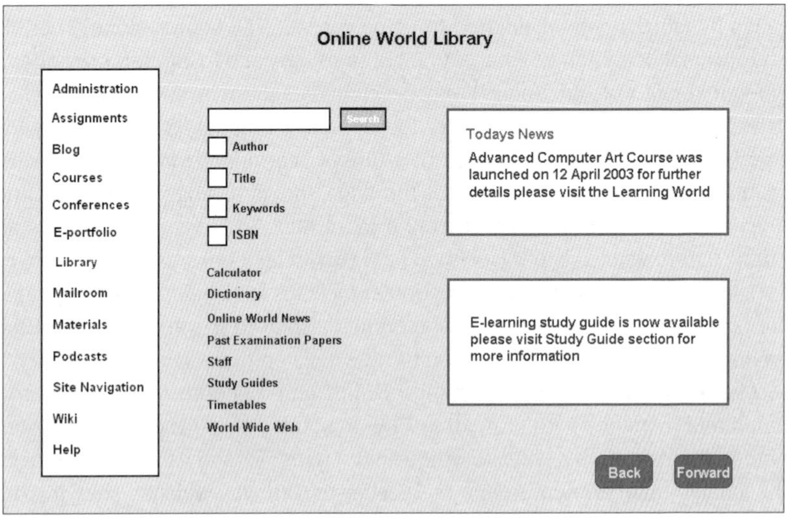

**Figure 4.2**   Example Virtual Learning Environment library

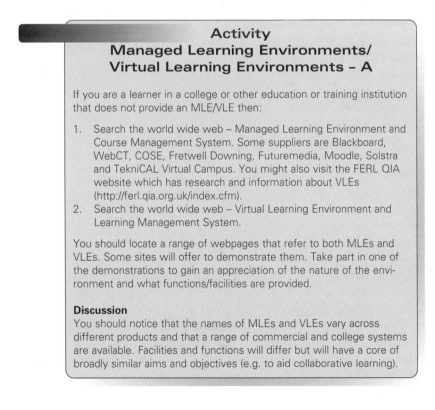

**Figure 4.3**  Excellence Gateway (Quality Improvement Agency)

## Activity
## Managed Learning Environments/
## Virtual Learning Environments – A

If you are a learner in a college or other education or training institution that does not provide an MLE/VLE then:

1.  Search the world wide web – Managed Learning Environment and Course Management System. Some suppliers are Blackboard, WebCT, COSE, Fretwell Downing, Futuremedia, Moodle, Solstra and TekniCAL Virtual Campus. You might also visit the FERL QIA website which has research and information about VLEs (http://ferl.qia.org.uk/index.cfm).
2.  Search the world wide web – Virtual Learning Environment and Learning Management System.

You should locate a range of webpages that refer to both MLEs and VLEs. Some sites will offer to demonstrate them. Take part in one of the demonstrations to gain an appreciation of the nature of the environment and what functions/facilities are provided.

### Discussion
You should notice that the names of MLEs and VLEs vary across different products and that a range of commercial and college systems are available. Facilities and functions will differ but will have a core of broadly similar aims and objectives (e.g. to aid collaborative learning).

## Activity
## Managed Learning Environments/
## Virtual Learning Environments – B

If you are a registered learner in a college or other education or training institution that does provide an MLE/VLE then:

1. Systematically explore the environment and make notes of each facility that you might want to use during your course.
2. You may find the environment has virtual guided tours to help you understand how to use the MLE/VLE, so take part in one.

**Discussion**
You should find lots of useful features that will help you with your learning. Often there are detailed elements which are helpful, such as other learners' lists of useful publications, access to past examination papers and examples of assignments. It is essential that you become a competent user of the MLE/VLE since it can provide you with an enormous amount of support.

Virtual Learning Environments and Management Learning Environments will often provide access to many facilities such as:

- e-Portfolios
- wikis
- blogs
- learning materials
- study suides
- forums and mailgroups

### Navigation

Each college or educational provider will configure their VLE in different ways and in some cases each department may also add or take away features. Individual tutors may also make changes to specific courses. You cannot therefore take for granted that the navigation and structure of the environment will be the same as any you have experienced before. You need to invest some time exploring the environment and become familiar with the structure. It is normal initially to be confused but this will disappear once you become familiar with the structure, layout and presentation.

Figure 4.4 shows an example of a course page within a VLE. In order to have navigated to this point you will probably have had to log in to the system using a password and user name. This may have taken you to a general introduction such as presented in Figure 4.1 or in some cases the

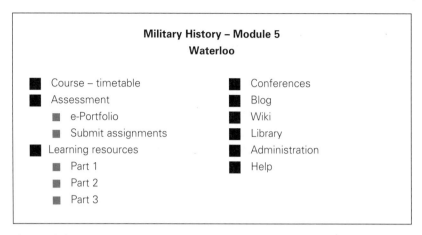

**Figure 4.4**    Course page

system directs you immediately to the course page since it recognises your password as a student on this particular course. You will notice that some options on the general and course displays are the same, such as blog, wiki and e-portfolio. These are facilities that are available to all students and the link will often take you to a general page in which you are asked to log in to that particular system. In most systems there are multiple ways of reaching a particular facility. It is good practice to have only three steps to reach any point within a VLE but not all systems are designed in this way.

The course page offers you 14 options to choose from. In many systems you may find a lot more choices. You will need to explore them early in the course so that you do not miss important resources. In this case you have access to:

- Course – timetable – tells you how the module is organised and when assignments are due;
- assessment – provides details of how you will be assessed as well as links to your e-portfolio system and the assignment submission facilities;
- Learning Resources — links to online information, reading lists, details of activities and anything else you will need are provided for each module;
- Conferences – links you to the different forums that relate to the course (Figure 4.5);
- Blog, Wiki and Library – take you to the relevant institutional system;

- Administration – this is course-related while Administration in Figures 4.2 and 4.2 is probably college-wide (there are no rules about this type of decision and you will need to find out by trail and error how your college system works);
- Help – support with the system.

Figure 4.5 illustrates the conference system for this specific course. It shows seven different forums. You may find that you have far more to use. Often people get carried away with conference forums and have too many. Each forum will have its own messages and you have to visit them separately to receive and send messages. This means that to keep up to date with discussions you need to manage your time and visit them regularly. It is a simple mistake to miss an important message.

In this structure (Figure 4.5) you have:

- Café – general socialising;
- Technical Issues – to discuss with your peers any problems and to seek their support, which is often very effective since they will have experienced the problem;
- Administration – normally for college staff to post messages about the course (e.g. the date of the final examination);
- Assignments – allows you to discuss the assessment;
- Parts 1, 2 and 3 – discussion forums relating to each element of the course.

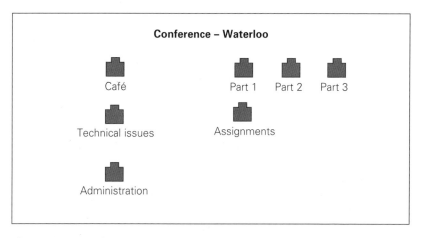

**Figure 4.5**   Conferences

As the course progresses the messages become an important resource. If you have a technical problem a useful first step in solving it is to search the technical forum to see if someone has already had the same difficulty and solved it. In a similar way answers to other questions relating to assignments, administration and the course may be found in the messages. If the answer is not present then the second step is to send a message to the relevant forum and ask for help. However, this system only works if everyone not only asks questions but also offers solutions. You need to participate.

The potential complexity of forums, systems and materials available within a VLE is huge. It can be an enormous help to you but only if you become a competent and confident user of the system. This requires that you spend time learning to navigate the environment, that you actively participate in the forums, blogs, wikis and e-portfolios and that you plan your time in orde to be able to visit regularly.

## World wide web

The world wide web is a vast resource for any learner studying almost any subject. There are many sites that can be helpful to you including:

- biographies;
- libraries and bookshops;
- dictionaries;
- electronic journals;
- online databases.

The world wide web is essentially a huge information library. It is important when using information from the world wide web to reference the source. Appendix D provides some guidance on referencing online sources. However, some colleges will have their own preferred approach to the format of online citations and an example is shown below.

Clarke, A, 3 May 2007, Re-Study Skills.(online). Available from study-skills@studymail.ac.uk. (accessed on 3 May 2007).

### Biographies

There is a wide variety of websites concerned with biographical information about famous people including:

- www.biography.com/ – many thousands of biographies including video material;

- www.s9.com/biography/ – a wiki biographical dictionary that allows you to edit the entries;
- http://aabd.chadwyck.com/ – African-American biographical database

## Libraries and bookshops

Books are probably the major learning resource for any student. Your tutors will often provide you with reading lists of articles, books and journals that you should study. The major practical issue is locating the books and other resources. It is now common practice for college libraries and learning centres to have their catalogues available electronically. The library databases are available for you to search in order to locate the books you are seeking. The catalogue will often tell you if the book is available or if it has been borrowed by another student, where the book is physically situated and for how long you can borrow it. Some colleges have placed their catalogues online so that you can carry out your search from your home or local centre without the need to travel. As well as the college library, there are also online libraries.

You may also seek to buy books. The world wide web is rich in online bookshops that often have an enormous range of stock and in some cases they are linked to second-hand bookshops enabling you to find used or out-of-print titles. Some online bookshops are:

- http://bookshop.blackwell.co.uk/;
- www.abebooks.com/;
- www.amazon.com/;
- www.waterstones.com/.

Online bookshops will provide not only a range of ways to search for items but also services such as:

- a description of the book (e.g. length, cost and publisher) and in some cases examples of the book's content;
- readers' reviews.

The activity below will provide you with some experience of using an online library. It is always useful to explore your own college library's electronic and online facilities.

## Activity
## Library

Visit the Internet Public Library (www.ipl.org/ – Internet Public Library) and explore the resource. Follow some of the links and investigate what is available.

**Discussion**

Your own experience is likely to be different owing to the dynamic nature of the world wide web, but I noticed many different features of the home page:

- ready-reference items (e.g. almanacs, dictionaries and encyclopaedias);
- reading room;
- subject collection;
- special collections (blogs);
- poetry wiki.

When I linked to the encyclopaedias item, I was taken to a list of online resources that related to them. I found sites covering a range of different information (e.g. philosophy to physics).

The reading room gave me access to links relating to books, magazines and newspapers. In turn, each of these items offered a list of subjects (e.g. arts and humanities to science and technology).

I clicked on the education subject collection and was presented with a list of sub-headings from which I chose adult education. This linked me to a list of websites related to adult education and by following the links I discovered the Canadian Office of Learning Technology site and their publications which I could download or print in some cases.

The special collections had an item called blogs that provided access to a list of sites relating to blogging (e.g. blog hosts).

The poetry wiki offered a means of editing and entering poetry for teenagers.

What did you discover?

## Dictionaries

Dictionaries are useful for all learners and they can be located on the world wide web at sites such as:

- http://dictionary.reference.com/;
- www.askoxford.com/;
- www.m-w.com/;
- www.yourdictionary.com/.

## Activity
## Dictionaries

Visit http://dictionary.reference.com/, www.askoxford.com/ and any other dictionary sites. Compare the sites by seeking definitions for:

- serendipity;
- palliative;
- dendritic;
- reflex.

**Discussion**
I was able to find definitions for all four words, although in some cases I had to check associated words to understand the term fully. How did you do?

### Electronic journals (e-journals, webjournals or online journals)

There has recently been a large growth in the number of electronic journals covering a wide range of topics.Sometimes they are electronic versions of conventional paper ones but many are only available in electronic form. Some you can only access by subscription but many are free. e-Journals vary in presentation as much as conventional ones do. Some offer access to an archive of past editions and so provide a rich resource (e.g. http://scholar.lib.vt.edu/ejournals/JTE/ – Journal of Technology Education).

Many journals allow students to download or print a copy of articles but you should check the conditions under which this is provided.

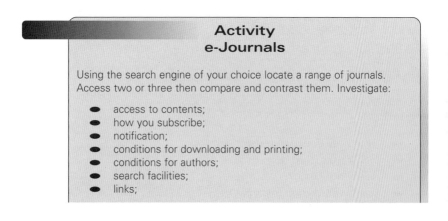

## Activity
## e-Journals

Using the search engine of your choice locate a range of journals. Access two or three then compare and contrast them. Investigate:

- access to contents;
- how you subscribe;
- notification;
- conditions for downloading and printing;
- conditions for authors;
- search facilities;
- links;

**Discussion**

You should find that access to contents varies depending on whether the journal is free or only available by subscription. Sometimes you only have access to abstracts or sample articles rather than the whole text but in many cases you can view the whole journal.

Subscription is usually by e-mail and will in some cases require a fee to be paid whereas others have no charge. Most will notify you by e-mail that a new edition is available so you can visit the website.

Most journals require you to adhere to their conditions for accessing, downloading or printing content (e.g. the copy is for personal use and the source must be acknowledged).

Many provide detailed guidance for prospective authors which can be useful for readers in that they provide evidence on which to judge the quality and objectivity of the papers (e.g. all submissions will be reviewed by three independent members of the editorial committee).

Some journals allow you access to past editions and in some cases there is a search engine to help you locate papers relating to a particular subject.

Many journal sites offer links to other related websites.

e-Journals are a very useful resource.

If you are a registered student at an educational institution you will find that access to many subscription journals is provided as part of your course and you will be given passwords to gain access to them.

## Online databases

Many sites provide users with databases of useful information. There are two main types:

- full-text;
- bibliographic.

Full-text databases provide you with a copy of the whole entry, often in the form of articles from online or conventional journals or research papers. Bibliographic databases hold the details of the publication with a short summary of its contents. This enables you to locate the item through a library or bookshop. Both types of database are often provided by college or national library services, while access to some is by subscription. That said, many colleges are subscribers so check which ones your college has linked to.

## Activity
## Investigating online databases and resources

ERIC – Educational Resource Information Center (www.eric.ed.gov/) is a major online resource containing bibliographic and full-text databases, lists of journals, publications and many other resources.

Visit the site and explore the possibilities offered by the resource. In particular:

1. Consider what help is provided (e.g. Frequently Asked Questions – FAQs).
2. Use the internal search engine to investigate the database – try searching using the different options and see the results of searching for 'e-learning skills'.
3. Find a publication relevant to your course.
4. Explore the journal index to locate relevant publications.
5. Explore the rest of the site.

Continue until you are confident that you can use the resource.

**Discussion**
1. While searching a resource such as ERIC, you will notice that you need to use the site's own search engine in a similar way that you would to locate information on the world wide web. If you search for e-learning skills without any qualifying criteria you will locate the maximum number of hits but a few optional criteria will limit results to a more manageable total.
2. You will have noticed that in order to print and read full-text documents, you need to employ Adobe Acrobat reader. This is freely available from Adobe and numerous other sites including ERIC.
3. You are able to save and print ERIC documents.

Online databases are important resources.

## Downloading

The world wide web offers a variety of opportunities to download files containing documents or other resources. The process is straightforward – normally you only have to double-click on the downloaded file on the website to start the process. Your operating system will ask you where you want to save the file to or if you want to open it. Figure 4.6 illustrates saving a file that you have downloaded. You should select which folder to save the file into and change the file's name to one which is meaningful to you. When you have a large number of files it is easy to forget a name or a location, so try always to use memorable names.

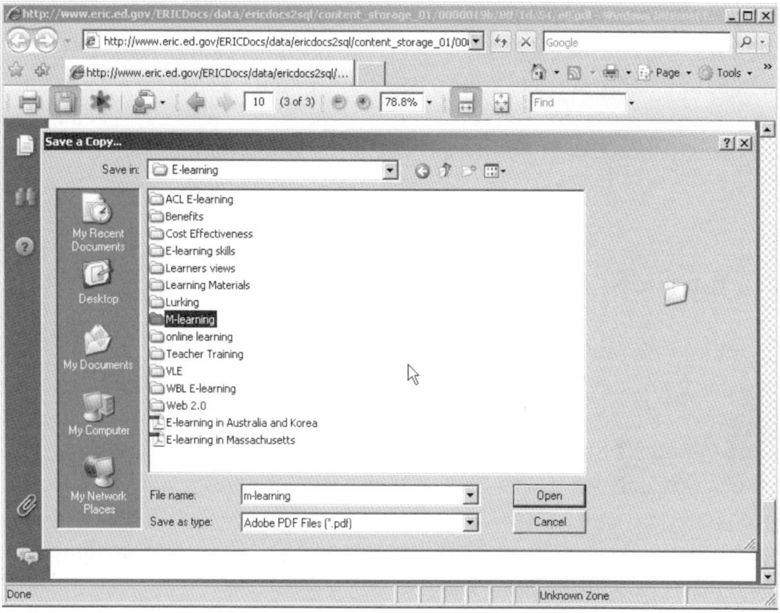

**Figure 4.6**   Downloading a file – Save as Window (Windows XP®)

Downloading is straightforward but should never be attempted unless you are confident that your virus protection software is up to date and that the site you are downloading from is likely to take precautions against virus infection.

In order to read a file you must have the application that created it or a compatible one on your system.

### Reading online documents

There are already many e-books and other electronic documents available on the world wide web and intranets. In order to read these publications, you often need the use of specific reader applications, usually freely available from their producers. Two major suppliers of e-book applications are Adobe and Microsoft and both provide free reading applications, providing you agree to abide by their licence agreements. They are available from:

- www.adobe.com/support/downloads/main.html
- www.microsoft.com/reader/default.asp

In each case the licence agreement that governs the use of the products is available on the website.

**Frequently Asked Questions**

Often websites include a section called 'Frequently Asked Questions'. These attempt to identify the questions that visitors to the site will be asking and to provide model answers for them. They can be a valuable asset because you can quickly locate the information you are seeking during your visit to the site.

### ● Intranets/extranets

An intranet is an organisation's own miniature world wide web. It is normally a private area which only authorised people are allowed to access. A majority of large companies and many small and medium-sized ones have created intranets for their employees. Many colleges have also built intranets for their students whereas many of their facilities can have an online presence. Students can access the intranet from a college computer or from home, usually through the college website and by using a user identification (User ID) code and a password. Some colleges and employers call their intranets portals or managed learning environments.

College intranets will often provide facilities such as:

- library catalogue;
- learning resources;
- administration;
- careers advice;
- assessment records;
- course details;
- course timetables.

If you are a learner in a college or other education/training institution that provides an intranet, it is important to make yourself aware of the facilities that it offers you (e.g. biographies of tutors, introductions to other students, other learners' lists of useful publications, access to past examination papers and examples of assignments). In some cases the help or other facilities will provide an introduction to the intranet.

Extranets lie somewhere between the complete open access of the internet and the closed world of an intranet. An extranet is designed to be an intranet which is open to outside users through the use of a password and an agreed user identification. They are often used to facilitate group work so that individuals who are geographically spread can co-operate on a joint project.

## WebQuests

WebQuests were developed at San Diego State University (Dodge and March, 1995). They are, as the name suggests, about undertaking a task using the information available on the world wide web to achieve a set objective. They can take a variety of forms from a task lasting a few hours to one taking weeks or even months. It is normal to provide the learner with the sources of information (i.e. links) so that it is not about searching the web but rather comparing, contrasting, integrating and analysing information. Usually the author of the quest provides assistance with how to proceed with the investigation. In some cases the learner is asked to take on a particular role or the quest is designed as a group activity. The use of WebQuests is growing rapidly and they are being used at all levels of education.

---

### Activity
### WebQuests

Using a search engine of your choice, carry out a search on the term 'WebQuest'. You will locate a variety of sites. Some will provide you with examples of different WebQuests. Compare and contrast the different examples you have located and produce a list of the different topics used for the quests for both adults and children.

**Discussion**
My search using the keyword WebQuest on the Google search engine gave 3,020,000 hits which I reduced to 467,000 by searching within the original hits with the keyword example. I considered the pages within the top 30 webpage hits. This produced a large number of examples for school children and students including: natural history, geography, weather, sport, industry, environment, politics, astronomy, space travel, modern and ancient history, music, biology, animals, archaeology, art, mathematics, languages, reading, etc.

WebQuests clearly can be employed in almost every possible subject.

---

## Learning materials

In e-Learning courses and programmes, a key role is often played by the learning materials which can take a wide variety of forms and serve a number of purposes. Table 4.3 describes a range of learning materials and how to use them.

| Learning materials | How to use them | Comments |
|---|---|---|
| Study guide | A study guide will provide you with guidance from the course design team about how to obtain the most from the course. It will often explain the suggested route through the course materials, details of assessment and good practice. | It is useful to read the guide at the start of the course and to review your progress regularly against it. It can help you plan your learning. |
| Course website | Course websites often will provide information about:<br>1. outcomes of the course;<br>2. course timetable;<br>3. assessment methods;<br>4. suggested materials;<br>5. suggested links to other websites.<br>Changes to the course are often posted to the course site. | It useful to visit the site regularly to check for messages and new developments. |
| World wide web | Almost every topic is available on the world wide web. It should become a natural reaction to any question to search the web for information.<br>Remember to record useful sites, wikis and blogs using the Internet Explorer's® Favorites feature.<br>Subscribe to useful RSS feeds. | Search skills are a key requirement of any e-learner. Take every opportunity to practise. Although information on almost all subjects is available, its quality needs to be carefully assessed. Some e-learning courses will have identified suitable world wide web resources to save you time and to assure you of their suitability. |

| | | |
|---|---|---|
| Interactive learning materials (computer-based materials) | These materials are specifically created to help you learn. They are designed to help you realise specific learning outcomes and often clearly state what you should achieve by using them. Well-designed materials will engage you and help you to assess your own progress through tasks and questions. | It is useful to take a few moments to ensure you understand the structure of the interactive materials. Many packages have an introduction to help you employ them effectively. |
| Open-learning packs (paper-based materials) | These materials are specifically created to help you learn. They are designed to enable you to complete specific learning outcomes and often clearly state what you should achieve by using them.<br><br>Most open-learning packs are paper-based materials which can be carried with you and studied when you have time. | It is useful to take a few moments to ensure you understand the structure of the materials. Large packs will often have several booklets, video/audio tapes and other materials. A few moments spent studying them is a useful investment to avoid later confusion. Many packages have an introduction or study guide to help you employ them effectively. |
| Textbooks | Textbooks are designed to provide an explanation of the whole or a part of the syllabus you are studying. | You can use a textbook in a variety of ways, for example, as a reference into which you dip when you are unsure. |
| Learning resources | Learning resources can take a variety of different forms including:<br>1. lecture notes;<br>2. reading lists;<br>3. lists of websites; | The diverse nature of resources makes it difficult to generalise about using them. However, a key factor is to identify those parts which are most useful to you so that you can use those elements in revision or as content for essays/assignments. |

**Table 4.3**　Learning materials – *continued overleaf*

| Learning materials | How to use them | Comments |
|---|---|---|
| | 4. PowerPoint® presentation graphics program presentations;<br>5. videos;<br>6. examples of projects;<br>7. podcasts. | The use of learning resources is often called resource-based learning. It requires that the resources are effectively integrated to help you to achieve the desired objectives. They also need to be supported with tutorials, peer discussions and feedback. |
| Problem-based learning | Problem-based learning is based on the concept that if you learn by doing then you will retain the experience more effectively.<br>The approach is based on asking you to solve a problem which is either provided for you or which you identify for yourself. You will often be working with other students.<br>The learning resources are provided and can take any form. | This is a powerful way of learning and especially useful in an organisational context where you are attempting to solve a business problem. |
| Case studies | These are a series of case studies of actual events which you are asked to study. They can be associated with any subject but are often linked to business management. | The aim is to provide you with more experience by giving you access to case studies of events outside your current practice. To gain the most benefit requires that the case studies be fairly detailed. You should study them systematically, seeking common factors, and identify good practice to transfer to new situations. |

| Podcasts | These are audio and video materials and provide material in many forms such as: <br> 1. Lectures; <br> 2. Interviews; <br> 3. Discussions. | Short recordings can help illustrate topics and can be saved so you can listen to or view them several times and use them for revision. |
| Video lectures | These are short lectures filmed using a screen cam, edited from a longer video of a lecture or produced in other ways. | Short videos allow the tutor to provide brief inputs on difficult topics. They are useful in that they can be saved so you can view them several times and use them for revision. |
| Screen captures | There are several applications that allow you to capture activities on a computer screen and play them back. | These are essentially demonstrations of how to carry out a particular task using a software application. You should use them in a similar way. They have the advantage of being able to be viewed many times. |

**Table 4.3** *continued*

There is a worldwide effort by many universities to offer online free access to some or all their learning materials. The Massachusetts Institute of Technology was the first to allow individuals to use their materials online. The Open University was the first in Great Britain. It launched Open Learn (http://openlearn.open.ac.uk/) in 2006 and aims to offer 5 per cent of all its materials through the website. This amounts to over 3000 hours of content and is still growing.

Many educational and training providers offer some degree of access to free online content.

## Blended learning

Many colleges, company training department and other educational institutions are integrating e-learning approaches with more traditional methods. This can take a variety of forms such as:

- conventional lectures with teaching notes and visual aids placed on the college intranet for you to access;
- using digital cameras to record practical work for your portfolio of evidence;
- all assignments submitted in an electronic format and feedback provided in the form of annotation;
- e-mail and conferencing with tutors in place of face-to-face tutorials;
- collaborative assignments based on using a wiki to produce an agreed report;
- simulations of laboratory experiments as part of a conventional science course;
- distance-learning course with regular face-to-face meetings;
- individual blogs to develop a diary of your learning experience.

There are a huge number of possibilities and it is useful before you start any course to enquire about the methods that will be employed. The growth in blended learning is very rapid and probably exceeds pure e-learning approaches.

## Summary

### 1. Places to learn

You can take part in e-learning in a number of locations including:

- learning centres – colleges, training facilities and community sites have centres;
- cybercafés – these take a variety of forms (e.g. internet kiosks and coffee bars);
- mobile – laptop computers and PDAs combined with a mobile phone or wireless connections allow you access to the internet almost anywhere;
- home – create a suitable learning environment that is organised with your books, papers and other learning tools;
- workplace – at your desk or within the company's learning centre.

### 2. Synchronous learning (e.g. audio or video conferencing)

Video and audio conferencing are synchronous approaches to e-learning. The technology varies from high-quality, large-screen images usually viewed by a group of learners to individual learners interacting through to a small, low quality image on a personal computer.

Conferencing can take several forms such as:

- a group of students interacting together with a remote tutor;
- several groups of students in different locations interacting with a remote tutor;
- individual students at many different locations interacting with a remote tutor;
- large groups of students listening to a remote expert.

To obtain the best results it is important that conferencing be organised and chaired. Special arrangements are sometimes required to allow learners to ask questions.

Synchronous conferencing learning is broadly similar to traditional classroom approaches.

3.  **Groupware**
    Groupware is a form of synchronous interacting using an application that several participants can share. They can each take it in turn to control the application. This is often used to undertake a group project.

4.  **Managed Learning Environment (MLE) or Course Management System (CMS)**
    This is an online integration of a variety of systems to form an online environment. MLEs vary considerably but may offer:

    - an administration system including financial, attendance and registration records;
    - course information including learning resources, assessment systems (e-portfolios), library, support and advice;
    - communication systems such as e-mail, blogs, conferencing, chat rooms, bulletin boards and wikis.

5.  **Virtual Learning Environment (VLE) or Learning Management System (LMS)**
    A Virtual Learning Environment (VLE) essentially has those elements of an MLE that are intended to support and deliver the online learning. VLEs can be integrated into MLEs but sometimes stand alone. There is no standard definition of an MLE or VLE.

6.  **World wide web**
    The world wide web is essentially a huge information library that provides resources such as:

    - libraries and bookshops – catalogues and books online including second-hand and out-of-print publications;
    - electronic journals – there are many different journals, some are electronic copies of paper based journals while others are only published online;

- online databases;
- full-text – copies of the publication are available;
- bibliographic – summaries/abstracts of publications.

The world wide web can provide document files for you to download along with e-books and other electronic documents. You should only download information if you have up-to-date virus protection. Some e-publications require specific reader applications.

### 7. Intranets/extranets

Many colleges and companies have intranets which are essentially websites on the organisation's own network. These provide learners with access to facilities and information. An extranet is an intranet which is open to outside users through use of a password and an agreed user identification.

### 8. WebQuests

WebQuests involve using the information available on the world wide web to achieve a set objective. Learners are often provided with the sources of information so they can concentrate on comparing, contrasting, integrating and analysing the data.

### 9. Learning materials

Learning materials are an important part of e-learning. A wide variety are used, including traditional forms, online information, podcasts and interactive multimedia.

### 10. Blended learning

Blended learning is the integration of e-learning approaches with more traditional methods.

# 5  e-Learning Skills

To be successful, e-learners require well-developed learning skills. This chapter aims to help you identify those skills required of an e-learner. It will look at learning styles and strategies and how they relate to e-learning. A key factor in any skill is awareness of your own performance in relation to it. You need to recognise what you are doing and how well you are doing it. This will help you to improve your performance. All skills need practice in order to be developed and extended.

### ● Initial experience

It is likely that you will go through a number of stages in your experience of e-learning. Initially, you are likely to feel unsure about what to do and how to use the resources available to you. This is not likely to last very long, especially if you have a tutor since he or she will be working to help you gain confidence and to understand the e-learning environment. You should start by communicating with other learners and your tutor using e-mail, instant messaging, chat rooms or other methods. The more you can communicate, the quicker you will feel comfortable and confident. You need to gain an understanding of your subject, the environment, your tutor and the other learners. The best way of developing this is to ask questions, explore the subject content, reflect on the learning material and consider the answers.

Once you feel comfortable, try to:

- develop your relationship with other learners and your tutor through communication technology;
- explore the learning environment – what is available (e.g. information about the assessment, learning content, etc.);
- collaborate with other learners;
- locate resources on the world wide web.

## Time management

One of the major benefits of e-learning is the freedom it gives you to learn at a time that fits best into your life. However, the price of this freedom is that you must choose when to learn. In conventional courses, you are given a timetable of classes you must attend and assignments you need to complete. This largely determines when you study. An e-learning course is likely to tell you, for example, that an estimated 150 hours of studying are required over a 22-week period (i.e. approximately seven hours a week) with, say, three assignments that provide 50 per cent of the total marks required for the course, but the details of when you learn is left up to you. You can study as many hours a week as you like. You could do seven hours one day each week, one hour a day or any combination that suits you. Some e-learning courses do not set a fixed period for completion, although these will often not lead to a qualification. You have an open-ended course and only need to complete the content. The greatest risk of this type of programme is that you fall behind or fail to finish.

The timetable for a conventional course provides a structure that is supportive but limiting. e-Learning increases the freedom but reduces the supportive structure. You must make the most of the freedom and replace the missing structure with your own.

In order to do this you should:

- Consider the course structure – what do you need to do to complete the course (e.g. assignments, marks, forums, collaborative activities, examinations or other assessments)?
- Analyse your own objectives and personal timetable (e.g. when do you want to finish the course?).
- Balance your different priorities against each other (e.g. childcare compared to study time; hours of employment – long work days make studying at weekends the only option; limited access to computer technology).
- Reflect on your personal learning preferences – you may prefer to study at night or in the early morning.
- Recognise good learning practice – it is poor practice to study for many hours without a break. It is better to study regularly, even if each session is relatively short, than to occasionally study for an extended period
- e-Learning courses are often based around discussion forums, blogs and collaborative activities. These all need to be considered in planning your time.

- Ensure your health and safety (e.g. eating and drinking at the computer is poor practice, not least because you do not get a break but also because liquids and electrical equipment do not mix).
- Consider family responsibilities – you must integrate your studies into the needs of your family (e.g. childcare).

Outlook® software provides a number of features that enable you to organise and control your time. Figure 5.1 shows you the Calendar view. This lets you maintain an electronic diary of your studies. You can change your view of the calendar to show a single day, a five-day week, a seven-day week or a month by selecting the View menu (Figure 5.1). In addition to a calendar, there is a task pad to create a to-do list. These two functions offer a way of arranging your learning in a systematic way. Many organisations' Managed Learning Environments also provide calendars to which course tutors will add key dates, so it is useful to explore what your institution offers.

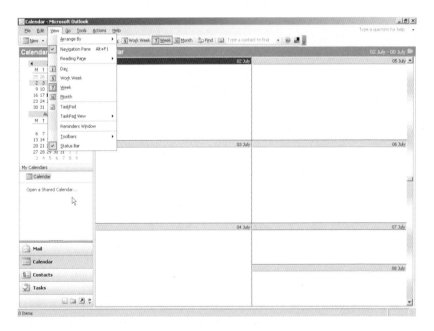

**Figure 5.1** Outlook® software Calendar view

# Activity
## Creating a study timetable

For your own course devise a study timetable of significant aspects, such as a major assignment or your regular study pattern. Consider all the issues such as employment, preferences, social responsibilities, etc. Timetables can be helpful if they reflect your whole life and not simply the course.

**Discussion**

Figure 5.2 shows a simple example of a timetable developed using Outlook® software. It is based on completing an assignment to write an essay about General Grant's career and involves allowing:

1. two periods to research the background for the essay;
2. four periods to write notes;
3. one period to prepare the essay;
4. one period to write the initial draft;
5. one period to revise and finalise the essay.

I have also allowed three days for unforeseen difficulties before the assignment has to be submitted.

Within the timetable I have also added when I will check my e-mail. This shows a regular pattern of every other day. It is good practice to maintain contact with your peers and tutors even when you are busy with an assignment. Personally, I check my e-mail every day and sometimes more than once when I am busy. Many people assume you will respond to e-mail messages immediately.

To make it more useful you should add your employment, family and other responsibilities since these will tell you if your study plan is realistic.

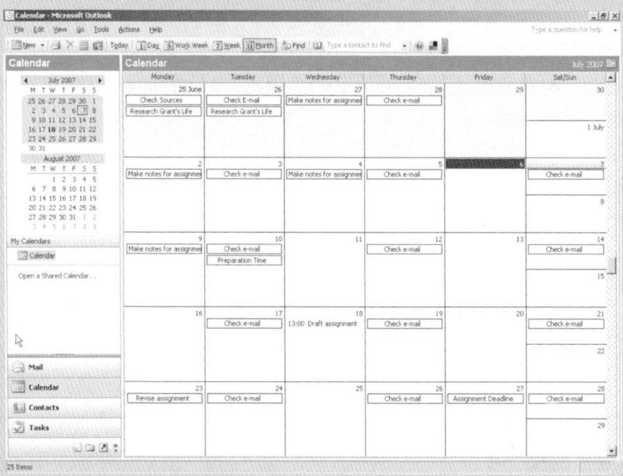

**Figure 5.2**   Timetable

For many people the attraction of an online or e-learning course is the increased freedom to choose when you study. However, this means that you need to manage your time more and some of the features of e-learning require that you regularly participate. Many courses will want you to take part in a range of online forums. To benefit from discussion forums requires regular participation and a systematic approach to reading messages. How often you visit depends on the nature of the discussion and the course but it is not unusual to have to visit several times a week.

Collaborative exercises are also a normal part of online and e-learning courses. Collaboration involves each participant compromising to ensure that the task is completed successfully. Each participant will have different time pressures and as part of the exercise you will need to agree a common timetable and then follow it. Time management is, therefore, not just about your own life and study balance, it is also about your peers.

## Acceptance of responsibility

All courses assume that you will accept responsibility for your actions but they will often provide structures to ensure that you cannot fall short simply because you forget a deadline or something similar. e-Learning courses also provide structural devices to help you but since you are often studying at a distance from your peers and tutors, many of the informal systems, such as colleagues reminding you, are different. Tutors will frequently offer help or reminders at the end of lectures or workshops, but this is not so easily duplicated at a distance. e-Learning courses also offer more freedom and choice so you are able to decide when to undertake particular tasks. This all combines to move responsibility on to you. Freedom comes at a price. You must understand:

- the course structure and standards (e.g. alternatives);
- course conditions (e.g. who can grant an extension to a deadline and under what circumstances);
- assessment conditions (e.g. pass marks, assessment methods – balance of continuous assessment and examinations);
- deadlines.

It is important at the start of the course to make yourself aware of these issues.

Acceptance of responsibility also includes realising your own personal objectives and standards. This can be expressed in a number of different ways, such as aiming to reach a standard that will equip you for a particular career.

## Activity
## Reviewing the structure of the course

Identify key dates and priorities – how are you going to ensure that you are able to satisfy fully the needs of the course? Write down an approach that will help you meet all the objectives.

**Discussion**

There are several different approaches that you might want to follow. One is to develop the things-to-do method which involves writing a list of things to do in relation to each key item in the course structure. Review the list regularly and cross off each step. Figure 5.3 illustrates the use of Outlook® software to produce a list of tasks that need to be done in relation to preparing to write an essay about General Grant.

You may simply mark up a calendar or diary with key dates and tasks to act as a reminder. Outlook® software provides the means to give yourself electronic reminders.

How does your approach differ from these suggestions?

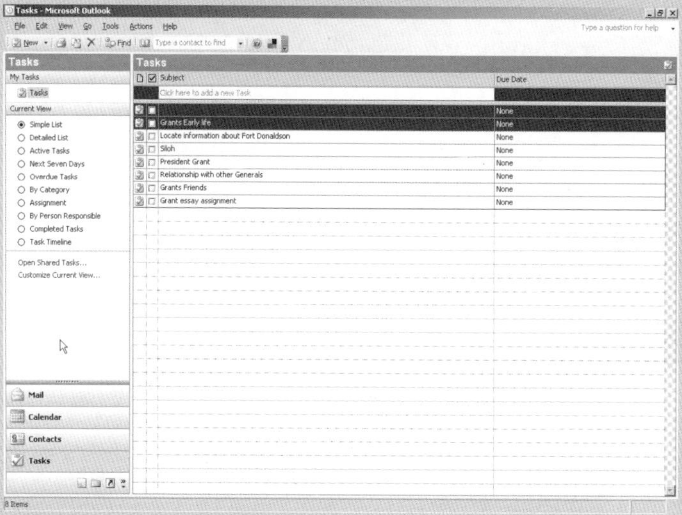

**Figure 5.3**   Tasks

## Planning

You have almost certainly met students who always seem to finish an assignment at the last moment. You may even behave in this way yourself. It is poor practice. Almost certainly your performance will be reduced if you do not plan ahead. Planning will improve your results, you will be more productive and you will reduce your stress.

Planning involves:

- looking ahead:
    - what does the course require you to do over the next term?
    - what subjects will you be studying?
    - what assessments will you need to undertake?
- identifying critical points (e.g. two assessments close together – how can you prepare for both?);
- setting your goals – what you want to achieve;
- producing your personal action plan:
    - when you will study;
    - starting your reading early enough;
    - starting your preparation for an essay;
- organising yourself:
    - creating records/files of your work;
    - balancing your life – good life/study balance;
- monitoring your performance;
- adjusting your plans.

---

### Activity
### Planning an assignment

Consider an assignment you need to complete:

1. When does it need to be submitted (i.e. the date)?
2. Working backwards, consider how long you will need to complete the assignment:

    - Do you have all the information you will need or do you have to locate it?
    - What research will you need to undertake?
    - How long will it take to write?
    - Are there any compulsory elements (e.g. it is a group activity and you need to agree with the other members what each of you will do)?

3.  Decide on your writing process:

    - outline notes;
    - initial draft;
    - proofread/spell and grammar check;
    - final draft.

If you have a real assignment, plan your timetable considering the issues above. If you don't then plan an essay of three thousand words about the main trends in the information society (e.g. employment changes, new skills, social changes, entertainment, etc.). It is due in four weeks' time.

**Discussion**
I have considered the task of planning an essay on the main trends in the information society, which needs to be submitted in four weeks' time.

1.  I do not have all the information that I will need. I must search the world wide web, library catalogue, bibliographic database or e-journals and then read, analyse and make notes about what I find. I estimate that this will take a whole day and perhaps longer if I find a lot of information. I will need to split the task, since a whole day reading and researching is probably too much at one time.
2.  With a good set of notes I think I could write a three-thousand word initial draft in two or three sessions of three hours. I doubt I could do more than one session on any one day.
3.  Proofreading and checking will take about three hours but again I will need to break it up since I cannot redraft in a single session.
4.  The final draft will take about three hours.

This tells me I need to divide the work on the assignment into about eight sessions. I have four weeks over which to plan these. I will almost certainly have other tasks to do and a reasonable pattern is likely to be:

1.  research and notes – two sessions during week 1;
2.  initial draft – three sessions of three hours during week 2;
3.  proofreading – two sessions during week 3;
4.  final draft – one session during week 3 or 4 (allows some time if things go wrong).

A task such as writing an essay, which can be difficult for many students, can benefit from planning. Many learners who do not plan will find themselves in week 4 trying to fit everything in and subjecting themselves to intense pressure and the possibility of a poor assignment.

### Self-assessment

There are lots of ways of judging your own progress. Some are formal (e.g. marks achieved) while others are informal (e.g. comparing your own understanding with that of your peers). The informal methods are often part of discussions before or after a lecture or other learning activities where you can compare your own reactions with those of your peers. When you are studying at a distance from your colleagues or you rarely meet them, then many of these informal methods are not apparently available to you. However, while it can require confidence to ask questions, e-mail provides a means of communicating with all your peers in a far more systematic and potentially effective way than a brief chat at the end of a presentation.

In traditional learning courses a key responsibility of the tutor is to ensure that you are aware of your progress. Tutors will often speak to each learner individually to highlight good work and any weaknesses, misunderstandings and confusion. In e-learning this responsibility is moved to you. Tutors are still responsible for providing feedback but this is likely to have changed from a verbal face-to-face process to written feedback. Face-to-face allows you to ask straighforward questions immediately about your performance, whereas written feedback requires that you make the additional effort of contacting the tutor. It is important to ask for clarification if the feedback leaves you uncertain.

It is useful to keep records of all forms of feedback as this will make it easier to judge your progress. Consider the comments on your work given by both your tutor and your peers (e.g. on your blog entries and e-portfolio evidence). It will help you identify and address subject areas that need more work and where you are making progress to address problem areas.

A wide range of assessment approaches are used within e-learning materials. They include (Clarke, 2001b; Race, 1994):

- multiple-choice questions;
- true or false questions;
- sorting information into order;
- matching pieces of information together;
- filling in the gaps.

These methods are also used in more conventional paper-based learning materials but some are uniquely used in online or e-learning assessment such as:

- taking part in a virtual journey or exploring an environment;
- using a simulation;

- developing an electronic portfolio;
- keeping a blog learning diary;
- creating a group document using a wiki.

Many assessments are intended to help you check your own understanding rather than forming part of the formal assessment process. They will often give you the opportunity to take the assessment more than once. To take advantage of this type of assessment, it is useful to keep records of patterns that show your strengths and weaknesses.

You should regularly review your peers' blogs to compare their efforts with your own. The comments made on your blog by your fellow students can also be very helpful in assessing your own progress. Your tutor will often offer feedback on your e-portfolio evidence. This can help you to judge the strengths and weaknesses of your evidence.

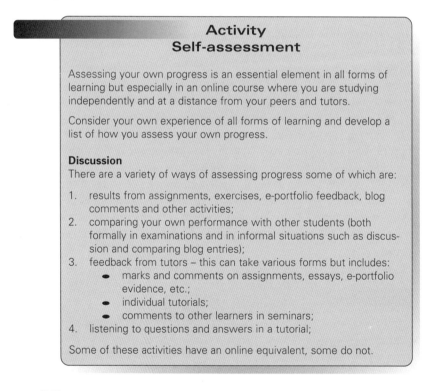

## Activity
## Self-assessment

Assessing your own progress is an essential element in all forms of learning but especially in an online course where you are studying independently and at a distance from your peers and tutors.

Consider your own experience of all forms of learning and develop a list of how you assess your own progress.

**Discussion**
There are a variety of ways of assessing progress some of which are:

1. results from assignments, exercises, e-portfolio feedback, blog comments and other activities;
2. comparing your own performance with other students (both formally in examinations and in informal situations such as discussion and comparing blog entries);
3. feedback from tutors – this can take various forms but includes:
   - marks and comments on assignments, essays, e-portfolio evidence, etc.;
   - individual tutorials;
   - comments to other learners in seminars;
4. listening to questions and answers in a tutorial;

Some of these activities have an online equivalent, some do not.

## Portfolios

A widely used assessment method is the portfolio – that is, a collection of evidence to demonstrate your skills, understanding and competency in a particular subject. The evidence is defined by the awarding body or the educational institution so that each learner's portfolio can be compared. It is often aligned with the detailed requirements of the course or qualification being undertaken. Typical evidence requirements are:

- examples of work undertaken (e.g. letters you have sent to show that you can lay out and present an effective communication, minutes taken by you and copies of papers you have written, orders placed after a sales demonstration, photographs of work completed such as window displays, products constructed, etc.);
- supervisors', tutors' or mentors' witness statements (e.g. a colleague describing how you undertook a particular task);
- observations undertaken by objective observers (e.g. assessment of your performance in carrying out an experiment).

ICT provides the opportunity to develop electronic portfolios which can take a variety of forms. A simple collection of evidence would include:

- copies of word-processed documents (e.g. creative writers);
- digital photographs (e.g. artists, craftsmen and gardeners);
- e-mails (e.g. to show your participation in group tasks);
- audio and video evidence of your competence (e.g. musicians).

In some cases e-portfolios could be a personal website designed to show the person's skills, knowledge, competencies and achievements. This type of portfolio is essentially a living document of the person's achievements. The portfolio can be updated and enhanced from anywhere, thus becoming a dynamic document. A significant difference between e-portfolios and traditional ones is the opportunity for your tutor to offer feedback on items of evidence.

## Activity
## e-Portfolios

Using a search engine of your own choice, locate a variety of sites covering the use and development of e-portfolios and consider how they are being employed.

**Discussion**
My initial approach to this search was to use the simple term e-portfolio. Then I added the word learning (i.e. e-portfolio learning). I found a large number of webpages showing e-portfolios being used

internationally and in a variety of ways. Several sites offered the opportunity to see examples of student portfolios.

Different ideas for e-portfolios covered:

1. showing your personal continuous professional development in a dynamic way as you are a lifelong learner;
2. helping artists and performers to exhibit their skills and achievements through digital music, video and photographs;
3. providing templates for particular courses, topics or subjects to assist learners to produce their portfolios;
4. showing student progress since they are dynamic and will change as the course continues;
5. reducing the costs of conventional portfolios;
6. providing standards for e-portfolios so that learners' work can be compared and assessed.

There were lots of other ideas and concepts being explored and developed, indicating the large degree of interest in this approach.

## Virtual experiments

The potential to create virtual environments for learners to explore, carry out experiments and undertake tasks is being exploited in e-learning courses. The practical issues of health and safety for students with no experience of a laboratory, the cost of operating laboratories and the potential for practical work to go wrong have all encouraged the development of virtual experiments.

Virtual experiments enable you to experience even more than if you carried them out in a real laboratory, since you can revise the experience to explore all the possibilities and do so without leaving your home or learning centre.

### Activity
### Undertaking a virtual experiment

Identify a virtual experiment that you can use then undertake it. Reflect on the experience.

Examples:

Try the genetics experiments available on the Channel 4 Television website www.channel4.com/learning/microsites/G/genetics/ activities/ shockwave-bug.html
(This experiment requires Macromedia Shockwave Player, which is available free through the site.)

Virtual micrometer – learn how to use a micrometer: http://members.shaw.ca/ron.blond/Micrometer.APPLET/

> Schlumberger Science Lab offers a range of experiments for you to try:
>
> www.seed.slb.com/en/scictr/lab/index_virtual.htm
>
> **Discussion**
> Your experience will depend on the experiment you have chosen but you may have found that you are able to explore more options than you could have done for real. It may have allowed you to recover from errors which in an actual experiment would have cost you time and forced you to start again.
>
> What did you experience? How does it compare with your previous experience of undertaking actual experiments? Did you learn a lot about the subject?
>
> If you have time, try carrying out several different experiments.

## Formal assessment

All the self-assessment methods that we have considered can be used for more formal assessment by your college, employer or the qualification awarding body. Some other ways of assessing your performance that you may encounter are:

- video and audio conferencing;
- remote control or monitoring.

The examiner and student can be separated in space but linked through video or audio conferencing which can be used to provide a form of oral or demonstration assessment. The student is asked to make a presentation, complete a task or take part in a role play. The examiner can watch or listen to the student and then ask questions.

Remote control or monitoring is often part of technical courses and allows the examiner to view the students' computer display while they are carrying out a task. This enables them to assess progress directly, offer feedback or take control of the computer and demonstrate how to carry out the task.

## Evaluation

Another aspect of assessment is consideration of the effectiveness of the e-learning course. This will almost certainly involve you, if only to ask you what you liked or disliked about the programme.

If your college or employer is seeking to evaluate the e-learning course, you may, for example, be asked to complete a final questionnaire about your views of the course, or to take part in evaluation interviews. e-Learning is a relatively new approach so it is perhaps more likely to be evaluated than other more conventional approaches.

## Problem solving

All forms of learning require that students deal with the many practical problems that emerge. e-Learning students are often working physically alone and so dependent on information and communication technology.

### Technical problems

Technology can be confusing and frustrating when it does not work. This does not mean that you need to become a computer technician to be a successful e-learner but you do need to know where to find help to solve the problem. In many cases technical problems can be quickly solved and as your experience grows you will be able to deal with them yourself. It is rare to have to return your computer or other equipment back to the supplier in order to have it fixed. This section aims to help you access assistance, particularly if you are studying at a distance from your college or at home. However, if you only use equipment belonging to your college or employer, it is likely that you need only report that the machine is not working correctly.

If the technology goes wrong at home then you can feel isolated and vulnerable. Good technical support is vital to e-learning and many educational providers offer telephone and other forms of helpline. At an early stage in your course you need to find out precisely what is on offer and how to access the help. In some cases technical assistance will only be available between certain hours and on specific days (e.g. 9 a.m. to 5 p.m. Monday to Friday).

In many cases the help system is a telephone line with a technical specialist who can help diagnose the problem and suggest solutions. You need to be willing and able to undertake the solution in the case of hardware faults. This will often mean sending the computer back to the supplier (it is good practice to keep the original packing). With software faults, it will probably require reinstalling applications. The specialist will talk you through the process but you need to be able to carry out his/her advice.

Help desks will often only provide support for products they have supplied. A college helpdesk will provide advice on the Managed Learning Environment and associated products but will not help you with your own computer. You will need to contact the supplier's help desk for assistance with your own equipment.

Online communication problems are often difficult to diagnose and will involve trying out ideas. This is difficult if you only have a single telephone. How can you test a solution while talking to the helpline and using it to connect to the internet? It will help if you have two lines or a mobile phone so that you can continue to discuss the problem while trying out solutions. Many internet service providers offer technical support as an alternative to your educational provider. The scope of the technical help will depend on your contract and can involve additional costs, so you need to check your contract. In some cases it will be 24 hours a day, every day of the year.

Some helplines also offer a website containing solutions to standard problems or informing you of problems outside your control (e.g. that college computer servers have broken down). It is useful to check online sources before telephoning the technical support team. To take advantage of all forms of technical support you need to be prepared. Some useful things to do are:

- Have all your documentation accessible:
  - user identification (helplines will only help if you can show you are a registered student or customer);
  - computer handbooks/users' manuals/warranties/guarantees (e.g. computer, monitor, modem and printers).
- Write down a precise description of what is going wrong, including any error messages that have appeared.
- Keep a notebook with a record of what you have tried.
- Label the many cables and connections on your computer system and thus avoid becoming confused.
- Become familiar with the operating system and diagnostic information so you can follow the technical helpline's advice.
- Keep all your installation disks, those containing equipment drivers and other software, near to your computer in an ordered way so you can rapidly locate them.
- Although it may seem obvious, it is always worth checking that your power connections are correct and that all other connections are firm.

## Activity
## Windows® operating system

Windows® operating system provides help and support to users, enabling you to become familiar with the system. You will benefit from technical assistance if you understand the fundamentals about your operating system. All versions of Windows® operating system offer a help system; some provide a troubleshooting option and some a guided tour to the system.

Explore the help system provided by your operating system.

**Discussion**

I explored the Help and Support system provided by Microsoft XP Home Edition®. Figure 5.4 shows the Help window containing an option to help you fix a problem. Figure 5.5 shows the display if you select the Fix a Problem option. A list of problem types lets you choose a category. The process systematically asks you to identify precisely what is wrong. This is done by offering you lists of options (questions) for you to select and then focus on the problem itself. Eventually you will be offered advice to help you solve the problem. You can print this advice and it is useful to keep a copy either for future reference or to explain to the technical helpline.

Other options in the Help and Support system will offer you a tour or tutorial of the operating system (see Figure 5.6). This is a good way to gain familiarity with your operating system.

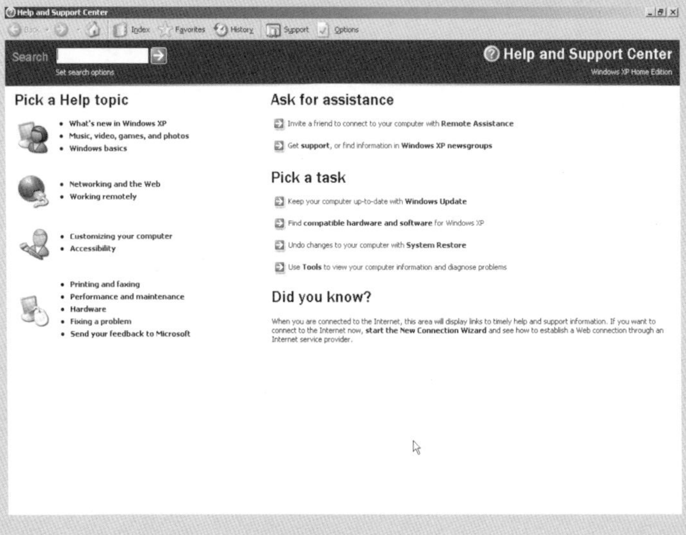

**Figure 5.4**   Windows XP help system

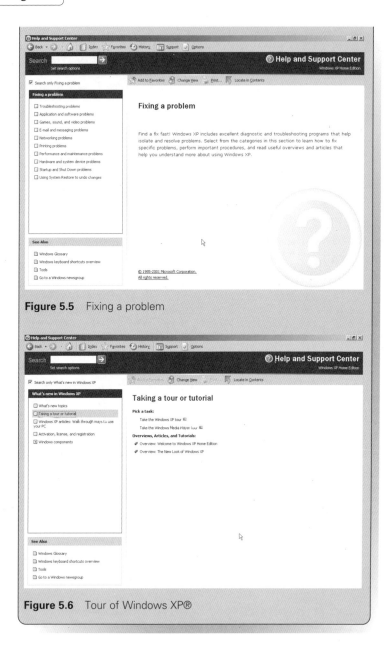

**Figure 5.5** Fixing a problem

**Figure 5.6** Tour of Windows XP®

## Other forms of problems

Using technology involves getting used to solving problems but many aspects of learning also involve unravelling dilemmas. You need to able to:

- identify the real problem (i.e. not the symptoms);
- analyse the evidence systematically;
- consider if there is a pattern or an exception to the rule;
- review the solution;
- apply your experience (i.e. learning from similar problems you have already encountered).

## Activity
## Solving problems?

Consider how you approached some recent problems. They can be anything, such as your car failing to start, poor results from a piece of work you were sure was well done or a misunderstanding with someone. Think through a range of problems and write down how you handled them.

**Discussion**
A standard approach to problem solving can be summarised as follows:

1. Identify the problem (e.g. flat battery, wet engine or poor connection).
2. Get the facts – find out as much information as you can about the problem.
3. Analyse the evidence.
4. Decide on a solution (e.g. charge battery, telephone breakdown service or fix the connection).
5. Check the solution.

What is your approach?

Problems can be solved in a variety of ways. Some approaches are:

- Trial and error – although this appears to rely on good luck to provide the solution, if you systematically make changes and notice the effects of each change then it can be useful. However, it does depend on making changes logically and noting the effects, otherwise it becomes simple guesswork. It can also take a lot of time.

- Serendipity – essentially you are hoping that some inspiration occurs to provide a solution.
- Analysis – this is essentially the approach adopted in the activity of gathering the facts, analysing the evidence, balancing the information to arrive at a solution and finally reviewing the solution.
- Creativity – there are a variety of techniques that can be employed to solve problems creatively, such as brainstorming.
- Rule book – this is a standard approach where you follow the procedure (e.g. soldiers are often encouraged to follow the rule book which is essentially the experience of earlier soldiers written down for the benefits of others).

## Coping with stress

Everyone finds learning stressful at times – perhaps you are facing an examination, have left it too late to finish an assignment or simply find the subject difficult to understand. e-Learning provides more freedom to study when you want, at the pace that suits you and at your preferred location. This can also mean trying to learn in the family home with various distractions surrounding you, combining your studies with your family responsibilities and studying for long hours when perhaps you should be relaxing or even sleeping. It is vital for your health to establish a good life/study balance. If you are also working then the balance becomes even more complex because you have to consider work, life and learning.

A key factor in coping with stress is to try to identify the cause and to remove it. If you have family responsibilities combined with a heavy learning burden you will almost certainly feel stressed from time to time. If you find yourself with a deadline to meet and have to work many more hours (perhaps all night) to get the work done then you are going to experience substantial pressure.

Some ways to cope with stress are shown below:

- Before you start your course, find out what is expected of you. Consider your own personal circumstances and judge if you can deal with that amount of commitment. Many courses will provide you with guidance about how much time you should expect to study each week.
- Planning your work will reduce stress by avoiding some of the crises that generate pressure. Give yourself sufficient time to complete assignments without last-minute panics.

- e-Learning provides you with more freedom to study but does expect you to take more responsibility for your learning. Use the freedom to plan your studies and reduce the pressure.
- Give yourself a sound study pattern with regular breaks, rest and meal breaks. It may sound great to study all night but it is both poor learning practice and unhealthy. It is better to study for shorter periods but regularly. An hour a day is likely to be more effective than seven hours once a week.
- Different learning tasks need different study patterns, so be flexible. It is unreasonable to expect yourself to be able to read books for a whole day and become concerned that you are unproductive. You are likely to achieve better results if you try to work on a range of different tasks.
- Monitor your life/study balance to ensure that you are not neglecting your learning in favour of a busy social life or, equally, ignoring relaxation in favour of studying.
- Online learning can be very isolating and this can add stress. At an early stage of the course, try to make contact with other learners so that you develop relationships and give yourself some peer support. Problems can often be reduced by some friendly discussion.
- Ask for help when you have a problem. Many tutors comment that they can be more helpful to their students if they are informed earlier of difficulties but frequently they are asked for assistance too late.
- Assessment makes most learners anxious. The key is to prepare yourself adequately for the test by planning ahead to give yourself enough time to revise or complete the assessed task.

## Activity
## Life, work and study balance

Over a typical week keep a detailed record of how you spend your time. This should include:

1. all activities you spend time on – with your family, eating, relaxing, sleeping, studying and working;
2. when you undertake each activity (e.g. 1 a.m. to 2 a.m. – writing essay).

Present your analysis as a calendar with a timetable, for example:

```
Date:          Sunday 29 June
8 a.m.         Breakfast
8.30 a.m.      Walk to local shop
8.45 a.m.      Read newspaper.
```

Analyse the record to identify how much time you spend:

1. studying;
2. working;
3. relaxing/social life;
4. sleeping.

What is the balance?

**Discussion**
It is difficult to say what makes a good balance of life, work and study. Everyone has a different mix of family responsibilities, work pressures and learning activities to combine but you should be able to see a distinct pattern. The key is that everything is in moderation and extremes are rare. Some features to be concerned about are shown below:

1. You have very little social life.
2. All your studying takes place late at night.
3. You do not see your family on many days (e.g. Monday to Friday).
4. You get less than eight hours' sleep a night.
5. You get little or no exercise.
6. You are not studying regularly.

## ● Motivation

There are many reasons for undertaking an e-learning course. You might want:

- to get a better job;
- to give yourself more job security;
- to change your life;
- to learn about a subject that fascinates you.

Whatever the reasons for learning, almost all students find that there are times when they are miserable, irritated with their own performance or the technology (especially true in e-learning) or simply unsure if they are doing the right course. A motivated learner will overcome problems and difficulties while a demotivated one will be hindered by even the smallest of barriers.

When motivation is low, it is important to take action to improve your enthusiasm. Try some of the following steps:

- Have a break – a few hours away from studying can often work wonders whereas trying to force yourself to study when motivation is low will often achieve little.
- Remember why you are doing this course – there is nothing like recalling your original motivation to disperse the doubts.
- Consider what you have already achieved, what you will gain by completing the course and how little there is still to do.
- e-Mail your tutor and ask for help.
- e-Mail other learners and see how they feel – they are in the best position to understand what you are experiencing.
- Discuss how you feel with your family – often their support is vital to successful learning.

### Activity
### Motivation

Consider the course of study you are currently undertaking and write a list of the reasons for studying.

Next consider when your motivation is low – what demotivates you and what helps you overcome these periods.

**Discussion**
At one stage in my life I undertook nine years' part-time study while completing master's and doctorate courses. My reasons for this long period of effort were:

1. a real interest in the subjects I was studying;
2. developing expertise in areas relevant to my career;
3. developing my own self-esteem;
4. discovering my own strengths.

The factors that demotivated me always seemed to be centred around poor or slow progress. In my case success made me want to achieve more while a delay or an obstacle often discouraged me. I overcame these periods by taking a break from the frustration to reflect on what had gone wrong. I was often able to see a new way of overcoming the barrier.

### ● **Reflection**

Reflection is an important learning skill in all forms and types of learning. It will help you gain a new insight into yourself and the subjects you are studying. Everyone can reflect on experiences in an informal and haphazard way. To gain the maximum benefit, it is useful to approach it in a systematic and considered way.

Normally reflection requires peace and relaxation, yet many people are able to reflect on a bus or train. You need some mental space and that is often available during a journey. Other ways of gaining the space are to:

- take a walk in the countryside or even in a town although there are more potential distractions and interruptions in an urban area;
- listen to some favourite music – headphones are an effective way of cutting yourself off from the world;
- sit in the sun by yourself;
- find a quiet place (e.g. library);
- make notes about the subject and later review them;
- keep a learning diary;
- add your reflections on a topic to your e-portfolio.

Many courses increasing offer the opportunity to develop a blog of your personal reflections. A blog has an important advantage over a conventional diary in that you can share it with your peers and tutors. They can then add comments so that you gain other perspectives of your feelings and experiences. You can also read your peers' blogs which may help your reflection.

You will sometimes be required to produce reflections on a topic, such as a paper or book you have read, for inclusions in your e-portfolio. Your tutor is free to offer you feedback on the work so that you gain another viewpoint on your approach to reflection. This can help you improve your ability to reflect.

When you reflect you are trying to:

- consider new experiences in the context of what you already know;
- fit new knowledge into the existing understanding that you have about the subject;
- analyse your e-learning experience, perhaps by comparing it with your previous experiences of learning in more traditional ways.

Reflection helps you to understand new information, fit it into what you already know and change your own opinions.

## Activity
### Reflecting on reflection

Consider your own efforts to think through issues – that is, how you have found reflecting? What is the best way for you to concentrate on thinking through a set of ideas, compare different experiences or understand an issue? What environment do you need in order to reflect effectively? How must you approach the task?

**Discussion**
Personally, I am able to reflect in different settings, depending on my personal motivation and the subject that I am considering. My best environment for reflecting on new knowledge is to take a walk with a notebook and focus on the different aspects as I stroll. As ideas or concepts occur to me, I stop and make a few notes so that I do not forget them.

Alternatively, I can reflect by attempting to write a short piece explaining my thoughts, ideas and reflections on a specific issue. In a sense, I need a focus such as writing a blog entry to allow me to reflect.

You may find that you need a particular setting such as a quiet room or library in order to reflect. You may need to take notes and look at these a little later. Many people find that a short break after reflecting gives them new insights into the topic. It is useful to know your own reflection preferences so that you can get the maximum benefit from the experience.

## Listening

You will have spent many years listening to teachers and lecturers. Listening in e-learning has new dimensions, such as listening to recorded materials in the form of podcasts and taking part in audio conferences.

### Podcasts

You can listen to a podcast on your computer or on a portable device when you are away from home. At home you will be listening in an environment of your choice so you can eliminate or reduce distractions and concentrate on the recording. However, listening on the move means that while you have the advantage of fitting in study time when it is convenient, you also have lots of potential distractions.

It is useful when listening to:

- minimise the possibility of distractions;
- take notes if you can while you listen or write them down later;

- before you start to listen, prepare yourself by thinking about the topic and recalling what you already know and any items that you would particular like to know more about;
- as you listen, try to identify the key points of the material – a speaker will often give you clues by using words like important, vital, main, critical and significant.

Podcasts allow you to stop, start and replay them so don't just listen but take part, by controlling the presentation of the material. Most podcasts are sound only but there are also vodcasts which employ video material. The key issues in watching a vodcast are essentially the same as listening but with the extra possibilities that visual clues give you to help you identify key points (e.g. speakers emphasise with their hands or use body language).

### Audio conferences

An audio conference places a great emphasis on your ability to concentrate on what the other participants are saying. Unlike a podcast, you cannot control how long they will last nor can you replay them. You need to be able to concentrate for a long time. Three key factors will help you concentrate:

1. *Preparation*: prepare for the conference so that you know what you would like to say and what you hope to learn.
2. *Notes*: take notes, starting with recording who the other participants are, and then try to note each key issue as it is raised. You can gain a lot by listening to the discussion.
3. *Participation*: take part in the discussion – ask questions, make comments and build on points other people have made. The more you contribute, the more you will gain.

### Research skills

Research skills form a part of all courses. You may only wish to find out the answer to a question, find examples to help you write an essay or revise a topic for an examination but all these things involve locating and evaluating information. Earlier you considered how to search for information on the world wide web and this is a key skill which has various associated activities. The list in Table 5.1 below outlines some good practices to help your research activities.

One approach extensively employed when the world wide web was relatively new was to e-mail a famous or well-known researcher or author with

| Practice | Explanation | Discussion |
|---|---|---|
| 1. Questioning | The first step is to develop/consider the question that your research is seeking to answer. | You may feel that the question is obvious but try to write a precise statement of it. Some time spent considering the actual question you want to address will save you time later. |
| 2. Planning | Before you start to research your subject consider what you are looking to find:<br>• general information introducing the subject;<br>• surveys – quantitative or qualitative;<br>• research reports;<br>• particular authors. | It is very tempting to go immediately online and to start searching. However, this is likely to be less effective than spending a few minutes considering exactly what it is you are seeking. |
| 3. Search terms | You need to consider a range of terms and alternatives that you might use.<br>Consider the use of the Boolean terms to refine your search:<br>• OR;<br>• AND;<br>• NOT.<br>Everyone has a favourite search engine but it is often beneficial to employ more than one to provide a comparison. | There are two alternative approaches to searching:<br>1. Start broad and focus.<br>It is often useful to start your search with general terms, especially if it is a new subject or topic since this will capture the most sources. Subsequent searches can focus on the precise area of your interest. You might want to consider a series of searches, each one building on the previous one.<br>2. Start focused and broaden if you cannot locate sufficient sources. |

**Table 5.1**   Research activities – *continued overleaf*

| Practice | Explanation | Discussion |
|---|---|---|
| 4. Assessing the quality of the information | Who is the author? Is biographical information provided? Who owns the site (e.g. consider the domain)? Are they appropriate for the information provided? Is it a personal site? Is it simply an individual's opinion? What references are incorporated within the information? What links are provided from the page? Are they good quality pages? When was the site last updated? | The earlier section on the quality of world wide web information should be consulted. |
| 5. Reviewing the results of the search | You need to review the outcome of your search since this will indicate not only the success of your efforts but also suggest other keywords and sites to refine your search | Reflection and review are important elements in any research process. |
| 6. Saving results and searches | You will frequently need to repeat searches, so keep records of the outcomes and search terms. | Keeping records is a vital element in research. You must be able to find information later that was previously very helpful to you. |

**Table 5.1** *continued*

a question. This was very successful when they received only an occasional message but nowadays all users of e-mail receive large numbers of messages. You are unlikely to receive any response except an occasional acknowledgement. However, many researchers and authors have developed personal websites and/or blogs including details of their publications, ideas and new projects. These are very useful when you are seeking information. In a similar way, many research groups have created websites to disseminate the outcomes of their projects.

## Activity
## Research skills

Consider searching for information about online assessment:

1. Plan your research – what would you like to find?
2. What search terms will you use and what engines?

Carry out the search and record the most successful results (e.g. webpages etc.)

**Discussion**
My initial step was to check out the scale of the task by simply searching the world wide web using three different search engines – Google, Yahoo and MSN. The results indicated that there is a massive number of webpages linked to the subject (i.e. online assessment):

- Google – 176,000,000 pages;
- Yahoo – 52,900,000 pages;
- MSN – 1,675,618 pages.

To make the search more concentrated, I amended the terms to e-learning online assessment and reduced the number of pages significantly:

- Google – 1,970,000 pages;
- Yahoo – 1,590,000 pages;
- MSN – 463,923 pages.

I next reviewed the top ten pages from all three engines and found that Google, MSN and Yahoo had two in common while MSN had four in common with Yahoo.

My next step would have been to explore the ten sites to help refine my search terms.

What did you do and what were the outcomes?

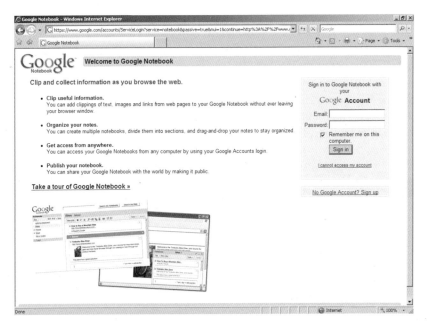

**Figure 5.7**   Google Notebook

When you are researching online you will often need to take notes of what you find. Google provides a useful notebook. It allows you to add text, pictures and links and to organise the notebook contents. It is online so that you can use it wherever you can access the internet and it even enables you to allow other people to view the notebook contents. This is illustrated in Figure 5.7.

## Main sources of dissatisfaction

Hara and Koling (2000) have identified two major sources of frustration for e-learners. They are:

1. *Technical problems:* All forms of technical problems can be a nuisance and severely distract you from your studies. There are several ways of dealing with them:

   - College helpdesk – your college may provide a student helpline to assist you with software and hardware problems. However, in some cases this is limited to the software and hardware they have supplied with the course.

- Warranty – your equipment may be covered by a warranty from the suppliers which will often include a telephone helpline, although sometimes you have to pay extra for the call. The initial step is almost always a telephone diagnostic process to identify the problem. In addition, an engineer may call if the problem is too difficult to resolve over the telephone or they may collect your equipment to repair at their centre. You need to study warranties. Ideally you need one which guarantees how long they will take to come out and repair your equipment. Many simply offer to take away and repair the equipment with no time limit.

- Applications – many technical problems arise from applications. Many major application suppliers provide websites with technical advice and some (e.g. Microsoft® software) build troubleshooting features into their products.

- Peers – many course forums provide a self-help discussion forum for you to ask questions about technical issues so that your colleagues can offer assistance.

2. *Teaching problems:* there are several ways of dealing with teaching problems:

    - e-Learning programmes will usually provide you with a personal tutor, mentor or learning supporter. They are the first place to seek support and help with teaching and learning problems.

    - If you are new to e-learning it is often difficult to judge if the problem is with the teaching or yourself. The easiest way is to ask your fellow students. What do they think?

    - Your college will almost certainly have a complaints procedure if the problem is serious. This will often be available on the course website.

## Summary

### 1. Initial experience
You are recommended during your initial experience of e-learning to:

- participate in all communication activities to develop your relationship with other learners and your tutor;

- explore the learning environment – discover what help is available – look for learning materials, study guides, library facilities and other resources.

## 2.  Time management

A major benefit of e-learning is the freedom to learn when it is best for you but this comes at the price of being responsible for managing your own time. Some ways to help you manage your time are:

- using Outlook® software and similar applications;
- considering the course requirements and structure (e.g. assignments, marks, examinations or other assessments);
- analysing your own objectives, personal timetable and learning preferences;
- balancing your priorities against each other (e.g. family and work responsibilities);
- considering good learning and health practice;
- devising your own study timetable and reviewing it at intervals.

## 3.  Acceptance of responsibility

e-Learning assumes that you accept more responsibility for your studies than do traditional learning methods giving you more freedom of how and when to learn. It is important to:

- understand at the start the course structure, standards and conditions (e.g. deadlines and assessment);
- Outlook® messaging software and similar applications can be helpful with planning studies (e.g. To Do lists).

## 4.  Planning

Planning will improve your results and productivity and reduce your stress. It involves:

- looking ahead;
- identifying critical points;
- setting goals;

- producing a personal action plan;
- organising yourself;
- plan assignments and other components as well as the overall course.

## 5.   Self-assessment

You are responsible for monitoring your own progress. It is important to:

- compare your own progress/understanding with that of your colleagues – contact them early in the course and try to establish a culture of self-help;
- question any feedback to ensure you have a clear understanding of your strengths and weaknesses;
- use interactive materials to test yourself;
- reflect on all forms of feedback that you receive;
- keep records of feedback/performance so you can identify patterns of strengths and weaknesses;
- use e-Portfolios are a means of dynamically showing your skills, understanding and competency;
- use comments on your blog entries and compare your blog with those of your peers to help you self-assess;
- use virtual experiments to help you revise and experience a large range of experiments.

## 6.   Problem solving

When using technical equipment you will occasionally encounter problems with the hardware or software, so be aware that:

- courses will provide assistance to solve these problems and you need to know how you can access it;
- technical specialists will often talk you through the troubleshooting process with both hardware and software problems;
- online communication problems often require two telephone lines so that the technical support can check the connection to the internet while you are talking to them;

- both your internet service and educational provider can provide technical support (the degree of support will depend on your contracts);
- helpline websites often present solutions to standard problems or provide background information;
- it is useful to have all your documents, handbooks, passwords and tools close to your computer;
- it is important to make notes of exactly what is not working, and especially any error messages;
- you should always disconnect the equipment from the power supply;
- operating systems often have extensive help systems.

**7.   Coping with stress**

Stress can affect all learners at some time during their course but there are a variety of ways of helping yourself to cope with this:

- e-Learning provides more freedom to study but does expect you to take more responsibility for your learning. Use the freedom to plan your studies and reduce the pressure.
- Establish a good life/study balance (i.e. rest, relaxation, work and family).
- Remove the causes of stress.
- Plan your studies and your life.
- Build relationships with your fellow learners.
- Ask your tutor for help if you need it.

**8.   Motivation**

Motivation is critical for success in most courses. Everyone becomes demotivated at some stage. The key is not to ignore the problem but to take action to overcome the feelings (e.g. take a break, consider what you have already achieved and reflect on why you are doing the course).

**9.   Reflection**

If you are able to reflect effectively on your own experiences and understanding you will gain a significant learning benefit. Reflection requires:

- a systematic and considered approach;
- mental space (e.g. peace and quiet).

## 10.   Listening

Listening in e-learning will often involve recorded materials (e.g. podcasts) and audio conferences. It is useful when listening to recorded material to:

- minimise distractions;
- take notes;
- prepare;
- identify the key points.

Podcasts allow you to stop, start and replay them.
Three key factors of a successful audio conference are:

- preparation;
- taking notes;
- participation.

## 11.   Research skills

Research skills are useful in almost all learning programmes and are vital for the efficient and effective use of the world wide web as an information source. Research requires you to:

- plan your investigation;
- search for information, perhaps using the web (e.g. identify appropriate keywords);
- assess the quality of the information you find;
- review your approach – has it been effective? – should you try another way?
- save your keywords and outcomes as you may want to repeat it.

# 6 Developing Skills

This chapter continues the development of skills discussed in Chapter 5. It will focus on providing a range of activities to extend your e-learning skills.

## ● Time management

There is often a considerable difference between how you think you use your time and how you actually do. It is important to be aware of this difference since it will help you plan and manage your time. The activity below asks you to monitor how you spend your time over a week-long period.

### Activity
### Monitoring your use of time

Over a period of a week, keep detailed records of how you spend your time. Figure 6.1 gives an example of a table which may help you keep your records but feel free to modify it to suit your own pattern. It is simply a breakdown of a day spent studying, showing learning, breaks and social activities. You may want to add comments on whether you felt the learning went well (e.g. you could concentrate and achieved good results), or on travel or any other significant action that requires your time.

**Discussion**
Most people underestimate how much time they spend simply doing nothing or doing what could loosely be called social activities. Equally, it is essential to take regular breaks. Your productivity will be improved if you do this. It is not sensible to try and study for many hours continuously. Make a drink, take a walk or simply watch the television. A regular pattern of short spells of study is often very productive.

Assess how you spend your time. If your course provides guidance on how many hours you should study, compare the actual with the theory. Are you spending your valuable time sensibly? Are you giving enough time to the most important work? Are you meeting your deadlines? Are you getting enough sleep? Are you studying at the most effective time (i.e. when you are alert)?

| | Date | | 21-Jul-07 | | |
|---|---|---|---|---|---|
| | Start Time | Finish Time | Activity | Notes | Total |
| | | | | | |
| | 8:00 | 10:00 | Reading and making notes | | 2.0 hours |
| | 10:00 | 10:30 | Break | | 0.5 hours |
| | 10:30 | 13:00 | Research on the Internet | Sources for essay on Napoleon | 2.5 hours |
| | 13:00 | 14:30 | Break | | 1.5 hours |
| | 14:30 | 17:00 | Library | Visit to library to locate some books and journals | 2.5 hours |
| | 17:00 | 20:00 | Break | Dinner – doing nothing | 2.5 hours |
| | 20:00 | 22:00 | Television | Watching football match | 2.0 hours |
| | 22:00 | 23:30 | Listening to music | | 1.5 hours |
| | 23:30 | | Bed | | |
| | | | | | |
| **Summary** | | | | | |
| | | | | | |
| **Study Time** | | | | | 6.5 hours |
| **Breaks** | | | | | 4.5 hours |
| **Social Activities** | | | | | 3.5 hours |

**Figure 6.1**  Monitoring

Are you finding that studying at certain times (e.g. evening) is difficult? Perhaps you are easy to distract at that time. It is often a good idea, if you are finding that a particular time is poor for studying, to switch to another (e.g. from evenings to mornings after breakfast).

## Activity
## To Do lists

A very useful task to assist control and management of your time is making a To Do list. Simply list all the things you need to do and then place them in order of importance. This gives you a sequence of actions to further your studies and helps you make effective use of your time.

Write a To Do list of what you need to achieve over the next few weeks or months.

### Discussion

I have produced my own list below with an explanation of why it is important:

1.   Write the essay – the deadline is only two weeks away and it is worth 20 per cent of the continuous assessment for the course.

2.  Locate the set books for the course – I need some of them almost immediately and it could take time since some of the books may need to be ordered.
3.  Check the assessment criteria for the final examination – although this is some time ahead I need to consider my planning.
4.  e-Mail all the other members of my co-operative learning group to check if anyone else is finding understanding the course's fourth activity difficulty – although the deadline for the activity is some weeks away people often do not reply immediately and I need to clarify what I have to do.
5.  Buy another memory stick – not very important but I keep forgetting to do this.

Sometimes my lists are far longer and I frequently list tasks in the wrong order but usually I get everything done without last-minute panics.

## Acceptance of responsibility

In a traditional course, the responsibility for your learning is to some extent taken by your tutors who will often organise the learning around assessment deadlines, plan time for revision and generally direct your attention to what they regard as critical activities. This process, although helpful, often conditions you to react to their initiatives rather than encouraging you to be proactive.

One way of developing a more personal responsibility for your own learning is to take the lead. The next two activities are based on your volunteering to take responsibility for your own and, to some extent, other people's learning.

### Activity
### Volunteers to lead a group task

Collaborating with other learners to carry out a task is a frequent e-learning activity. It involves dividing responsibility for the component parts of the task between the group and asking people to take responsibility for roles such as leading the group.

In the next group activity, volunteer to lead. While you undertake the task, keep a record/diary of what happens and reflect on the process and your own learning.

**Discussion**
Your experience will be unique to the circumstances of your group and the task but you may have experienced the following:

1. It was easy to volunteer. Everyone accepted you – often people are reluctant to take responsibility so are happy if someone else comes forward.
2. It was not so easy getting agreement on everyone taking a fair share of the work but you were pleased that a timetable was agreed.
3. Some group members failed to meet their targets. In some cases, members did not seem to have done anything, others had done a lot but not what was agreed and a few had completed their agreed tasks.
4. You spent a lot of effort encouraging members to keep to the agreement. This was not always successful.
5. You worked harder than you imagined.
6. You found yourself filling some of the gaps.
7. Other group members helped by taking on extra work.

Overall, you have probably learnt a great deal about the problems of co-ordinating a group without any authority to compel. However, there is a lot of satisfaction in achieving the end result. You are surprised as much by who helped as by who did not pull their weight.

Hopefully you have learnt a good deal about yourself and how you should behave in a learning group.

Another typical e-learning activity is online or mailgroup discussions. Many people are often reluctant to take part. A useful way of developing your own acceptance of responsibility is to play an active part in an online discussion.

## Activity
## Participating in an online discussion

Prepare yourself to take part in a discussion that you start and to which you make a significant contribution. Remember that a discussion is more that just giving your own views. It requires other learners to take part and you need to be prepared to help others to contribute. While you are involved in the discussion, keep a record/diary of what happens and reflect on the process and your own learning.

**Discussion**
Your own experience will be different from these reflections since it will be unique, based on the topic and the membership of the discussion group. However, you may have encountered:

1. a slow response to your original message;
2. responses that seemed only marginally related to your contribution;

3. responses that showed considerable understanding of the issues and made you feel inadequate and reluctant to reply for fear of showing your own lack of knowledge;
4. the need to e-mail other learners directly to ask a specific question about their contribution;
5. the need to e-mail other learners to encourage them to take part;
6. messages that related to much earlier contributions, taking the discussion off on a tangent;
7. messages sent directly to you asking for clarification or encouraging you to keep contributing;
8. contributions that were unconnected to the topic.

Numerous other things may have happened. Hopefully, you have gained confidence in your ability to contribute to discussions and have learnt a lot about yourself.

## Planning

Planning is a continuous process and impacts on many other e-learning skills in that it can:

- help reduce your stress since you have fewer crises due to a lack of foresight;
- contribute to your time management;
- make you realise the issues you need to take responsibility for;
- make you aware of when assessments are due;
- give you adequate time to resolve difficulties and problems;
- provide you with sufficient time to reflect on your learning;
- help motivate you by making the learning process smoother;

Planning should be at the heart of your e-learning skills.

### Activity
### Planning your revision

Revision for your assessment requires careful planning. Consider in the context of your own e-learning course what you need to do in order to be prepared for the examination.

**Discussion**
There are many ways of planning for your revision. Some issues are:

1.  Consider the overall timetable for the course. When are the assessments due and how much time have you available for revision?
2.  Preparation for revision needs to start at the beginning of the course. Your notes are partially aimed at providing you with a set of explanations suitable for revisions months later. Plan time for checking your initial notes in order to annotate and fill in any gaps.
3.  Do not expect too much from yourself – give yourself breaks and plenty of time.
4.  What methods do you employ during revision (e.g. completing past examination papers, editing your notes, reading, listening to podcasts, etc.)? Make the process interesting. If you are bored then you will find it difficult to revise effectively.
5.  Reflect on your planning and identify what went well and what you would want to change for next time.

Planning is a key activity but all plans need to be flexible and can be improved.

# Activity
## Planning a research project

In the context of your own e-learning course, consider how you would plan a research project. If your course does not include a project, then plan another aspect of the work such as an assignment.

**Discussion**
One approach to planning a project is:

1.  Consider what the aim of the project is. Some colleges will provide guidelines if the project is a major part of the course (e.g. final-year project).
2.  How much time is recommended by the college for the project? When do you need to begin? What part in the overall assessment of the e-learning course is played by the research? How is the research marked? You need to be well informed to plan effectively.
3.  Identify your aims and objectives. What do you hope to achieve? Is it realistic?
4.  How will you undertake the research? What methods will you use?
5.  What scale of literature review will you undertake?
6.  Does research involve:
    - a survey;
    - interviews;
    - experiments.
    If you are going to carry out a survey then you will need to design your questions, pilot the questionnaire and revise it. All approaches will need design effort and validation.

7. Consider how long each element of the project will take and the relationship of the elements to each other (i.e. do they need to be done sequentially or can you do them in parallel?).
8. How long will it take to write the research report? You need to allow time for it to be proofread and revised.

It is often useful to produce a visual plan. An example is shown in Figure 6.2.

| | January–February | March | March | April–June | July | August–September | |
|---|---|---|---|---|---|---|---|
| | Gathering Information | | | | | | |
| | | Aims & Objectives | | | | | |
| | | | Methods | | | | |
| | | | | Literature Review | | | |
| | | | | | Survey | | |
| | | | | | | Writing Report | |

**Figure 6.2** Visual plan

## Self-assessment

## Activity
## Involving your tutor

In all forms of learning your tutor is a vital resource. In e-learning you need to involve your tutors in judging how you are progressing. Consider how you can make use of them. Write a short list.

**Discussion**
There are many ways of involving your tutor. They include:

1. Feedback – your tutor will provide feedback on your assignments. This can take a variety of forms but is often provided as overall comments and grades combined with annotation of your assignment. You need to read the feedback carefully and ask questions. If you are unsure, then contact your tutor and ask for clarification.
2. Questions – you can ask your tutor for help at any time during the course. He or she can explain difficult concepts, offer advice and suggest alternative approaches to your learning.
3. Comparison – to assist your self-assessment, ask your tutor how your work compares with that of other students. Your grade is important but it is very helpful if you know how everyone else has done.

## Activity
## Involving your peers

In all forms of learning discussing your studies with your peers is a useful resource. They can help you assess your progress, often by comparing your efforts with theirs. Consider how you can make the best use of them.

**Discussion**
Ways of involving your peers can include the following:

1. Respond to your peers' questions and requests for help and generally be positive. They will hopefully help you when you ask for assistance.
2. Be open about your own assessment and suggest that everyone will benefit if there is some form of sharing of marks or comments. Ask your peers to read and comment on your blog.
3. Suggest establishing a self-help group where everyone can pose questions, ask for support with particular topics, etc. The more you offer help, the more assistance you are likely to receive (see plagiarism section).
4. Remember that although a message sent to a mailgroup is forwarded to all participants, you can send individual e-mails to your colleagues as well. This allows you to respond directly and privately to single learners.

It is likely that your college, employer or the training provider organising the e-learning programme will encourage mutual support, so respond positively to their efforts

## Activity
## Making yourself more effective

How can you make yourself more effective at assessing your own progress? Write a list of actions you might take.

**Discussion**
There are a number of possibilities including:

1. Records – it is useful to keep a record of feedback, marks and other assessment comments so that you can identify trends and patterns.
2. Communication – it is important to assess informal feedback, so you need to encourage discussion with your peers and tutors. You should be proactive in encouraging an exchange of views, ideas and reflections. These will help you assess yourself against your colleagues and the standards of the tutors.

3. Documents – you should have read all the course information so that you are well prepared (i.e. you know the course timetable and understand the assessment criteria and rules governing the educational institution).
4. Feedback – offer feedback to your colleagues and encourage them to comment on your work in blogs, wikis or your e-portfolio. Try to reflect on their feedback and compare comments made to colleagues with those made about your own work.

There are probably further items. What did your list include?

## Problem solving

There are many sources of assistance for solving technical problems available on the world wide web. Often suppliers of hardware and software provide technical advice on their websites.

### Activity
### Contacting a technical helpline

If you found that you had a problem with your computer and you needed to contact your technical helpline, perhaps as part of the supplier's warranty, how would you go about it? List the things that you would expect the support service to want from you in order to diagnose the problem.

**Discussion**
This is based on my own recent experience when contacting my supplier's helpline:

1. You need proof that you are a bona fide customer who can call the helpline. You are often supplied with a code number or password to show this. Copies of purchase documents (e.g. receipts) are also important.
2. You should have your operating system code number (i.e. the number you enter when installing the system to show it is a legal copy). You may need this if you have to reinstall the operating system.
3. You will sometimes be given a recovery CD-ROM to help you reinstall the system back to its original settings. This is useful when you have a significant failure. You should not use it unless you are certain you understand what to do.
4. Have on hand your system and software documents (e.g. guides, manuals, etc).
5. Keep copies of your original operating system software in case you need to reinstall it. If you suspect the problem is connected

with other applications, it is a good idea to have copies of those ready too.
6.   You may need screwdrivers and other tools in case you are asked to open the computer to check items.
7.   Have a pen and paper to make notes.

What other items did you have on your list? In simple terms, you need to be organised and keep your application's software and documentation in a safe place so that it is to hand when things go wrong.

## Activity
## Suppliers' websites

Hardware, software and service suppliers (e.g. internet service suppliers) often provide a range of sources of assistance when you have a problem or, perhaps more importantly, to help you prevent trouble. Identify a variety of suppliers' sites and visit them to identify what assistance they provide.

### Discussion

I visited suppliers of computer equipment and applications and also an internet service provider. Your own experience may be different due to the dynamic nature of the world wide web and the different suppliers. I visited the sites for Apple, Microsoft and Demon, respectively. They offered a wide variety of information and services such as:

1.   technical information about equipment, applications and connectivity (e.g. different broadband connections);
2.   access to software that you can download – this is often new versions of applications (e.g. e-mail editors and browsers), extensions to existing products or fixes for technical problems (often called patches);
3.   news about viruses or other important issues;
4.   information about local suppliers, sources of help and new developments;
5.   other items.

All the sites offered comprehensive assistance for users which should assist in solving or preventing problems.

There are also support forums linked to particular products where other users will be able to answer your queries if you send them a message.

What did you discover?

## Activity
## Buying software

Select something you would like to do if you had sufficient funds (e.g. upgrade your office applications, change operating systems or buy a programming language to help you learn how to programme). Identify all the factors that you need to consider when buying the chosen application for your computer. Many software suppliers offer special deals for students and teachers, so investigate whether you can get an educational discount. If you are sponsored by your employers, they may well have rules about the purchase of hardware and software (e.g. central purchase or loaning you equipment for the duration of the course).

Write a description of the process to ensure you purchase a suitable package.

**Discussion**
It is important to approach the task systematically – identifying the basic information you need and then considering more complex matters. Some possible questions to answer are:

1.  What is the specification of your computer system (e.g. processor, random access memory (RAM), storage capacity, CD-ROM drive, etc.)?
2.  What are the recommended requirements for your new application?
3.  What is the cost of the new application?
4.  Do you need the full version of the application or can you use an upgrade because you have an earlier version of the software?
5.  Are there any discounts for buying online? Can you download the application? Do you have to pay a delivery charge?
6.  How do you install the application?
7.  What users' reviews are available? Some suppliers of applications provide users' reviews of their products.

Your own list may be different, but the key to solving problems is to approach the task systematically.

## Coping with stress

Stress can be part of everyone's life. It is vital to ensure that your approach to learning minimises its influence and that you live a balanced, healthy life.

## Activity
## Study/life balance

Previously you considered how you spent your time over a week. The following activity aims to help you improve your study/life balance. A good balance is about working smarter rather than harder. Earlier you monitored how you used your time to become an improved time manager. Now consider how you could reduce the pressure on yourself by working smarter. Write a list of actions.

**Discussion**
There are both small and large actions to help you work smarter. They include:

1.  Planning and organising your time
    *For example*: If you are going to visit the library, consider what books or other resources you will need later in the course for future assignments and locate them alongside your immediate needs. Try to think ahead and organise yourself as early as possible.
2.  Study time – everyone has preferences about when they like to carry our particular tasks. Plan your work around your preferred times and be realistic about what you can achieve.
    *For example*: Trying to write an essay after a 12-hour working day is unlikely to be successful.
3.  Waste – effort is sometimes wasted by a lack of personal preparation.
    *For example*: You start an assignment and then realise that you have forgotten to bring a key book with you. Plan ahead and prepare yourself to make the most of your time.
4.  Priorities – consider carefully what you have to do and list them in order of importance and urgency. To Do lists are very useful to prioritise actions as well as ensuring that you do not forget them.

What items does your own list contain?

## Activity
## Healthy life

A healthy lifestyle is likely to help you control your study and life pressures. Write a list of what you feel would constitute a healthy lifestyle.

**Discussion**
I believe that a healthy lifestyle includes the following:

1.  A balanced diet – it is important to ensure you have a healthy diet. This is likely to include five portions of fruit and vegetables every

> day and minimising the consumption of saturated fats (see e.g. https://www.healthspace.nhs.uk/).
>
> 2.  Regular exercise – keeping fit generally requires that you regularly undertake short spells of exercise (i.e. 20 or 30 minutes) which leave you slightly out of breath. I like to walk briskly for 30 minutes each day and find walking an excellent way to relax after a busy day.
> 3.  Sleep – a regular pattern of sufficient sleep is important to help you study.
> 4.  Reduced anxiety – adjust your study pattern to reduce, or ideally remove, stress. Time pressure is often a key part of study stress so start your work as early as possible and plan how to undertake it. Do not be a source of your own time problems – organise yourself.
> 5.  Support – seek help and assistance from your tutors, peers and family. This will help put your problems in perspective, solve them or at least reduce their intensity.
>
> What items does your own list contain?

## Motivation

People are motivated by different things but one factor that encourages most people is success. Success brings rewards such as a more interesting career, higher pay or increased self-esteem.

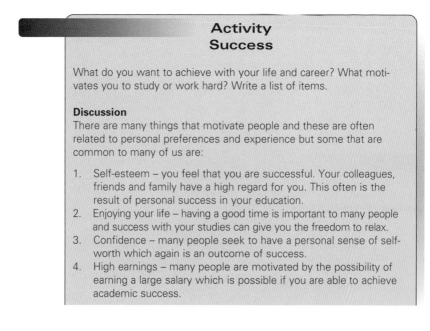

### Activity
### Success

What do you want to achieve with your life and career? What motivates you to study or work hard? Write a list of items.

**Discussion**
There are many things that motivate people and these are often related to personal preferences and experience but some that are common to many of us are:

1.  Self-esteem – you feel that you are successful. Your colleagues, friends and family have a high regard for you. This often is the result of personal success in your education.
2.  Enjoying your life – having a good time is important to many people and success with your studies can give you the freedom to relax.
3.  Confidence – many people seek to have a personal sense of self-worth which again is an outcome of success.
4.  High earnings – many people are motivated by the possibility of earning a large salary which is possible if you are able to achieve academic success.

> 5. Security – educational achievement can result in developing a career which will ensure that financial accomplishment is an outcome.
> 6. Personal achievement – some people are motivated by the possibility of self-improvement.
> 7. Rewards – when you complete a task on time then give yourself a reward (e.g. a bar of chocolate, a book or a visit to the theatre).
>
> What motivates you?

## Reflection

A useful way to develop your reflection skills is to keep a learning diary which will help you to consider your learning in a systematic and ordered way. You will be able to compare and contrast each experience, your own behaviour and how you could improve your performance in the future.

A learning diary can take a variety of forms and what you reflect on in its pages is more important than how it is structured. It can simply be a calendar diary where each day you record your experiences and what you learned from them or you could develop a more complex structure. You can present your diary as a blog that you can choose to reveal to your colleagues. This has the advantage that you can receive feedback on your entries. Personal reflections are often aided by feedback. You could reflect on books or papers that you have read so that your peers can comment from their viewpoint.

You may, however, opt for a private diary. You might begin by considering your past experiences of the subjects being studied and your personal strengths and weaknesses in relation to them. You might list each strength and weakness, the components that make them up and actions to improve the situation. an example is shown below.

Writing

*Weakness*  1. Spelling  – I make simple errors – my ideas flow too fast for me to write them down, so I make mistakes

2. Grammar – I make simple errors – in part, I am thinking too quickly but also I do not understand some of the rules of grammar

*Action*

I will spell check everything I write and then ask John if he will read the more important pieces and explain what is wrong with the grammar so that I can learn the rules.

## Activity
## Keeping a learning diary

To help reflect on your own learning and experience, keep a diary of what you have learnt and the experience of learning. Establish a learning diary and keep a daily record for three or four weeks. Consider your experiences both during and at the end of the period. What do you need to change to maintain a useful learning diary and continue your records? The diary can take any form but it may be useful to present it as a personal blog.

### Discussion

*Personal diary*
A learning diary can be a very personal activity and students record different aspects of their experience. I like to make a daily note of:

1.   What I have done.
2.   How I felt the experience helped me and why.
3.   How long I spent on each part of the tasks.
4.   What I learnt from the experience about learning and studying.
5.   What I need to improve.

I have used a variety of ways to maintain records including a standard diary with one page for each day, a loose-leaf folder, a word-processed document and the diary in Outlook® software. It does not matter what you employ, it is the process of keeping the diary that will help. Figure 6.3 gives an example daily sheet.

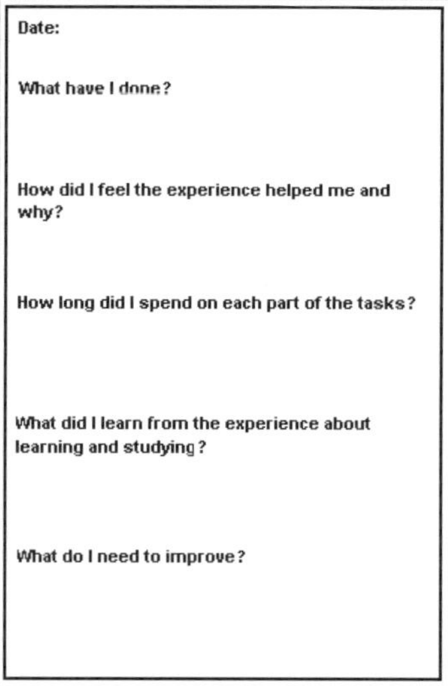

Date:

What have I done?

How did I feel the experience helped me and why?

How long did I spend on each part of the tasks?

What did I learn from the experience about learning and studying?

What do I need to improve?

**Figure 6.3**   Learning diary

*Blog*
A learning diary can be a public activity whereby you seek comments from peers. I like to present:

1.  What I have been studying (e.g. papers and books read or activities carried out).
2.  How the different information sources and activities undertaken influenced my views. I try to compare and contrast the new information with my existing understanding.
3.  Occasionally I present my own review of a paper or book.
4.  I encourage colleagues to add their own comments to my daily blog entry.
    I also like to read and add comments to my colleagues' blogs since that provides me with a valuable comparison with my own reflections.

What did you discover about your own learning and the experience of keeping a diary?

## Activity
## Reflecting on online skills

You have probably had considerable experience of learning in different situations and using a variety of methods. Consider your experience of traditional forms of learning such as the lecture, tutorial, relationships with your classmates and using a library. Reflect on this experience and try to identify what experience, skills and knowledge would be most useful in an e-learning course.

**Discussion**
Some experience from traditional forms of learning that might be useful in e-learning are:

-   Lectures – note-taking is a useful learning skill in all types of study, especially the ability to annotate them from independent study. Listening to a podcast or participating in an audio conference requires the skills of concentration, preparation and note-taking which are similar to those needed to listen to a lecture.
-   Tutorials – asking questions to clarify your understanding and listening to the answers to other learners' questions are useful if they can be transferred to an e-learning environment (e.g. e-mail communication and blog comment).
-   Relationships – all forms of learning are enhanced by the support of other learners. Being a team player who is willing to contribute to the benefit of everyone is a positive skill area.
-   Reading – reading is part of all courses and for e-learning rapid browsing to locate key points is vital.

- Revision – planning your studies is a useful skill in all forms of learning and particularly in e-learning since you have more responsibility for your own studies and freedom to choose when you learn.
- Organisation – organising your notes, assignments and study materials is a skill that you will need in developing an e-portfolio.
- Library – the experience of finding books and journals may well transfer to searching for information on the world wide web.

What experience did you identify that would be useful in e-learning?

## Listening

Listening requires concentration and motivation. It can be helpful to use recording since it allows you to study at times when it would otherwise be difficult (e.g. when walking).

### Activity
### Listening to a podcast

Identify a source of podcasts and download one or more that interest you. Listen to them as you would normally do (e.g. using an iPod as you travel or a desktop computer at home). How easy or difficult was it to understand the contents?

**Discussion**
The experience will be different depending on the specific podcast you are listening to, but some issues that may have arisen are shown below:

1. The quality and structure of the material will vary. Some will simply be 30 minutes of conversation between two people or an hour-long recording of a lecture. Both of these will not have been structured for listening to that is, the recording will not have been broken down into short sections to aid understanding.
2. It is difficult to concentrate when the material is so long that you need to pause the material and have a break.
3. Writing some notes helps you concentrate and identify the key points.
4. It is a good use of time to study as you travel.

The experience will depend on how motivated you are about the podcast's contents.

What was your experience like?

## ● Research skills

A significant talent for any learner is the ability to locate and analyse information. This is often called research and is a fundamental set of skills for any student or trainee. All subjects and careers require the capacity to investigate. The world wide web provides an astonishing information resource but does require the ability to locate and judge the quality of content.

---

### Activity
### Research: blended e-learning methods

Consider how you would learn more about the use of blended e-learning approaches. You may search the world wide web or visit a library, or both.

**Discussion**
My initial step was to search the world wide web using the term 'blended e-learning'. The Google search engine identified 2,230,000 pages. Visiting some of the top twenty pages produced several definitions of blended e-learning, all of which were broadly similar – blended e-learning being a combination of e-learning or online learning approaches with traditional/ face-to-face methods. The pages suggested the following:

1. Integrating the different methods was the key factor.
2. Online learning is referred to on many pages rather than e-learning, so what is the difference?
3. Other terms used include web-based methods, courseware, collaboration software and EPSS.

This initial search indicates the importance of defining terms and understanding the differences between them. It provides information to undertake a variety of other searches.

What did you discover?

There are many other subjects you could consider such as:

1. student retention in online learning;
2. social networking – compare what you find with alternative terms such as web 2.0;
3. digital divide.

Compare the information from the different sources and try to identify which are the key factors that make you decide the information is valid and reliable.

## Continuous development

e-Learning covers a new set of approaches. Few people would claim that their skills do not need to improve, develop and be enhanced, so it is important to take a long-term approach to your e-learning skills and try to adopt a continuous improvement strategy to developing them. The following activity asks you to judge your current level of skill and identify opportunities for improvement.

### Activity
### Online learning skills assessment

Table 6.1 provides a structure for you to assess your current level of skill, what future level you would like to achieve and what opportunities you aim to take in order to develop your skills.

**Table 6.1**   Online learning skills assessment

| Skill | Current skill level | Opportunities to develop skill |
|---|---|---|
| **Time management**<br>1. Achieving deadlines<br>2. Balancing different priorities<br>3. Personal organisation<br>4. Looking forward | | |
| **Acceptance of responsibility**<br>1. Understanding of course structure and standards<br>2. Personal objectives and standards | | |
| **Planning**<br>1. Setting goals<br>2. Producing action plan<br>3. Monitoring performance<br>4. Adjusting plans | | |
| **Self-assessment**<br>1. Identifying strengths and weaknesses<br>2. Reflecting on feedback<br>3. Seeking feedback | | |
| **Problem solving**<br>1. Identifying real problems (i.e. not the symptoms) | | |

| Skill | Current skill level | Opportunities to develop skill |
|---|---|---|
| 2. Systematic approach to solving problems<br>3. Reviewing solution and learning from experience | | |
| **Coping with stress**<br>1. Awareness of causes<br>2. Study/life balance<br>3. Reducing pressure | | |
| **Motivation**<br>1. Recognising personal motivation<br>2. Setting objectives | | |
| **Reflection**<br>1. Analysing e-learning experience<br>2. Comparing different approaches/experiences such as blogging with a conventional diary | | |
| **Listening**<br>1. Concentrating on materials to identify key issues<br>2. Being an active listener (e.g. pausing, replaying, etc.)<br>3. Taking notes | | |
| **Research**<br>1. Searching for information<br>2. Comparing information sources to decide which is more reliable | | |

## Discussion

An example analysis of a learner's e-learning skills is shown in Table 6.2 and is intended to provide you with a comparison.

**Table 6.2**  Personalised online learning skills assessment

| Skill | Current skill level | Opportunities to develop skill |
|---|---|---|
| **Time management**<br>1. Achieving deadlines<br>2. Balancing different priorities | I usually meet deadlines but have a clear tendency to try to do too much. | I will draw up a personal study timetable. |

| Skill | Current skill level | Opportunities to develop skill |
|---|---|---|
| 3. Personal organisation<br>4. Looking forward | I normally look ahead to check for deadlines. | |
| **Acceptance of responsibility**<br>1. Understanding of course structure and standards | I read the study guide at the start of the course. | I will make a poster of the course timetable for my room to remind me about deadlines. |
| 2. Personal objectives and standards | I normally do not set myself formal objectives or consider personal standards. I simply aim to pass the assessment. | I will set distinct standards for my work and will monitor my achievements. |
| **Planning**<br>1. Setting goals<br>2. Producing action plan<br>3. Monitoring performance<br>4. Adjusting plans | I tend to react to pressure and often do not plan my studies. | I will look ahead and plan my learning so that there are no crises.<br>I will keep records of my work. |
| **Self-assessment**<br>1. Identifying strengths and weaknesses<br>2. Reflecting on feedback | At the moment I only consider the marks and rarely study the feedback. | I will carefully read comments and ask my tutor to clarify what I need to do to improve my performance.<br>I will try to consider my performance systematically. |
| 3. Seeking feedback | I read comments from peers and tutors on blogs and e-portfolios | I will read colleagues' blogs and add my comments to encourage them to reciprocate. |
| **Problem solving**<br>1. Identifying real problem (i.e. not the symptoms)<br>2. Systematic approach to solving problem<br>3. Reviewing solution and learning from experience | I haphazardly solve problems as I encounter them.<br>I only occasionally review what has happened. | I will focus on learning from the software problems that I encounter by using text books, college helpline and supplier websites.<br>I will keep records of what were the best approaches. |
| **Coping with stress**<br>1. Awareness of causes<br>2. Study/life balance<br>3. Reducing pressure | I am sometimes anxious about my course. | I will review what makes me anxious and in addition I will consider my study pattern. |

| Skill | Current skill level | Opportunities to develop skill |
|---|---|---|
| **Motivation**<br>1. Recognising personal motivation<br>2. Setting objectives | I rarely consider my long-term motives. | I will write a list of reasons for wanting to be successful and stick them on the wall by my desk to remind me when problems are encountered. |
| **Reflection**<br>1. Analysing e-learning experience<br>2. Comparing different approaches/ experiences | Although I think about the course, this is in a relatively unsystematic way. | I will keep a learning diary of how I feel and what I experience. I will attempt to write down my feelings each day as well as recording what I have done. |
| **Listening**<br>1. Concentrating on materials to identify key issues<br>2. Being an active listener (e.g. pausing, replaying, etc.)<br>3. Taking notes | I am used to listening to music when I travel. I have not listened to learning materials. | I will download some relevant podcasts and listen to them while travelling. |
| **Research**<br>1. Searching for information<br>2. Comparing information sources to decide which is more reliable | I have little experience of research. | I will seek to apply a systematic, planned approach to my investigations. |

It is a good practice to plan to improve your skills and you should regularly review your progress.

# Summary

## 1.  Time management

Some key recommendations to help you improve your time management are:

- Monitor your use of time (e.g. over a period of a week, keep detailed records of how you spend your time).

- To Do lists – these assist you in controlling and managing your time.

## 2.  Acceptance of responsibility

Some key recommendations to help you improve your acceptance of responsibility are:

- Volunteer to lead a group task – collaborating with other learners to carry out a task is a frequent e-learning activity. While you undertake the task, keep a record/diary of what happens and reflect on the process and your own learning.
- Participate in an online discussion – keep a record/diary of what happens during a discussion and reflect on the process and your own learning.

## 3.  Planning

Some key recommendations to help you improve your planning skills are:

- Plan your revision – in the context of your own e-learning course plan what you need to do in order to be prepared for the examination.
- Planning a research project or assignment – in the context of your own e-learning course, consider how you would plan a research project or assignment.

## 4.  Self-assessment

Some key recommendations to help you improve your self-assessment are:

- Involve your tutor – your tutor is a vital resource so involve them in your learning
- Involve your peers – consider how you can make the best use of them.
- Assess yourself – how can you make yourself more effective at assessing your own progress?

## 5.  Problem solving

Some key recommendations to help you improve your problem-solving skills are:

- Contacting a technical helpline – what do you need in order to help the support service to diagnose your problem.
- Suppliers' websites – hardware, software and service suppliers often provide a range of sources of assistance when you have a problem or to help you prevent trouble.
- Buying software – what are all the factors that you need to consider when buying a chosen application for your computer?

### 6. Coping with stress

Some key recommendations to help you improve your ability to handle stress are:

- Study/life balance – a good balance is about working smarter rather than harder. Consider how you could reduce the pressure on yourself.
- Healthy life – a healthy lifestyle is likely to help you control your study/life pressures.

### 7. Motivation

It is important to understand what you want to achieve with your life and career so that you can identify what motivates you to study or work hard.

### 8. Reflection

Some key recommendations to help you improve your skills of reflection are:

- Keep a learning diary – to help reflect on your own learning and experience, keep a diary of what you have learnt and the experience of learning.
- Reflecting on online skills – consider your experience of traditional forms of learning and compare them with the e-learning skills you will need.

### 9. Listening

Compare listening to a podcast on your iPod as you travel or on a desktop computer at home. Where do you find it easier to understand?

**10. Research skills**

It is important to practise your research skills in order to improve them.

**11. Continuous development**

e-Learning covers a new set of approaches. it is important to assess your current level of skill and identify opportunities for improvement.

# 7 e-Assessment

The use of technology to assist and deliver assessment has been growing across all education and training sectors for several years. It takes a variety of forms and is used for both formative and summative assessment. Formative assessment is normally linked to providing you with feedback on your progress and is often not part of the overall marks that you achieve during the course. It is intended to help you improve your performance. Summative assessment often takes place at the end of the course or of a specific module of the programme and is intended to provide a final assessment of your progress. Formative assessment may offer you the opportunity to test yourself.

There are many different ways that technology can assist with formative and summative assessment such as:

- providing a showcase for your achievements;
- helping you to reflect and self-assess;
- offering you feedback on your performance;
- presenting evidence of your competency.

## Tests

The rapid growth in e-assessment has been due to the use of onscreen and, in some cases, online assessment based around multiple-choice questions. There are obvious limits to what you can assess with this type of question but the advantages are significant. The assessment often:

- is on demand so you can take the assessment when you feel ready;
- allows you to test yourself (i.e. formative self-assessment);
- provides your results immediately.

There are several ways to present multiple-choice questions but two that are widely used are:

1.  presenting you with a question and a number of alternative answers from which you choose the right one;
2.  presenting you with a question and a series of alternative answers but only one at a time. You need to reject an answer before seeing the next.

In both cases, questions can involve showing you still images or video in order to enrich the scenario.

Although multiple choice is probably the most used form of on-screen test, there are other types such as:

*   true or false – selecting between alternatives;
*   text entry – entering your answer (these are limited to short answers at the moment);
*   matching items – the question offers two lists and you have to match items together;
*   dragging and dropping – using the mouse pointer to drag items around the screen to place them in appropriate spots;
*   visual choices – usually a variation of one of the other types involving selecting from pictures or diagrams;
*   filling in the gaps – entering text into gaps left in a document or statement.

Some students find these types of test quite intimidating. It is important, if you find tests stressful, that you actively work on ways to reduce their effects. The key is to gain experience of completing these tests. Take every opportunity to practise them. Many learning centres will provide you with self-assessments so that you can do this. Actively work on improving your ability to take tests.

The main ways of improving your ability to answer these types of assessment are as follows:

*   Carefully read the instructions – these types of assessment often appear so straightforward that you feel you know what is required, so it is easy to get a poor result from misunderstanding the instructions.
*   Read each question carefully and study each alternative answer. It is easy to make errors as a result of over-confidence. Often alternative answers are very similar.
*   Practise doing the tests as much as you can. Learning centres and computer-based learning materials often offer the opportunity to test yourself.

- Many computerised tests and assessments offer some form of feedback that can help you understand the nature of the test. Some will allow you a second attempt so consider the feedback carefully.

## Classroom voting systems

There are now classroom voting systems that allow a group of students to respond to questions or offer opinions. These are normally wireless hand-held devices that communicate with a central computer and present the overall response on a large screen or through a video projector. They are frequently used to encourage groups to interact with each other by revealing their voting patterns.

Their role is to offer formative feedback whereby you can see what your peers' views or answers to questions are. It is helpful to know how your own performance compares to that of your colleagues.

There are various ways of using voting systems but one is to present the class with a question that relates to the curriculum and ask them to select, through the voting devices, an answer from a selection of options. Students who voted for a particular answer are asked to explain their choice. This allows a discussion of topics to occur naturally and for everyone not only to realise what is the right answer but also why it is the right one. Voting systems are normally fun to use.

## Self-assessment

Self assessment is an important element in learning. It has become associated with technology through the development of more portable forms of equipment and the availability of web 2.0 technologies that let you create content. In adult education, there is considerable interest in recording progress and achievement with ICT (Clark and Hussain-Ahmed, 2006).

Using ICT to assist self-assessment has many useful benefits in that it allows you to integrate assessment into the learning experience, reduce the time required for assessment, create a potentially long-lasting and portable record and make the process personal to your own needs.

The first step in any self-assessment process is to establish what are your aims and objectives. These will provide you with a standard to measure yourself against. You next need to select the appropriate technology to help you satisfy the objective. Technology provides a permanent record that you can review as often as you want, so allowing for reflection over time. Some ways of using ICT are shown below:

- Digital video recording a field trip will provide evidence of what you have observed and achieved. The recording can then be reviewed and reflected on at your leisure to gauge your achievement.
- Digitally recording an interview, discussion becomes a means of reflecting and keeping a record.
- Recording your efforts to speak a foreign language provides you with a means of listening to your pronunciation.
- The group can review a video or recording.
- Create a blog to record your feelings, views, impressions and anything else that you find useful. The blog allows you to reflect on the learning experience and share your conclusions with your peers. Blogs offer the opportunity to compare your own assessment of your progress with your peers' and tutors' comments.
- Create a portfolio of evidence on which you can reflect as a way of assessing your progress. The learning objectives of the course can form part of the evidence so that you can compare yourself against them.
- Wikis provide the means to collaborate on creating a document and thus to compare yourself with your collaborators.

## e-Portfolios

Portfolios have been used for many years in education and training. They are often linked to creative fields such as art and design and they have been employed extensively in vocational education and training as an alternative to traditional examinations or tests. Vocational learners collect evidence of their skills, knowledge and experience to demonstrate that they can competently undertake a profession. The evidence is aligned against defined standards for the particular vocation, often in the form of competency statements which define the skills, context and conditions in which the evidence must be linked.

e-Portfolios are essentially a development of the traditional portfolio in both the context of a focused application and a design to allow the learners to demonstrate their abilities. The main developments are that:

- the evidence is electronic and so can be stored easily over long periods;
- the evidence can be multimedia (e.g. sound and video);

- the evidence can be linked to online resources;
- other students and peers can contribute to online e-portfolios and so allow feedback to be incorporated;
- learners can add their own reflections on the evidence and course objectives;
- e-portfolio evidence can be organised into different formats to meet different needs;
- content can be edited, linked and merged;
- e-portfolio evidence can be presented in different ways to meet different needs;
- e-portfolio evidence is easily searched due to its electronic nature.

In contrast, traditional portfolios are often inflexible, large, bulky and difficult to maintain over long periods.

The e-portfolio definition below is based on one provided by Wikipedia:

An electronic portfolio, or e-portfolio, is usually an online collection of evidence (e.g. assignments, projects, images, multimedia, blog entries, wiki entries, sound files, witness statements and web links) gathered, organised and managed by a learner. Potentially, e-portfolios can be developed over a lifetime or significant period. They could begin during early schooling and follow learners through all their education, training and life experiences, serving to record achievement. However, they are often provided by colleges for specific courses with narrower objectives than life-long learning.

Figure 7.1 demonstrates an e-portfolio developed by the Open University called MyStuff. The figure shows the home page of the e-portfolio with a few items that I have added about myself.

There has been considerable discussion about the nature of an e-portfolio and it is likely that you will need different forms over a lifetime of use, such as:

- a structured repository to hold all your evidence of achievement gathered over many years;
- a specific collection of evidence to form an electronic curriculum vitae when applying for a particular job;
- a specific collection of evidence to demonstrate your competency or knowledge for a specific assessment (e.g. upgrading professional membership or achieving a qualification).

There are many different permutations and combinations that an e-portfolio of evidence could be used for. Products are already available that enable you to create a specific portfolio from a larger repository but there are also very specific applications designed for a specific qualification.

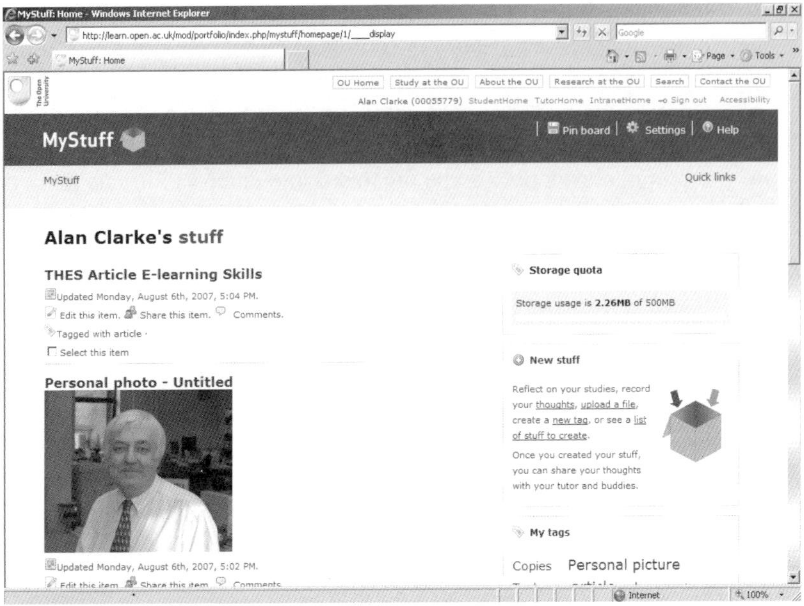

**Figure 7.1**   Open University MyStuff

## Learning and assessment

The emphasis in e-portfolios is often between a focus on formative assessment, aimed at aiding the learning process, and summative assessment. It is possible to achieve both outcomes but there are challenges in that summative assessment tends to want to standardise the structure and evidence of portfolios, making it easier for examiners to compare candidates and to judge quality. This will reduce the opportunities for creativity in the use and types of evidence that are acceptable.

Some colleges will use e-portfolios simply for summative assessment, others will concentrate on using them as a tool for learning and some will want to combine both aspects. You need to know what the course expects from you in your e-portfolio. At the start of the course, carefully study the requirements and begin to plan how you will meet them. If the emphasis is on summative assessment, then you must identify the evidence that you are going to need to provide in order to meet the course standards. Check if you can use the same evidence to meet different requirements or if the course expects a unique piece for each element of the assessment. In some cases there will be word limits on individual documents and the whole portfolio.

An emphasis on learning will place a different stress on the use of the portfolio. You will probably need to show that you can:

- reflect on your work and learning;
- respond to feedback from tutors and peers;
- demonstrate the distance you have travelled, perhaps through an initial self-assessment combined with systematic consideration of what you have learnt;
- make links to personal blogs that are providing a learning diary or wikis used for collaborative learning.

## Staff roles

Staff roles will vary between educational institutions and the courses being studied. Often the key person is your tutor, who will often be one of your assessors or examiners. Your tutor will be able to guide you in using the portfolio and also provide feedback on your evidence, including your own reflections.

In vocational education and training there is also a person called a verifier. Verifiers help with the assessment process by checking the assessor's judgements, usually in relation to a specific standard. They assist with ensuring a consistent approach to the evidence being used in the portfolio.

## Contents of an e-portfolio

e-Portfolios can contain many different types of information such as:

- personal information (e.g. name, age, address, telephone number and e-mail address);
- education and training records (e.g. qualifications gained, professional memberships and courses attended);
- individual learning plan;
- learning objectives for a course you are studying;
- work experience (e.g. previous and current employment);
- reflective comments on each item of evidence and on overall content;
- coursework – assignments, projects and other outcomes;
- tutors' comments;
- managers' comments;
- peers' comments;
- other references;
- personal and professional objectives;
- personal values and interests;

- presentations, papers and reviews of publications;
- personal activities – volunteer work and professional development.

The evidence included in an e-portfolio should demonstrate skills, knowledge and attitudes which show your ability and experience. They can be very focused on a specific set of competences and the evidence that you have collected to show you are competent. Alternatively, they can hold information on all the items of content in our list and possibly more if you are organising an e-portfolio of your life-long achievement. It would then provide a repository of evidence from which you could select items to show your ability and experience, perhaps in the form of a curriculum vitae for a job or course.

## Developing an e-portfolio

There are numerous different types of portfolio, so probably the first task is to determine what your course requires you to do and how the e-portfolio works. Some options (Stefani, Mason and Pegler, 2007) are:

- showcase;
- development;
- reflective;
- assessment.

A showcase portfolio is aimed at providing you with the means of presenting your achievements. It is likely to be accessible to your peers, teachers and possibly other groups. In some ways it serves the same purpose as a traditional artist's portfolio of work.

A development portfolio aims to present your work in progress so that you can obtain feedback from your peers, yourself and tutors. The advice and guidance received are intended to help you improve your work.

A reflective portfolio is intended to help you consider your own work with the objective of enhancing and developing it. This may be a private system open only to you.

An assessment portfolio is essentially a means of providing evidence to demonstrate your ability to pass some form of test. In professional development this could be a list of competencies that are required to demonstrate a set standard of skills and knowledge.

Although the four types are presented as if they are quite separate, an e-portfolio often requires a combination of showcasing, development, reflection and assessment.

## Activity
## e-Portfolio use

Consider your own personal use of an e-portfolio. How would a detailed record of your learning achievements be helpful to you?

Write a list of potential uses to which you could put an e-portfolio of evidence of your achievements.

**Discussion**
An e-portfolio could serve a variety of purposes including:

1. helping to persuade an employer that you are competent;
2. providing evidence to obtain membership of a professional body;
3. helping you reflect on what you have achieved to decide on future education or career directions;
4. self-assessing your own knowledge and skills;
5. assisting your continuous professional development.

### Selecting evidence

The choice of evidence to meet an assessment standard is one of the most difficult factors in using an e-portfolio. It is vital to study the guidance on what is required. Often this will:

1. restrict the amount of evidence you can provide so you may want to choose items that cover more than one aspect;
2. provide limits on the context in which the evidence can be gathered from (e.g. individual task);
3. limit the age of the evidence (e.g. no more than two years old).

It is not always easy to decide, so, if in doubt, ask your tutor, who is one of the most useful resources that you have available to you.

## Activity
## Selecting evidence

Many students find choosing the evidence for their portfolio to be a challenge.

Consider what evidence you would include in a portfolio to show that you were competent to carry out a practical task such as changing a tyre, ironing, painting a door or sewing.

You can only select three items of evidence since, in practice, assessment is often controlled so as to ensure comparable results with other learners.

**Discussion**
There are lots of possibilities but a practical task is often very visual, so digital images or a short video might well provide powerful evidence of your ability. It would demonstrate your practical skills (e.g. safe approach, selection of the correct tools and efficient completion of the task) but would not demonstrate directly that you understand why you are doing the task in this way. Add a written statement detailing your approach to the task and explaining why you are using this particular approach. This would provide evidence of understanding. The final item would be a witness statement from a recognised experienced person who can independently verify that you have successfully completed the task in the context and conditions specified in the assessment. If you had selected changing a tyre, the witness could testify that you had changed one in the rain, at night, on a motorway, and so on.

The three items support different aspects of the task but are also mutually supportive. In some cases you need evidence that covers several aspects of the assessment. It is important to consider the assessment requirements carefully.

## Structure

In some simple versions of an e-portfolio, you will be provided with a structure such as a series of competency statements against which you provide evidence. However, in many cases you will have largely a blank canvas on which to create a structure. It is important to design your e-portfolio with your objective clearly in mind, such as providing evidence that you have the skills, knowledge and attitudes required to pass the assessment. An e-portfolio is a hyperlinked multimedia document which allows for rich, interesting interaction but it does have the potential to confuse. The purpose of the portfolio is lost if you confuse your assessors.

The structure of a portfolio is based on:

- hyperlinked documents and multimedia resources;
- hyperlinks to external online sources.

The key to good design is to provide a logical, straightforward structure that is based on the objective of the portfolio. This will help assessors and other readers to navigate, based on intuition which is in turn influenced by the objective. The portfolio needs to have an index to the contents or home page so that readers know what it contains. The various pieces of evidence need to be introduced and explained. You need to consider:

- the course structure;
- the assessment criteria;
- the nature of the evidence;
- the limits on the size and nature of the evidence.

Probably the least effective approach is simply to keep adding evidence as you create it. This will result in a pile of information with no logical structure except a timeline.

If you are starting a portfolio that is intended to last for many years and have a variety of purposes, then you will need to allow for change and the different roles the information may serve. You are, in effect, creating a repository that will provide evidence for several more specific portfolios of evidence (e.g. job applications).

## Quality

In any assessment process it is important to consider the presentation of your work. The examiner will be reading many portfolios, so it is important at least to avoid confusing him and at best to impress. It is important to consider:

- the structure of your evidence – offer it in a logical, systematic way, addressing the assessment;
- introducing each item and explaining why you have included it (don't assume that it is obvious);
- creating a picture for the examiner (e.g. you are a competent student who has invested a lot of effort).

Falchiknov (2005) offers an approach to judging the quality of an e-portfolio. Table 7.1 is based on Falchinov (2005). However, the flexibility of e-portfolios allows individual institutions to vary their requirements so it is important to check the standards of your own college or provider. The danger in providing a framework to judge quality is that the inter-relationship between the different aspects is reduced. A portfolio is intended to present a comprehensive picture of the learner in a particular context (e.g. skills and knowledge to meet a professional standard). The framework may limit the development of the picture and focus too much on the components.

| Issues | Good | Acceptable | Poor | Unacceptable |
|---|---|---|---|---|
| 1. Structure | Clear structure that aligns with the central objective The choice of evidence is explained | Structure is apparent and evidence is introduced | Some basic structure | No obvious organisation to help users assess evidence |
| 2. Selection of evidence | Evidence fully meets all the assessment criteria | Evidence has been selected to cover assessment criteria | Some reasons apparent for choice of evidence | Random collection of evidence |
| 3. Focus | Evidence is mutually supportive and chosen to provide a comprehensive picture of the learner's skills, knowledge and attitudes in accordance with assessment criteria | Coherent collection of evidence which partially fits together to form a partial picture of the learner's skills, knowledge and attitudes in accordance with assessment criteria | Collection of individual items with little interconnection and only partial links to the assessment criteria | No obvious links between items of evidence |
| 4. Learner | Clear image of a reflective learner provided | Learner's reflections are apparent and a partial picture of them is presented | Difficult to identify learner's skills or character | Anonymous |

**Table 7.1**   e-Portfolio quality

Table 7.1 indicates some of the key aspects of an e-portfolio but others may also be important, such as:

- the range of media included (e.g. sound, video and text);
- the range of sources of evidence (e.g. witness statements, personal reflections and assessed materials).

These may form part of an individual college's assessment criteria, as may the overall size of the portfolio. For a summative assessment, you are likely to have a maximum size (e.g. word length, minutes of video and sound) to provide for comparisons between students to be more easily made.

## Online sources of evidence

It is possible in many e-portfolios to provide evidence through hyperlinks to online sites. This is a natural step with any online or electronic portfolio. However, consider the following:

1. *Websites*: websites are dynamic and continuously changing so there is always a risk of broken links or changed content. Ensure that your evidence is available to your examiner. You may need to make a copy of the online content and add it directly to the portfolio.
2. *Virtual Learning Environment*: e-Portfolios are often part of the college's virtual learning environment (VLE) so that you make links to your content stored in the VLE, such as a personal blog, wiki or podcast. This is normally safe in that these sources are under your control. However, if you intend to keep the evidence long term, then you will need to ensure you have copies, since colleges will probably not guarantee life-long access.
3. *Blogs*: Blogs can take several forms but in a learning context it will probably be a personal learning diary or webpage. A diary can demonstrate your ability to reflect on the content and processes of the course. You can create a private diary or one into which you allow access to a selected group of people such as your tutor and peers. They will often be free to add comments to your entries. You can use copies of entries with or without comments as evidence in your e-portfolio or provide a link. Blog entries will often serve to demonstrate your ability to reflect. A personal webpage can obviously serve a variety of purposes such as a commentary on some aspect of course content.
4. *Wikis*: wikis will often be provided as part of the VLE so that you can collaborate with other students to produce a joint document. They are

relatively straightforward to use and groups of students separated in time and space can work together. Wikis can provide evidence of collaborative working, of a completed document or both the process and content. If the wiki is within the college VLE, then a link from your portfolio will be effective.

5. *Podcasts*: podcasts that you have created can be evidence of your ability to produce them or an alternative way of providing evidence of your understanding of the subject of the podcast. This is no different from including an essay in your portfolio except for the possibility that you can provide a link to the online content.

6. *Forums*: discussion forums are a key element in communication but extracts from the messages can be useful evidence to demonstrate your understanding of issues, your communication skills and how you have participated in the course. Often e-learning courses include an assessment of your participation.

7. *Acknowledgements*: when using evidence that includes material created with others, you must acknowledge their contribution and seek their permission to use the work. If the content includes references to published sources, you must follow the normal conventions for providing a full reference so that it can be located.

## Ownership

One of the key factors in all forms of portfolio is the question of who owns it. It is important that at the start of a course employing e-portfolios you determine the ownership of the content. Does the approach followed allow you to take the contents of your portfolio with you when you leave? A major aspect of e-portfolios is that they can be life-long so that we create a record of personal achievement over our entire lives. It is doubtful that any institute will provide storage of and access to an e-portfolio over many decades. You therefore need to make sure that the contents of the portfolio can be transferred when you leave.

## Examples

e-Portfolios can be used in a variety of ways so it is important to review as many different types and approaches as possible. The following activity (Examples of e-portfolios) provides an opportunity to compare and contrast a wide range.

## Activity
## Examples of e-Portfolios

Institutions and individuals have provided access to e-portfolios on their websites. Search the world wide web and compare and contrast the examples you locate.

**Discussion**
I quickly located four websites which offered examples of completed portfolios and one which provided a demo of an open source e-portfolio system (www.mahara.org/). The completed examples ranged from specific portfolios, built as part of a course leading to a qualification, to more life-long collections. They covered schoolchildren, university students and researchers. Their structure and content varied greatly, as did their level of sophistication. This all served to demonstrate the flexibility and potential of e-portfolios.

Four websites which offered examples of completed portofolios were:

http://ict.edexcel.org.uk/home/eportfolios/samples/ – these are portfolios of young people who are taking the Edexcel GCSE in Applied ICT
http://electronicportfolios.com/ALI/samples.html – Dr Helen Barrett's examples of e-portfolios
www.portfolios.com/ – artists' and photographers' e-portfolios
www.ed.uiuc.edu/courses/ci335/eport_examples/index.html – US college students' portfolios

The one website offering a demo of an open source e-portfolio system was:

www.mahara.org/

What did you conclude?

## Summary

### 1.   Formative and summative assessment

e-Assessment can provide both formative and summative assessment. Formative assessment normally takes the form of feedback while summative assessment is the final formal test of your success at the end of the course or a specific module.

### 2.   Tests

e-Assessment in the form of onscreen and online assessment is growing rapidly. It is often based around the multiple-choice question. e-Assessment offers on-demand, self-testing and immediate feedback/results.

### 3.   Classroom voting systems

Classroom voting systems allow students to respond to questions or offer opinions. They use wireless hand-held-devices that enable the overall response to be presented to the whole group. The aim is to encourage group interaction and it is thus a type of formative feedback where you can compare yourself to the whole group.

### 4.   Self-assessment

Technology can assist self-assessment by allowing the integration of assessment with the learning experience, reducing assessment time, creating a record and personalising the process. There are numerous ways of using technology, such as digital video or sound recording, creating a blog, developing an e-portfolio and producing a wiki.

### 5.   e-Portfolios

e-Portfolios extend the traditional portfolio by allowing you to store evidence over a lifetime. They can include multimedia, can link to online resources, and can allow other students and peers to contribute and give feedback. Learners can add their own reflections and content can be edited, linked and merged. Evidence can be searched and presented in different ways to meet different needs.

The nature of an e-portfolio is likely to change over a lifetime and may take several forms, such as a structured repository of all your evidence of achievement, an electronic curriculum vitae and a specific collection of evidence to meet a precise need.

*Learning and assessment*: e-Portfolios can be used for both formative and summative assessment. There is a tension between the two roles in that summative assessment tends to want to standardise e-portfolios' structure and evidence. This tends to limit the possibilities for creativeness required for formative assessment.

*Staff roles*: staff roles will vary but the key person is normally your tutor, who will also be your examiner. Tutors will be able to guide you in using the portfolio and provide feedback on your evidence.

*Contents of an e-portfolio*: e-Portfolios can contain many different types of information, including personal information, education and training records, an individual learning plan, course learning objectives, work experience, reflective comments, coursework, tutors', managers' and peers' comments, references, personal and professional objectives, personal values and interests, presentations, papers and reviews of publications and personal activities.

*Developing an e-portfolio*: the main types of e-portfolios (Stefani, Mason and Pegler, 2007) are:

- showcase;
- development;
- reflective;
- assessment.

*Selecting evidence*: selecting evidence is one of the most difficult tasks. It is vital to study the guidance on what is required. This will often restrict the amount, type and age of the evidence that you can include.

*Structure*: in simple versions of e-portfolios, you will be provided with a defined structure. But more often you will have to create the structure yourself. A portfolio is based on hyperlinked documents, external sources and multimedia resources and is potentially very complex. A good design is to provide a logical straightforward structure based on the objective of the portfolio. You need to consider the course structure, assessment criteria, nature of evidence and limits on the size and nature of evidence.

*Quality*: you are seeking to impress, so the quality of your presentation and evidence is critical. It is important to consider the structure of your evidence, introducing and explaining each item and creating an overall picture through the selected evidence.

*Online sources of evidence*: it is natural to include links to other online sites in your e-portfolio. However, websites are dynamic and continuously changing so there is always a risk of broken links or changed content. You need to ensure that your evidence is available to your examiner.

e-Portfolios are often part of the college's Virtual

Learning Environment (VLE) so you make links to your content stored in the VLE such as a personal blogs, discussion forums, wikis or podcasts.

Evidence that was created with others must be acknowledged and the permission to use the work sought. A full reference for any publications cited must also be included. *Ownership*: it is important to determine who owns the e-portfolio (e.g. you or the college). Ascertain whether you can take the content with you when you leave or whether you have long-term access to it.

# 8 Communication Skills

Many e-learning programmes are based around the use of communication technologies and e-learners' success depends to a large extent on well-developed communication skills. This chapter will concentrate on:

- acceptable use;
- asynchronous communication;
- e-mail communication styles;
- mailgroups and newsgroups;
- forums;
- threaded discussions;
- 'lurking';
- blogs;
- synchronous communication;
- chat;
- audio conferencing;
- video conferencing.

A range of activities will be used to help develop your skills and understanding.

## Acceptable use

When you use the computer system in your college, learning centre or other public facility, it will be governed by its acceptable use policy which is essentially a set of conditions or rules that limit the use of the computer systems. Each location will have a different policy depending on its nature so it is important to check what you can do and the consequences of breaking the rules. Some centres and colleges may well stop you using their facilities if you are in breach of the rules. Some conditions which you may encounter will forbid you to:

- access pornographic or other offensive websites;
- download music;
- download offensive material.

These are easy to understand but some others may be perhaps more difficult:

- not to use a personal memory stick from your home;
- not to download files from websites.

Both of these conditions are related to the risk of infecting the system with viruses. Viruses can be transmitted across the internet, and moving files between computers without checking them for virus infection is a high-risk operation. Other conditions may forbid you to download copyrighted materials (e.g. software applications, videos and music) and may limit the size of files that you can download. You may also have a time limit on your use of a computer, combined with a requirement to book your use when you want to use it.

### Filtering

Filtering is essentially an automated way of enforcing the acceptable use policy. Software filtering systems enable the college or centre to limit what can be accessed and downloaded from the internet. Unfortunately some systems are relatively unsophisticated and so may block useful sites if they contain a word or phrase that has been used used to describe forbidden websites or resources.

### Other factors

There are numerous other factors to consider when using communication technologies and four of them are discussed in more detail below:

1. *Cultural differences*: online learning removes the geographical barriers that separate learners, meaning that you can study with people from a variety of other cultures. This is an excellent opportunity to gain access to a wide range of different perspectives and experience. However, to take advantage of it does require you to be tolerant of views different from your own. You can gain valuable new insights into the topics if ideas are explored rather than dismissed simply because they are different from your own. Reflect on the comments of your fellow learners and ask questions in order to develop common points of reference.
2. *Blogging*: blogging is essentially keeping an open diary or journal of your thoughts, ideas and experiences on a website. It has been described in many ways and certainly serves many different purposes. These can be very personal in that the bloggers are revealing their own views and feelings to the world. It is similar to issuing a personal

newsletter about your life. Some writers use their sites to comment on major developments, personal interests or the society in which they live. The section on writing blogs later in this chapter will take these issues further.

3. *Libel*: e-mail and other forms of online communication sometimes make people feel they are free to say anything in any way. The reality is that, like any other form of communication, you are governed by the law. You must write with the same care that you use in more traditional communication forms.

   Many organisations now add to all their e-mails a standard disclaimer to try and reduce the risk of offending people or breaking the laws of libel and defamation.

4. *Privacy and security*: many people are concerned that everything they store on a computer or send by e-mail can be intercepted or accessed by other people. In principle, this is probably true but it does assume that someone would take the trouble of identifying your message or can gain access to your computer. There are several steps that you can take to protect your messages and system:

   - Secure your home to prevent easy access to your computer. You may also want to install security devices to stop the removal of your computer by using metal cables or other methods to fix the machine to a desk.
   - Encrypt your files so that no one else can read them. This is very effective when you want to send confidential information by e-mail or store sensitive data on your system.
   - A password protecting your system is a straightforward and easy way of limiting access to your system. A good password is one that is very difficult to guess (e.g. a mixture of eight or more letters and numbers) and you should change it regularly.
   - Use a firewall – this is an application that stops hackers gaining access to your system.
   - Install an anti-spyware application that will check your system regularly for spyware monitoring your use of the system. Anti-spyware products can be set up to monitor your system continuously, checking new e-mails and ensuring no one gains access without your permission.
   - Install an anti-virus application that will check your system and incoming e-mail to ensure that you do not become infected with a virus.

## Asynchronous communication

Asynchronous communication methods such as e-mail are probably the main ones used online. They are very convenient in that:

- you do not need the sender and the recipient to be available at the same time;
- you can send a message to a large number of people at the same time;
- you can add an attachment to the message (e.g. a picture, word-processed file or spreadsheet);
- you can choose when to read messages;
- you can reply to all or a selection of the people who were sent the original message;
- you can forward the original message to other people;
- you can save the messages;
- your replies can contain the original message, thus containing a complete record of the communication.

In many learning programmes you will be involved in communicating with a number of other learners using e-mail. The way people read and send messages form complex patterns. Readers have widely different behaviours:

- Some people will read their e-mail messages every day or even many times a day.
- Some people read their e-mails in batches.
- Some people will be taking part in several mailgroups at the same time so will perhaps be receiving hundreds of e-mails every day.
- Some people will forward messages from other groups.
- Some people will reply to every message whereas others will very rarely reply.

These differences in behaviour often result in topics being relaunched after an interval because some learners have not read the message until a week or two after it was sent. Topics tend to become intertwined and several discussions are often mixed together. This makes the sequence of messages complex. You have only the written message (i.e. no body language, facial expression or tone of voice) to judge the meaning, so misunderstandings are more common that in face-to-face communication.

## ● e-Mail communication styles

e-Mail provides considerable freedom in the selection of how you would like to communicate. All communication methods have strengths and weaknesses and so far we have tended to consider the benefits of e-mail but one clear negative is the risk of offending people. Perhaps due to the short and informal way many people write e-mails, it is relatively easy to offend the recipients of the messages. This is probably increased by the speed and ease of sending e-mail which does not encourage people to reflect on their comments and thereby realise that they are being too aggressive. Netiquette was developed to combat this possibility by encouraging people to adopt rules of behaviour. A simple but useful rule is to never reply to any e-mail in anger. You will almost certainly provoke an argument if you do.

The key to producing a clear, polite e-mail is to:

- address your e-mail to the person – you can simply give the person's name, use 'Dear' or a similar phrase such as 'Hello';
- never be offensive or respond with anger to a message;
- treat everyone with respect;
- don't forward chain messages or send spam;
- don't use all capitals in your messages – it can be viewed as the equivalent of shouting;
- respect people's messages (e.g. don't copy messages to new recipients without permission);
- remember humour is difficult to communicate and can be easily misunderstood;
- use blank spaces or punctuation to make your communication clear – no punctuation may seem informal but it does not aid clarity;
- end your message with your name or a closing phrase such as 'Best wishes', 'Many thanks' or something similar.

Figure 8.1 shows a comparison of different ways of presenting an e-mail. You may say that you would never be so blunt, but I have seen far worse.

A second weakness is that the informal nature of e-mail encourages you to write in a casual and non-grammatical way. This is often seen as friendly but it is also sometimes difficult to understand. The presence of the original message is an encouragement to reply and annotating the sender's message is very useful on occasions. If you are working on a joint statement, then annotations will be helpful but always remember that embedding your answer in the original text may not make it easy to understand your points.

**Alternative 1**

Dear John

I would be grateful if I could borrow your
notes on the South Sea Bubble. They will be
very useful in helping me to complete my essay.

Many thanks.
Alan

**Alternative 2**
Send me your South Sea Bubble notes. I need them.

**Figure 8.1**　e-Mail politeness

The originator may not read the annotated reply for some days by which time their memory of the original message has faded. When you insert comments into the original message it is sometimes displayed in a different colour but, of course, this distinction will disappear if the e-mail is printed on a monochrome printer. Some e-mail users print out their communications.

The key to annotating an e-mail is to focus on making yourself clear and your comments understandable. Some simple steps to achieve these aims are:

- using blank lines to separate out your comments and the original text they relate to;
- introducing your message;
- giving a short summary to conclude your message.

Figure 8.2 compares an annotated and a sequential response to a message. Both are intended to be effective messages but in the annotated message you can see that the reply does not cover all the points made in the original message. A key part of the original message was 'but with evidence that we each contributed to a group investigation'. This is important to the students since they are going to be assessed on their work together and need to provide evidence of what they did. It is probably easier to compare an annotated reply to the original response than it is to compare a sequential reply. When replying to a message, an annotated approach makes it more straightforward to check that you have answered each point, since the original message is part of the reply.

**Original Message**

Hi Everyone

We need to form a group to investigate the nature of the digital divide. The course study guide suggests that we need to consider:

1. Is there a real divide in society?
2. If a divide exists, is it the equivalent of other social and economic divisions?
3. What are the key features of the digital divide?
4. What would we do to close the divide or at least stop it getting any larger?

We have two months to address the questions and we all need to submit an individual essay with our own response but with evidence that we each contributed to a group investigation. That seems a bit of a contradiction. We also have to say what we thought of the process of working together – I am unsure what that would involve. What does everyone think we should do – we need to get started quickly since two months is not long if we have to work together on this?

Cheers

Janet

**Annotated Reply**
[Text in this type is the original message; italic text is annotation.]

*Hi All*

*Here are some thoughts.*

Hi Everyone

We need to form a group to investigate the nature of the digital divide.

*I think we can form several small groups if we want to – there are 26 students on the course. That is too large to be a single group – why don't we divide into the groups that we had earlier for the learning object exercise?*

The course study guide suggests that we need to consider:

1. Is there a real divide in society?
2. If a divide exists, is it the equivalent of other social and economic divisions?
3. What are the key features of the digital divide?
4. What would we do to close the divide or at least stop it getting any larger?

**Figure 8.2** Annotation (1) – *continued overleaf*

*Again I would divide up the different objectives so we can get the most work done.*

We have two months to address the questions and we all need to submit an individual essay with our own response but with evidence that we each contributed to a group investigation. That seems a bit of a contradiction. We also have to say what we thought of the process of working together – I am unsure what that would involve.

*We should share all the evidence we located but then write our individual essays.*

What does everyone think we should do – we need to get started quickly since two months is not long if we have to work together on this?

*Can we have a quick vote on what to do – sort out who does what and get going?*

Cheers

Janet

*I hope these comments help.*

*Best wishes*

*Linda*

**Simple Reply**

*Hi All*

*Here are some thoughts*

I think we should form several small groups – there are 26 students on the course. That is too large to be a single group – why don't we divide into the groups that we had earlier for the learning object exercise? Then divide up the different objectives amongst the group so we can get the most work done.

We can share all the evidence we find before we write our own essays.

Can we have a quick vote on what to do – sort out who does what and get going?

I hope these comments help.

Best wishes

Linda

**Figure 8.2** *continued*

---

*Hi All*

*Here are some thoughts.*

Hi Everyone

We need to form a group to investigate the nature of the digital divide. *I think we can form several small groups if we want to – there are 26 students on the course. That is too large to be a single group – why don't we divide into the groups that we had earlier for the learning object exercise?* The course study guide suggests that we need to consider:

1.  Is there a real divide in society?
2.  If a divide exists is it the equivalent of other social and economic divisions?
3.  What are the key features of the digital divide?
4.  What would we do to close the divide or at least stop it getting any larger?

*Again I would divide up the different objectives so we can get the most work done.*

We have two months to address the questions and we all need to submit an individual essay with our own response but with evidence that we each contributed to a group investigation. That seems a bit of a contradiction. We also have to say what we thought of the process of working together – I am unsure what that would involve. *We should share all the evidence we located but then write our individual essays.* What does everyone think we should do – we need to get started quickly since two months is not long if we have to work together on this? *Can we have a quick vote on what to do – sort out who does what and get going?*

Cheers

Janet

*I hope these comments help.*

Best wishes
Linda

---

**Figure 8.3**   Annotation (2)

The presentation of an annotated response is important to avoid confusion and to communicate clearly. Figure 8.3 shows the same response with the layout removed. Do you think it is as clear? In practice the colour coding of the original and reply messages is often changed so that they become indistinguishable.

It is not a matter of which response is best. Both can be useful if used in an effective way. Concentrate on making your messages clear and ensure that you are understood.

### e-Mail signatures

Many e-mail systems allow you to establish a standard signature at the end of your messages. This can simply be your name or a short message. People use the signature function for a variety of purposes including advertising, disclaimers and humour. However, be careful since these can cause offence.

### ● Mailgroups and newsgroups

Mailgroups and newsgroups are communities of interest. If you are a member of one, you will have access to information about the subject on which it is based. You can send messages either to selected people or to all the members. The difference between them is that in a mailgroup the e-mails are sent to you whereas with newsgroups you have to visit them to receive the messages. There are newsgroups and mailgroups covering almost every topic. Often online courses will have specific associated mailgroups for registered students but in some cases you can gain valuable information by being a member of a general group.

You need to subscribe to a group in order to take part. They will normally want to know your e-mail address and your user name, although many people tend to enrol under a pen name. It is important not to disclose your personal details in a mailgroup. You do not know who else is taking part. Many newsgroups are known as usenet. Their names tell you in broad terms what they cover:

Alt – alternative (as the name suggests these are alternative views. You may find offensive material but they cover an enormous range of subjects);
Biz – business;
Comp – computer;
Sci – science;
Soc – social;
Talk – discussions about almost any topic;
News – newsgroups;
Rec – recreation;
Misc – miscellaneous.

Educational organisations will filter messages to remove offensive items from their network. In some cases this will mean that whole types of usenet newsgroups will not be allowed.

## Activity
## Newsgroups

Visit the Google search engine www.google.co.uk/ and select the Groups option to reveal a list of usenet discussion groups. Select a subject and explore some of the groups within it. You will be able to search the group for messages and to send yours if you want.

**Discussion**
You should have found that there are many groups to select from and that you can search to find messages relating to a particular aspect of the topic. You may see a link called Thread. If you click on a thread then you will be linked to the start of the discussion (i.e. when the debate or topic was raised). If you come to an interesting message you may well want to see how the discussion reached that point. Clicking on Thread is the way to find out.

## Forums

Mailgroups within a course are often called forums or conferences. They are frequently part of e-learning courses and can cover many topics associated with the course. There are often multiple forums that you can participate in, such as:

- Tutor groups – all the students have the same teacher or tutor. The group provides mutual support and allows the tutor to contact the whole group directly.
- Assignment groups – intended to allow discussion of specific assignments.
- Technical groups – provide self-help about technical issues associated with the course (e.g. how to add new content to an e-portfolio).
- Social groups – encourage social discussion and help students working at a distance to develop their relationships.

Forums are often moderated to assist the discussion. Many colleges provide access to them through their Virtual Learning Environments and once you have logged in, they are available to you. You are likely to need to visit several different forums in order to ensure that you are up to date with the course. This requires a disciplined approach and good time management.

## ● Registration

In order to join most mailgroups you need to register. You will usually be required to send an e-mail to a central address or visit the group website. Having provided your e-mail address as identification, often you will need to wait for the mailgroup to send you an e-mail with the induction materials explaining how to send messages (e.g. e-mail address), the conditions of participation (e.g. netiquette) and how to end your membership. The latter can be helpful, since until you begin to receive mailgroup messages, you are never completely sure if it is going to be useful. You should keep the mailgroup user instructions safe so you can communicate with the mailgroup administrator, end your membership or simply help others to join.

Large organisations (e.g. employers, universities and colleges) often not only restrict access to their online facilities to registered students but also prevent students accessing general mailgroups or newsgroups from their systems.

## ● Moderation

Many newsgroups and mailgroups are moderated – that is, your messages are read by the moderator who decides whether or not they should be posted. Forums are also moderated, but in this case the reason is not to check new messages but rather to facilitate discussion. Educational moderators often have a wider role whereby they will contribute to discussions, answer questions about the course, referee behaviour (e.g. stop arguments that breach the netiquette conditions) and suggest topics. They are essentially acting as facilitators to help learners gain the most from the discussion. An effective moderator does not prevent debate but assists participants by ensuring a fair exchange of ideas.

In many educational discussion groups, it is normal to ask a student to moderate or facilitate the group. The main aim of moderation is to encourage people to participate and to assist an in-depth discussion rather than a superficial exchange. The only means that a student moderator has to aid the discussion is his/her own messages. Some approaches that have been found to help are:

1. Scoping the parameters of the discussion:

   - What it will cover?
   - What is expected from the participants?
   - Netiquette rules.

This is normally more than a single message but does tend to be sent at the start of the discussion in order to focus participants and encourage contributions. An example is shown below:

The aim of the discussion is to consider what aids and hinders personal reflection. We need to agree a short summary by 17 July to submit as part of the assignment on reflection.

2. Questions – a useful way to get individuals and the group to contribute is to ask questions. These can either be follow-ups to a message sent to take the discussion further and encourage an individual to elaborate or sent to the whole group to introduce a new aspect to the debate. Questions can be asked at any time during the discussion and often form the structure of the debate. Two examples are shown below:

   ● That's an interesting point. What effect did that have on you?
   ● Has anyone had any experience of using a learning diary?

3. Direct message – it is sometimes necessary to send a direct e-mail to someone who is not contributing in order to encourage him/her to participate.

4. Summary – a useful method of gaining agreement is to summarise the discussion. It can promote a new level of discussion or simply act as a way of bringing it to a conclusion.

Although these methods are useful to a moderator they can also be employed by a member of a discussion group.

## Mailgroup digests and summaries

Mailgroups regularly publish a useful digest or summary of the discussion, enabling you to follow it without the burden of reading every message. The digest is usually published at certain intervals (e.g. weekly or monthly) so you can see if the debate is appropriate to you. Mailgroups will often archive all messages so if you realise a discussion is relevant then you can seek out and consider the individual messages. Some mailgroups, however, do not publish a digest or archive messages, so you should read the conditions under which the group operates to check what services it offers.

## Organisation

e-Mail systems provide you with some features to organise your e-mails. Mailgroups often send large numbers of messages and if you are a member of several you may find it difficult to cope with the volume. When receiving large numbers of messages, it is often a problem to identify what is important. Outlook® software allows you to:

- segregate e-mail into different folders so that you can separate e-mails from a particular mailgroup from other messages;
- automatically copy all messages you receive;
- remove spam e-mail messages;
- colour-code messages to help you identify different types.

These features can be accessed through Junk e-Mail, the Rules and Alerts tool and the Organise tool.

## New folders

The most straightforward step in organising your e-mails is to create new folders in which to store your messages from mailgroups, people or those relating to different subjects. To create a new folder select the File menu, highlight the Folder option to reveal a submenu and click on the New Folder option to open the Create New Folder window (Figure 8.4). This allows you to create a new folder and position it. It is often useful to create a series of folders within the inbox folder in order to keep all messages together in a

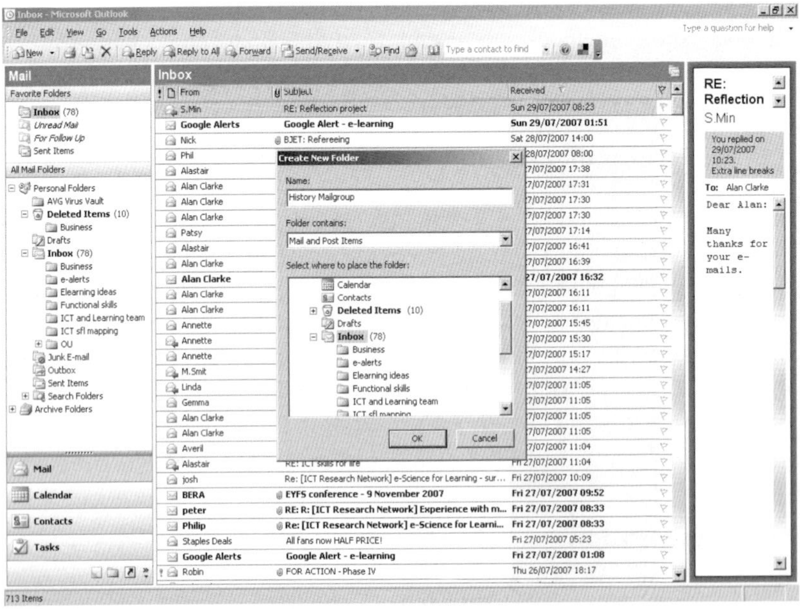

**Figure 8.4**   New folder

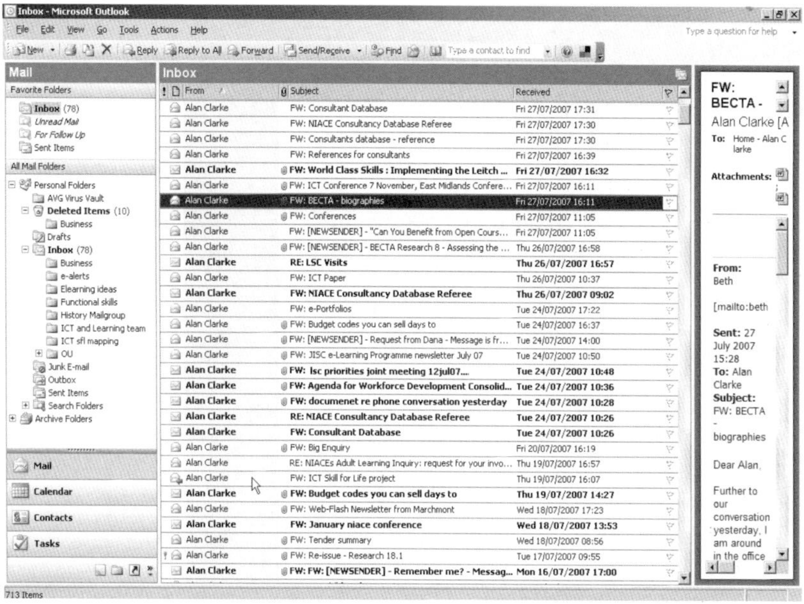

**Figure 8.5**   History folder

single master folder. Figure 8.5 shows that a folder called History Mailgroup Folder has been created within the inbox folder.

## Organizer

After creating new folders, your next step is to use the Organizer feature to send messages automatically to them. This will prevent your inbox from becoming crowded. One way of directing messages to particular folders is to use the Organize option in the Tools menu. This will open the Ways to Organize Inbox window (Figure 8.6). The current message in the inbox acts as an example of the type of message that you want to move into the selected folder (in this example, the History Mailgroup Folder).

You can also create new folders from the Ways to Organize Inbox. Click on the New Folder button in the top right-hand corner of the window. This will then open the Create New Folder window (Figure 8.4).

In the Ways to Organize Inbox is an option on the left-hand side of the window called Using Colors. This will colour-code messages, using the current one displayed as an example of the type you want to code (Figure 8.7). You can change the colours using the drop-down list in the colour box, so making it easy to identify different types of message (e.g. all messages from your tutor are coloured red).

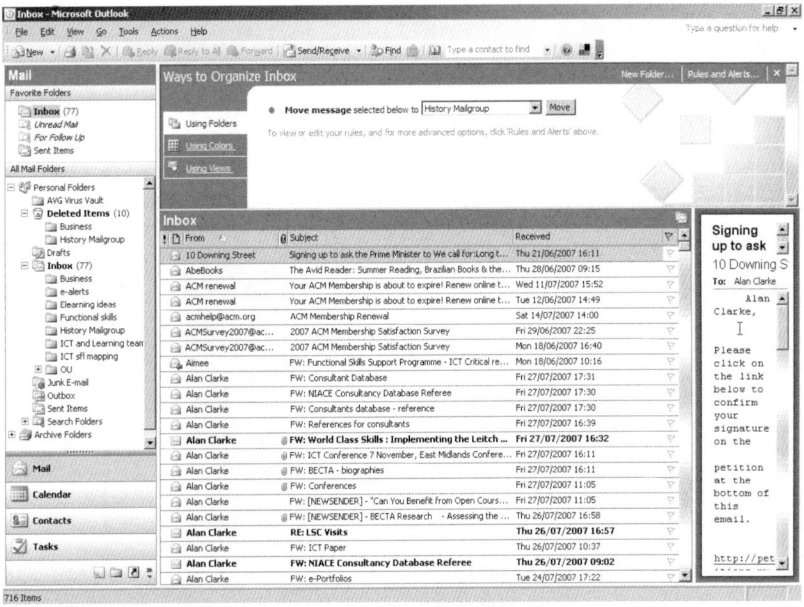

**Figure 8.6** Organize

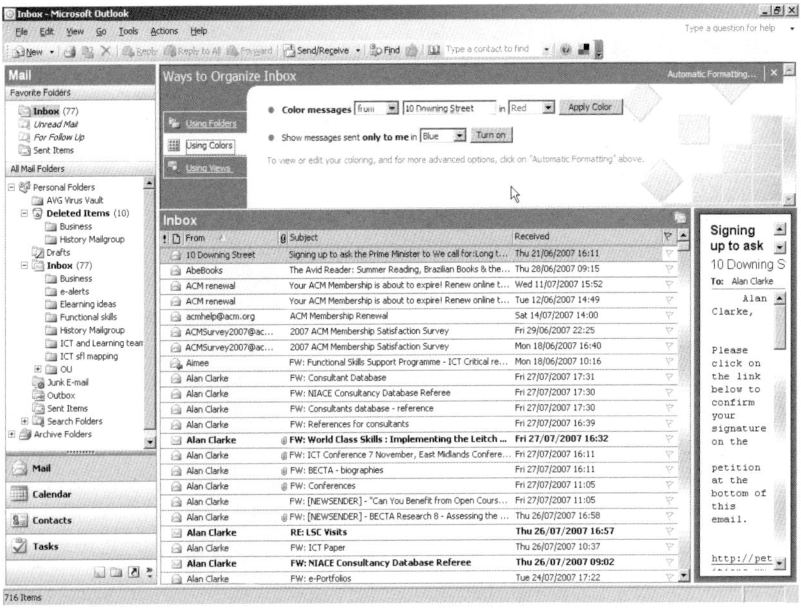

**Figure 8.7** Using Colors

A further option in the Ways to Organize Inbox is Using Views which, if you select it, will allow you to change the way your messages are displayed. You should explore the different options within the Ways to Organize Inbox to move messages to different folders, colour-code different types of message and change the display of your messages. The various versions of Outlook® software have different options.

## Rules and Alerts tool

Outlook® software (2003) contains a Rules and Alerts tool that lets you establish rules for handling your e-mail. You can establish rules to:

- send all messages relating to a particular issue or from a particular address to a folder automatically – this allows you to segregate your messages (e.g. so that you can keep your communications from your tutor);
- delete messages from particular addresses (e.g. spam).

The tool helps you to organise your messages. Figure 8.8 illustrates creating a new rule (i.e. Tools menu, Rules and Alerts option to reveal the Rules and Alerts window, select New Rule to open the Rules Wizard window).

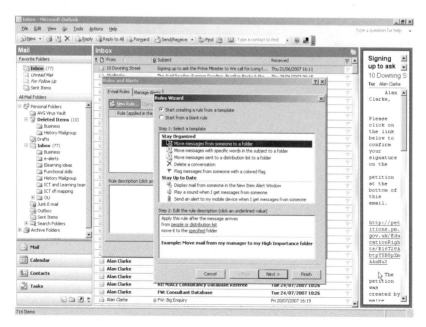

**Figure 8.8**   Rules Wizard

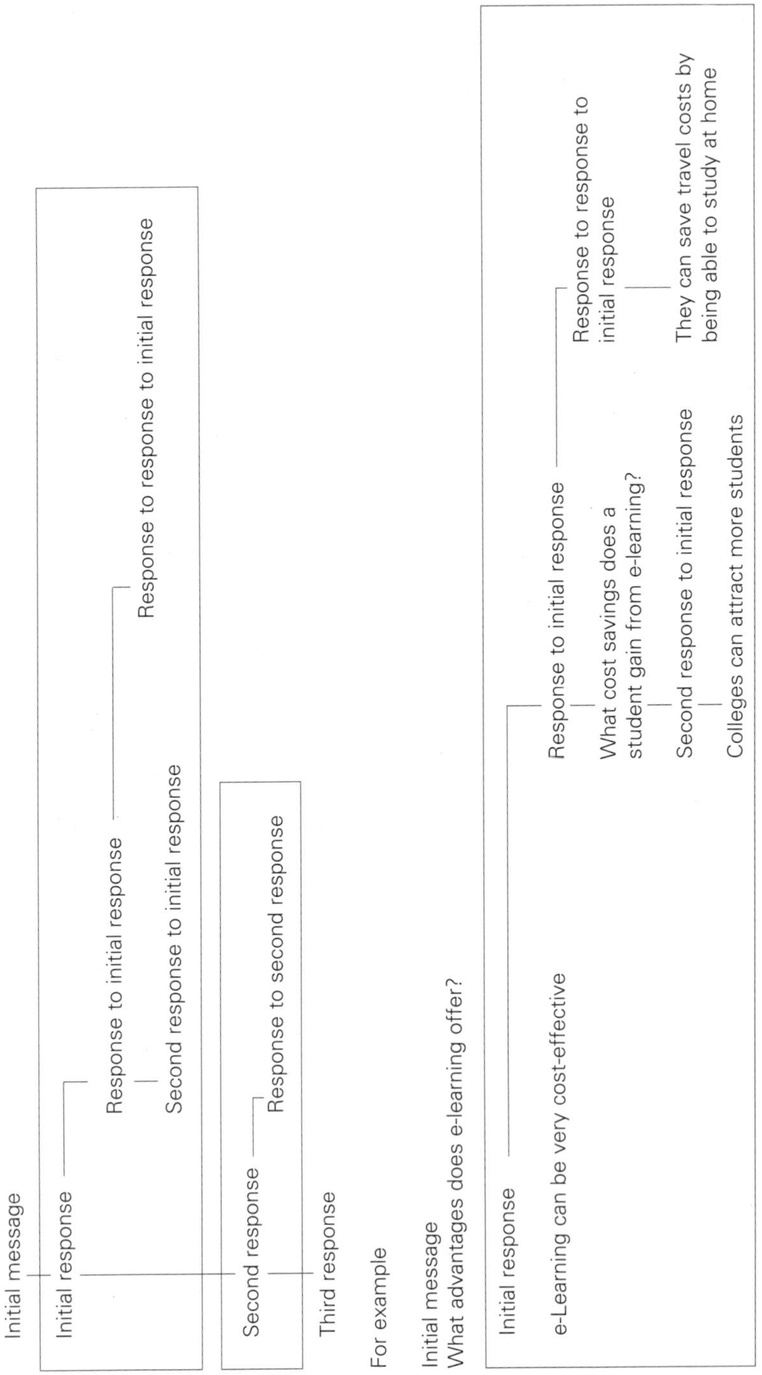

Initial message
Initial response ——
 Response to initial response ——
  Response to response to initial response
 Second response to initial response

Second response ——
 Response to second response

Third response

For example

Initial message
What advantages does e-learning offer?

Initial response ——
 e-Learning can be very cost-effective —
  Response to initial response —
   Response to response to
   initial response
  What cost savings does a
  student gain from e-learning?
   They can save travel costs by
   being able to study at home
 Second response to initial response
 Colleges can attract more students

**Figure 8.9** Threaded discussions

## ● Threaded discussion

In some mailgroups, newsgroups and other forms of online dialogue either the debate is shown as a threaded discussion or you will have the option of presenting the messages in this way. A threaded presentation demonstrates the sequences and relationships between messages. In Figure 8.9 you can see two threads. The initial message provoked three responses. Two of these then motivated people to reply to them, and so on. There are therefore two threads of discussion which are shown in the figure by being enclosed in a box.

It is possible to present these messages as a linear list without showing the relationship. The list is simply shown in date order, although often e-mail systems (e.g. Outlook® software) provide you with the choice of listing messages in other ways (e.g. unread). However, if you only occasionally read your messages (i.e. many arrive between visits) it is more difficult to understand the nature of the debate. While a threaded discussion makes it easier to understand the nature of the debate, it can initially be more confusing since the presentation is more complex. If you explore a threaded discussion you can analyse the contributions and relationships between messages. This is potentially a powerful aid to understanding the discussion. At a face-to-face debate it is often difficult to remember all the points made, answered or disputed. A threaded discussion provides you with the whole story.

A list presentation sometimes shows you that a message is a reply to an earlier message by changing the subject line in the e-mail. This helps the reader recognise a response but does not show the whole communication relationship (i.e. thread), for example:

| | |
|---|---|
| Initial message | Response |
| Secondment opportunity | Re: secondment opportunity |

If you are only an occasional participant in a discussion group, then it can take some time to catch up with the communications. However, an equivalent face-to-face debate would be almost impossible to understand if you missed a large part of the discussion. Online discussions do give you a complete record of the debate.

## Activity
## Threaded discussion

Consider your e-mail editor and see if you can change the display of messages to present a threaded view of them. The View menu item often contains options for presenting messages as a list or as a thread.

Explore the threaded messages and other ways of presenting the messages. Reflect on what the benefits of the different types of display are.

**Discussion**

To a large extent your experience will depend on the e-mail editor that you are using. However, if you have never considered a threaded display before, then at first it may not be obvious what the benefit is. You will probably be influenced by how different it is to a list display. Changing a familiar presentation can be uncomfortable for most people.

The major benefit is that you can quickly identify the relationships between different e-mails, which message initiated the discussion (thread) and how the messages relate to each other. This is important if you are trying to gain an insight into a new issue or to remind yourself of an argument. It is very useful if you only check the e-mails after an interval, whereby the order in which you read them could influence your understanding or alternatively confuse you. The thread shows you the order of the debate and how the discussion arrived at the present point.

Other ways of presenting the messages allow you to identify e-mails that you have not read, listing them by sender or by who they have been sent to and the date they were received. These can all be useful on occasions.

It can take time fully to appreciate a threaded presentation, so you may have to continue for a few days or even weeks.

What was your own experience?

## Lurking

Mailgroups, forums and other forms of online communication groups are a key part of many e-learning programmes. They mainly operate by sharing all the messages sent by any individual participant with everyone registered with the group. Sometimes a participant rarely or never sends messages to the group and this behaviour is known as 'lurking'. Nonnecke and Preece (2001) reported that the reasons for lurking varied and that it might meet individual needs, in that the individuals got what they wanted from the mail-group without having to post messages. This is perhaps the equivalent of not participating in a class while listening to the questions and answers from other students and tutors. You do gain an insight into the subject but you are not getting answers to your own questions.

To ask a question in a face-to-face class requires self-confidence. The fear is always that it is a stupid question and everyone will think that you are fool. Similar doubts occur in mailgroups and forums but there are significant differences. You have to write your question and can therefore check that it is a sensible one before posting it. In a face-to-face class you need to speak and everyone can see you, so if you hesitate or stumble over the words the whole class will know. In a mailgroup or a forum you can present yourself in any way you like.

Some e-learning programmes will assess your contribution to group activities such as mailgroups so you need to be able to send messages and join in the debate. If you are unsure then you should:

- prepare your messages away from the mailgroup;
- check them yourself or ask a friend to help;
- post the messages;
- respond to replies.

It is often best to send messages at an early stage in the group's formation when everyone is trying to be a part of it. Many messages have little punctuation and ignore grammatical rules so if you make an error, it is unlikely anyone will notice. Spelling mistakes are common but can be eliminated by using the spell checkers provided within e-mail applications.

### Activity
### Preparing contributions to mailgroups

Prepare your replies in response to these messages:

1. What do you find most difficult about studying?
2. What have you gained most from studying?
3. How would you describe yourself?

**Discussion**
My own responses to these questions are:

1. What do you find most difficult about studying?
   Most of my recent study (over the last fifteen years) has had to be combined with working full time. This means that I am always

trying to read text books, writing essays or researching in the evening or at weekends. I always seem to be trying to fit in too many things, squeezing my family responsibilities into the gaps, struggling to meet deadlines and satisfy my employers.

2. What have you gained most from studying?
   I have developed self-confidence. I have gained valuable skills such as writing for publication as well as developing an understanding of many subjects. This has helped me in my career and personal life.

3. How would you describe yourself?
   I am a middle-aged man of fifty-five years with grey hair. I have been married for nearly thirty-three years and have two adult sons. I work for a national educational charity trying to encourage people to use ICT to support and deliver learning.

If I had doubts about these messages I could ask a friend or family member to check them before posting.

## Blogging

Blogs are often described as diaries but there are several significant differences. As well as being public documents that your peers will read, blogs used as part of e-learning programmes often encourage readers to comment on the entries so that it becomes a form of discussion. Another important difference is that blog entries and comments can be used as e-portfolio evidence.

Blog entries are not essays but rather specific pieces of writing, often reflecting on something you have read or an activity you have participated in. In some cases, you may have been asked to write an entry as part of your course but more often you will have the more general task of reflecting on your learning. If you are hoping to use your blog as e-portfolio evidence, then it is appropriate to ensure that you give references for any publication you cite.

A blog entry is relatively short, ranging from a sentence or two to a few hundred words. They are often focused on a specific issue (e.g. reflecting on and reviewing a paper you have read) and they are your own personal views. A common error is to try too hard to produce fascinating, interesting and controversial prose. It is far more important that you write your own reflections, whether they are interesting or not. It is vital to consider what you want to put on your blog. It is always important to remember that it is the equivalent of publishing your words and you are creating a semi-permanent record (i.e. you can edit your words later but it is important to try to get it right first time). You should take your time and perhaps write a draft off-line before posting it. Reflection is often assisted by trying to write down your views, so producing a draft will help you to organise your thoughts.

My approach to writing blog entries is to:

1. make some general notes;
2. draft a reflective entry;
3. check the entry – proof read, spell check and contemplate the content.

An important way of improving your blog writing is to read as many of your colleagues' blogs as you can and consider their approach. You will gain an insight that simply writing will not give you.

## Reflection

Reflective writing and blogs are fundamentally linked together. Reflection is a key element in learning. It will help slot the experience into your overall understanding of the topic or related ones. Writing a reflective piece will help you reflect and therefore to learn. Reflection involves analysis, review, consideration of implications and relationships and questioning your own actions and decisions.

As part of your course you are likely to be reflecting on:

- a research or other paper that you have read, but you are not simply providing a précis;
- an activity you have participated in (e.g. a discussion group, an essay you have submitted or a presentation you have undertaken);
- how a group of ideas, bits of knowledge and experience relate to each other;
- what options are available to you (e.g. selecting your dissertation topic);
- ethical issues;
- implications of government policy or international trends.

Reflective writing is not about producing simple descriptions of activities or summaries but considering implications, your own feelings and actions and how they relate to other knowledge and experience.

## Commenting on blogs

Students are often asked to read and comment on their peers' blogs. This is helpful because you will learn a lot about the art and skills of reflective writing. In commenting on your colleagues, it is important to remember the normal rules of netiquette and always to be constructive, objective and helpful. It is critical to avoid offensive or angry comments. This applies no matter how much the blog has irritated you. Never respond when you are annoyed. Do not allow a comment on your own blog to provoke you into responding in kind.

## Activity
## Creating a learning diary

The Open University provides online access (http://openlearn.open.ac.uk/) to a wide range of learning materials and also offers the option of creating a learning diary.

Visit the site and consider the process of setting up a learning diary and the advice to prepare you for the activity.

Alternatively visit www.blogger.com/ and create your own blog.

**Discussion**
An effective learning diary needs to help you reflect on your learning experiences so you need to invest time in considering your experiences. Your entries should not simply be a description of the learning activity but more a consideration or critical review of it. It is important to compare and contrast the new experiences with your existing store of understanding.

## Synchronous communication

Synchronous communication requires that all the participants be involved at the same time. A telephone conversation is synchronous since both parties have to be present. If you leave a message on an answer machine then the communication is asynchronous. There are three main synchronous communication methods:

- chat;
- audio conferencing;
- video conferencing.

### Chat

Chat lets you communicate with one or more other people through text messages in real time. It is useful for having general discussions because topics can be changed quickly, so helping group formation amongst new students. It is often an enjoyable experience, breaking down the barriers between students. It is less effective for considering a topic in depth. It has been used for one-to-one tutorials.

There are a variety of chat systems including:

- Internet Relay Chat;
- Webpage Chat;
- Instant Message Chat.

Internet Relay Chat (IRC) was the original and it requires you to have a chat application installed on your computer. Instant Message Chat is essentially a simplified form of Internet Relay Chat requiring the use of a message client (i.e. a message application). Webpage Chat has the advantage that you participate through your browser so do not need an application to take part.

### Audio conferencing

The critical factor in all forms of audio conferencing is that you cannot see the other participants. This removes the richness associated with non-verbal communication (e.g. knowing when the other person wants to speak, disagrees with your comments or is simply not interested). In an audio conference, an effective chairperson is crucial to organise and control the communication. This is normally a tutor but occasionally students will need to arrange their own meetings.

Often audio conferences give each participant the opportunity to speak in turn. This can take a long time if everyone has a contribution to make and tends to make the event quite formal. For you to gain the most from an audio conference you need to:

- prepare in advance what you want to say and any questions you want to ask;
- keep a record of the discussion (e.g. simple notes or an audio recording);
- concentrate on the discussion – this can be difficult when you have no visual prompts.

Audio conferences are most useful when they concentrate on a distinct issue related to a limited topic. They allow a group of participants to reach a decision without the need to meet. Groups should not be too large, otherwise the conference can become cumbersome. A reasonable rule is not to exceed six participants. In e-learning they have been used effectively as a means of offering a tutorial to answer questions and discuss a topic.

They are not a spontaneous communication method since ad hoc comments will confuse or distract from the central theme and often it is not easy to recognise voices. It is good practice to introduce yourself when you make a contribution and to speak clearly and concisely. You should not interrupt other participants. At the start of the event it is sensible to agree the objectives so you should decide in advance what you want to achieve.

The key to successful audio conferencing is preparation. You should consider the following:

1.  Most audio conferences have a time limit so even if you have an equal share of the time, you will probably only have a few minutes in total and this will be made up of several short contributions during the conference. You need to consider how to make the best use of this time.
2.  It is important to consider your aims. What are you trying to achieve? In an audio conference you are more likely to achieve a limited goal than an ambitious one, so focus on your priorities.
3.  It is often useful to list all the points you would like to make and prioritise them.
4.  Listen to the discussion. In many cases, other contributors will raise some of your issues, saving you time and allowing you to raise other issues.
5.  Support other contributions. It takes very little time to say, 'I agree with . . . and would like to add . . .'.
6.  Before the conference starts, make sure you have everything you need (e.g. preparation notes, pens, notebook, etc.).

## Video conferencing

Video conferences have much in common with audio conferencing but they are not as limited in the amount of non-verbal communication available to participants.

The quality of the video varies considerably between different systems and there are a number of ways of organising the conference, such as:

- tutor remote from a group or several groups of learners;
- tutor located with a group; other remote individuals or groups of learners linked by video conference to them;
- everyone separated.

There are other permutations and combinations, meaning that the communication skills needed will vary depending on the structure of the conference.

Video conferencing can limit the opportunity that each participant has to contribute, rather like audio conferencing, but it is not quite as restrictive since you can see each other. The tendency is still to be formal and to organise contributions, which can make discussion lengthy. To gain the most from a video conference you need to:

- prepare in advance what you want to say and any questions you want to ask;
- keep a record of the discussion (e.g. simple notes);
- concentrate on the discussion – this is difficult when your view of participants will depend on camera quality and set-up (e.g. camera angles);
- remember that sometimes people can see you even when you are not speaking;
- remember that if you move then you may not be visible but probably can be heard.

Video conferences, like audio ones, are most useful when they concentrate on a distinct issue related to a limited topic. They allow a group of participants to reach a decision without the need to meet. Groups should not be too large as the conference will become cumbersome but the precise number depends on the technology and structure being employed unless a straightforward online lecture is being given. In e-learning, video conferences have been used effectively as a means of offering a tutorial to answer questions, presenting a seminar to develop a new theme or allowing a co-operative group to meet and discuss a topic.

Video conferences are not a spontaneous communication method since to be effective they need a large degree of organisation. It is good practice to introduce yourself when you make a contribution and to speak clearly and concisely. You should not interrupt other participants but it is sometimes possible to add comments once they have finished before the next formal contribution. At the start of the event it is sensible to agree the objectives, so you should prepare in advance what you want to achieve.

As with audio conferencing, the key to successful video conferencing is preparation. Some considerations are:

1.  Before the conference starts you should make sure you have everything you need and that the camera is positioned to show you. Ensure that you will not be interrupted.
2.  You are visible, so check that your dress is acceptable.
3.  Most video conferences have a time limit so you will have limited opportunities for participation and this will probably consist of several short contributions.

4. You should consider your aims and keep them specific and focused. In a video conference you are more likely to achieve a limited goal than an ambitious one.
5. You should list and prioritise the points that you would like to make.
6. Concentrate on the discussion. Other contributors will often cover your points, so leaving you free to raise other issues or add support to your peers.
7. Remember that you can use visual signals such as giving the thumbs up to show you agree.

## Assessing your communication skills

The activity below (Online learning communication skills assessment) provides an opportunity to assess your communication skills.

---

### Activity
### Online learning communication skills assessment

Table 8.1 provides a structure for you to assess your current level of skill and what opportunities you aim to take in order to develop your skills.

**Table 8.1** Online learning communication skills assessment

| Skill | Current skill level | Opportunities to develop skill |
|---|---|---|
| e-Mail<br>Mailgroups<br>Newsgroups<br>Blog<br>Chat<br>Audio conferencing<br>Video conferencing | | |

**Discussion**

**Table 8.2** Personalised online learning communication skills assessment

| Skill | Current skill level | Opportunities to develop skill |
|---|---|---|
| e-Mail | I have been using e-mail for several years. | I have never really used a threaded system. I will change the display of my e-mail editor to display the communication threads to |

| | | |
|---|---|---|
| | | learn more about this approach. |
| Mailgroups | Occasionally I have joined mailgroups but I have rarely sent messages. | I will join some mailgroups that are relevant to my course and try to participate regularly in the discussion. |
| Newsgroups | I have only occasionally joined a newsgroup and never for very long. | I will join some relevant newsgroups and review their value over a four-week period. |
| Blog | I have never used a blog or created a learning diary | I will visit a range of educational blogs in order to gain an appreciation of the writing styles and approaches taken. When I am confident I will start my own learning diary. |
| Chat | I have never used a chat room. | I will register with a chat service and take part in some sessions to explore them. |
| Audio conferencing | I have never taken part in an audio conference. | I will seek to participate in audio conferencing to gain an insight into this method. |
| Video conferencing | I have only taken part in one type of video conferencing where two groups meet through the technology. | I will seek to gain experience of other types of video conferencing especially participating at home via a low-speed line. |

## Summary

### 1.   Acceptable use

The use of public computer facilities is normally governed by an acceptable use policy which sets the rules that control how you use the system (e.g. when and how you can use technology and what you can do with it). Many public learning centres employ filtering software to limit your access to and use of the internet.

## 2. Some factors when using communication technologies

*Cultural differences*: online learning removes the geographical barriers that separate learners, giving you a chance to study with learners from many other cultures.

*Libel*: e-mail and other forms of online communication are governed by the laws of libel and defamation.

*Privacy and security*: there are several steps you can take to protect your messages and system including home security, encrypting files, using passwords and employing firewalls.

## 3. Asynchronous communication

e-Mail is an asynchronous communication method and probably the most widely used one. It has many advantages in that you can send messages at any time to one or many people with or without attachments. In a similar way, you have the freedom to read messages when it is convenient. People read and send messages in many different and complex ways.

## 4. e-Mail communication styles

It is relatively easy to offend people unintentionally, perhaps owing to the short and informal way many people write e-mails. This is probably increased by the speed and ease of an e-mail message. It is important always to send polite e-mails and never to respond in anger to a message.

Most e-mails are written in an informal style which is friendly but can sometimes be difficult to understand. It is important to concentrate on replying in a way that is clear to your receiver.

## 5. Mailgroups and newsgroups

Mailgroups and newsgroups are communities of interest that allow you to participate in discussions about their topic. Groups cover almost all subjects (e.g. business, computing and science). You need to register with a group in order to take part – this will involve giving your name and e-mail address. Many newsgroups and mailgroups are moderated. Moderators essentially referee the discussion although their role in education is to facilitate the debate.

### 6.  Organisation

You can receive very large numbers of e-mail, especially if you participate in mailgroups. Outlook® software and other e-mail systems provide various features to organise your e-mails, letting you save them, segregate different types of messages, create new folders and remove spam.

### 7.  Mailgroup digests and summaries

Many mailgroups publish a regular digest or summary of the discussion (e.g. weekly or monthly). It allows you to maintain an interest in the discussion without having to read the many individual messages. In any public forum you should never give your name or any personal details.

### 8.  Threaded discussion

In many forms of online discussion the debate can be shown as a threaded discussion. A threaded presentation shows you the sequences and relationships between messages, enabling you to understand the relationship between the different themes being discussed.

### 9.  Lurking

Many participants of mailgroups send very few messages. This behaviour is called lurking, and has been described as the equivalent of not asking questions in a class while listening to the questions and answers from other students and tutors.

### 10.  Blogging

Blogs are often described as diaries but they differ significantly in that they are public documents that your peers will read and comment on. Entries and comments may be used as e-portfolio evidence.

One approach to writing blog entries is to make some general notes, draft a reflective entry and then check it (e.g. spell check).

*Reflection:* reflective writing and blogs are fundamentally linked together. Reflective writing is not about producing simple descriptions of activities or summaries but rather about considering the implications about your own feelings and actions, and how they relate to other knowledge and experience.

*Commenting on blogs:* many courses ask that students read and comment on their peers' blogs. In commenting on your colleagues, it is important to remember the normal rules of netiquette and always to be constructive, objective and helpful.

## 11.   Synchronous communication

Synchronous communication requires that participants take part simultaneously. There are three main synchronous communication methods:

- *Chat*: chat allows you to communicate using text messages in real time, rather like a conversation. It has been used to simulate the types of informal communication had by learners meeting face-to-face.
- *Audio conferencing:* the critical factor in an audio conference is that you do not have the benefit of non-verbal communications. It is important to provide an organised and controlled event – this is mainly the role of the tutor.

  In order to gain the most benefit from an audio conference participants need to:

  - prepare in advance;
  - keep a record of the discussion;
  - concentrate on the discussion.

  Audio conferences are most useful:

  - when they concentrate on a limited topic;
  - when they limit participation to a small group;
  - when they focus on agreed objectives.

  The key to successful audio conferencing is preparation.

- *Video conferencing*: this is broadly similar to audio conferencing but not as limited in non-verbal communications. There are a wide variety of ways of organising a video conference such as:

- tutor remote from a group or several groups of learners;
- tutor located with a group, other remote individuals or groups of learners being linked by video conference to them;
- everyone separated.

Communication skills will vary depending on the structure of the conference. Some general points are that:

- they limit the opportunity for each participant to contribute;
- there is a tendency to be formal and highly organised.

In order to gain the most benefit from video conferencing you need to:

- prepare in advance;
- keep a record of the discussion;
- concentrate on the discussion;
- remember that sometimes people can see and hear you even when you are not contributing.

Video conferences are most useful when:

- they concentrate on a limited topic;
- they focus on decision-making;
- they limit participation to a small group;
- they provide a tutorial;
- they allow a co-operative group to meet.

The key to successful video conferencing is preparation.

# 9 Group and Co-operative Learning

This chapter will extend and build on Chapter 8 into consideration of group and co-operative learning. It will concentrate on:

- group working online (e.g. collaboration, contributions and organisation);
- co-operative learning;
- online seminars, discussions and conferences;
- video, audio and text conferencing;
- wikis;
- peer assessment.

## Group working online

Although e-learning is often described in terms of individualised study, a major element is group or collaborative learning. Face-to-face learning often involves group activities and there are similarities as well as differences with e-learning. The key benefits of group learning are:

- It encourages you to compare and contrast your own views, ideas and conclusions with other learners.
- With peer support you may be more willing to ask another learner rather than your tutor about elements of the subject you do not understand.
- It motivates you to explore new difficult areas with the additional support of the group.
- It allows you to develop new skills such as analysis, communication and assessment of evidence.
- It provides you with feedback.
- It helps you to develop your skills of reflection (e.g. peer comments on your blog).

In some courses, group work will be a compulsory part of the programme while others will encourage you to form groups to consider certain problems. You can, however, take the lead yourself and initiate the formation of a discussion group.

The largest difference between face-to-face and e-learning groups is immediacy. In a traditional group you can see your partners and any comments you make get immediate feedback. An e-learning group is normally linked through e-mail and often communication exchanges take days. They start and stop as different group members read their messages at different times. Unlike a face-to-face conversation where you listen to each contribution one at a time, with e-mail you will often read several messages together.

## Activity
## Reflect on the e-mail communication cycle

Consider the difference in time-scale between traditional and e-mail communication and how it would influence the work of a group.

**Discussion**
A number of thoughts on this type of communication cycle occurred to me:

1.  It is more difficult to get a quick decision because it is complicated getting agreement with e-mail without giving dead-lines. So perhaps you need to specify a date by which responses are required. However, this does reduce some of the freedom which may be a major motivator for people to take part in e-learning.

2.  Since there is a time delay in responding to an individual comment, it is likely that several different messages/ideas will be discussed in parallel. A face-to-face group will tend to be more sequential in its discussions, although no group is ever completely linear. The leader of an e-learning group will need to be aware of the parallel discussions.

3.  It is more intricate leading an e-learning group since a dispersed group is harder to influence. This is both an advantage and a disad-vantage since participants cannot be easily silenced whereas a traditional group can be dictated to by a single strong personality. e-Mail is far harder to dominate.

Traditional groups are usually quite small (i.e. six to eight people) and e-learning groups are often a similar size if focused on completing an assignment or project. However, if their purpose is much wider (e.g. a common interest) e-learning groups can be far larger, with groups of hundreds and even thousands existing.

## Group formation

All groups require time to coalesce into an effective unit and some never quite form a coherent whole. This is true of both face-to-face and e-learning groups. Face-to-face groups have the advantage of immediacy, while e-learning groups have time to think about responses, which is often beneficial. All new groups have a degree of uncertainty about them. When you are asked to join a group you should consider:

- What is the purpose of the group (e.g. what are its aims and objectives)?
- What is the time-scale for the group (i.e. deadlines)?
- What are you aiming to achieve (i.e. outcomes)?
- What role do you want to play in the group?

Even students who are usually confident will approach a new group with some doubts and anxiety. It is perfectly normal for you to feel uneasy at first. Everyone does. It is important not to let this natural nervousness stop you from participating and learning from the experience. Moderators should be aware that forming a group requires time and support. They should provide the motivation by explaining the group's purpose, ensuring that everyone understands what they are aiming to do and generally encouraging progress.

Group formation will slowly start to happen, with participants becoming more open and willing to express their opinions. It is important that when you notice this happening you should contribute fully. Sometimes at this point a degree of argument creeps into the group formation. People begin to position themselves to take on particular roles. The structure of the group begins to consolidate and accepted ways of working emerge from the discussion.

This type of process happens in both face-to-face and e-learning groups. The major difference is that a face-to-face group may form in a few hours whereas an e-learning group will usually take longer owing to the nature of e-mail and other means of online communication.

## Activity
## Problems with group formation

You will have taken part in many groups during your education, work and other experiences. Consider your own experience and identify what are the main problems of working in a group.

**Discussion**

Some of the main problems I have encountered in e-learning groups are:

1. In all types of group, both face-to-face and e-learning, there is often disagreement between participants. This can be about almost any aspect of the group's work and it can result in the group breaking down into sub-groups or even individuals who choose to undertake the task on their own. In e-learning programmes, participation in group activities is frequently assessed, so you will lose marks if you do not join in.
2. e-Learning provides learners with the choice of where, when and at what pace to take part, so in order to take part in group activities, some degree of compromise is needed. Some learners will be unwilling or unable to change their preferred ways of working, so their participation may be irregular. This can be frustrating if you are waiting for a team member to report in order to take the work forward.
3. Occasionally the group fails to complete a task. The reasons are often variable – perhaps as a result of arguments within the groups, because too few people are willing to make a contribution or simply because the task is too difficult.

## Comparing face-to-face with e-learning groups

Table 9.1 analyses and compares face-to-face and e-learning groups operation.

## Tutor's role

In e-learning, the tutor is often termed a moderator or an e-moderator. As the name suggests, the role is not that of the traditional tutor but rather as a facilitator of learning by moderating the discussion, providing advice about the objectives of the activity and being a resource for the group. The responsibility for the successful outcome of the group work rests with the participants. The moderator is a resource to assist you to reach the desired outcome.

| Element | Face-to-face | e-Learning |
|---|---|---|
| Environment | The activities can be relatively short. In some cases a few minutes is given to complete a simple task. However, it can also involve complex tasks requiring many meetings over several weeks or months. Meetings take place face-to-face in a room. | Normally not suitable for short group activities and requires days or weeks to complete the group task. Participants are in their own homes or a learning centre or other ICT access point. They often have not seen or met their group members. |
| Tutor's role | Facilitation, briefing and group support through face-to-face communication. Tutor is immediately available. | Facilitation, briefing and group support at a distance, usually through e-mail. Tutor is available after normal e-mail delays. |
| Communication | Communication is spoken and includes body language. Records have to be made by taking minutes so one participant will be pre-occupied by this task. Record is likely to be partial. Communication tends to be more whole group than individual. | Normally communication is by writing. Electronic discussion provides a means of keeping a full accurate record of the discussion without participants being distracted from the principle task. Communication tends to be more individual than whole group. |
| Focus | Face-to-face groups often concentrate on single issues. | e-Learning groups have the potential to consider more than a single topic and discussion of several simultaneous themes is normal. There is a danger of the group going off at a tangent. |
| Size of group | Ideally 6 to 8 people but often larger. | Often 6 to 8 people but far larger groups can be involved although usually on less focused issues. |
| Relationships | Normally a single group with no outside links to other groups. | Often groups will be linked to others. |

| | Face-to-face | E-learning |
|---|---|---|
| **Participation:** | | |
| 1. Frequency of contribution | The nature of the participation will be dependent on the confidence of the individual learners taking part. Dominant individuals may well influence the nature of the debate. | There are few barriers to participation. However, there is probably less peer pressure to join in than with a face-to-face group. Most new e-learners have some doubts about their initial contributions. It is normal to hesitate and be uncertain. Lurking or simply reading other people's messages while not contributing yourself is a common occurrence. Some educational groups assess your contribution, so you may have to participate. |
| 2. Size of contribution | Contributions are limited by the length of each meeting and the reaction of other members. You are more conscious of the reaction your contribution is making through non-verbal communication. | |
| **Subjects:** | | |
| 1. Introducing new subjects | Discussion tends to focus on a limited range of issues. Parallel discussions often fragment a face-to-face group. | Any subject can be raised at any time since everyone is free to send a message. This does tend to lead to many parallel discussions. |
| 2. Building on earlier contributions | Building on other people's contributions depends on whether the person is influential within the group. A quiet person's views may well be lost. Building on ideas is mostly immediate. | The record of the discussion and your own choice of when to read the messages allows you to build on previous contributions whenever you want to. This does often lead to discussions restarting about issues raised days or even weeks earlier. |
| 3. Duration of discussion | Discussions are limited by the time available for each meeting and are therefore disjointed. | Discussions are continuous and you are free to join in whenever it is appropriate to you. |
| Facilitator/moderator | It is important to agree who will act as the group's spokesperson, record-keeper and any other roles. This will ensure a record of conclusions is kept and someone takes on the role of ensuring that the task is achieved (i.e. you do not go off at a tangent). | In all groups it is important to define each person's role. It is often useful to ask someone to act as the group leader, facilitator or moderator. In many large online groups, a moderator is appointed who will often act as a referee, intervening if the discussion is aggressive or breeches netiquette rules. |

**Table 9.1**   Comparing face-to-face with e-learning groups – *continued overleaf*

| Element | Face-to-face | e-Learning |
|---|---|---|
| Records | Someone has to agree to make notes of what is agreed. These are often at best a limited record of the discussion and may miss key contributions. | The computer makes a record of all the contributions, so everyone has access to a full record of the group's discussion. |
| Review | Any review will be based mainly on the individual memory of the participants and the limited notes taken. | The full record of the discussion allows for a detailed review of the group's work to be undertaken. |
| Reflection | You can reflect on any experience but in a face-to-face group your reflection will be based on your memory and is likely to be more subjective. | As a full record of your contribution is available, you can undertake detailed objective reflection which will probably help you refine your arguments and approach. |
| Summarising | It is useful in any discussion to produce an agreed summary which will help the group come to agreements and focus their efforts. | The moderator will often produce a summary of the discussion at intervals. |
| Conclusion | The leader will need to propose to the group what he or she believes are the agreed conclusions. The other group members are then free to agree, disagree or build on the suggested conclusions. | Any proposed conclusion can be considered in depth and involve everyone in the debate. |

**Table 9.1**  *continued*

## Activity
## e-Learning group

Consider Table 9.1 comparing face-to-face and e-learning groups and also your own experience of working in a group. How would you ensure that you will gain most from the experience?

**Discussion**
Some of the things you might want to do are:

1.  Make sure you understand what you are being asked to do and that you understand the outcome required (e.g. some group activities are assessed to judge your personal contribution and peers are often asked to assess each other's actions).
2.  Volunteer to play an active role in the group, perhaps accepting the leadership of a sub-task or even the whole group. You will learn a great deal about the subject and people by taking on responsibility for a task. If you choose to play a minimum role then you will limit what you learn from the experience.
3.  e-Learning groups are not a series of meetings but a continuous process of communication so you need to organise yourself through:

    - regularly checking your e-mail, forum, bulletin board or other discussion list;
    - keeping records of the group (e.g. set up a folder to save messages and other documents);
    - planning your involvement (e.g. research time and reflection time to consider other participant contributions).

4.  Consider the depth of discussion. Are many of your exchanges simply responses or do they involve several ideas on a topic (e.g. genuine discussion rather than question and answer).
5.  Reflect on your own group role to improve your contribution.
6.  Be proactively helpful to other group members without interfering.

What did you conclude?

## Synchronous learning

Video conferencing and other forms of synchronous e-learning sometimes takes the form of a lecture to a large number of learners in varying locations, with the learners taking part in a group rather than as individuals. An expert may provide an hour-long presentation of some new development while a large number of people listen and watch, similar to a traditional lecture. In a traditional lecture it is possible to ask individual questions or for the lecturer to divide the audience into buzz groups to consider an issue or to decide on questions. These methods can also be used in video conferencing. Often individual learners are asked to write questions on cards which are then collected and sent to the speaker by e-mail, telephone, or another communication method. Buzz groups can also be employed to give feedback or to agree questions. In a large video conference this is slightly cumbersome but it does give some degree of interaction. While smaller events can be more effective, the large-scale approach has the significant advantage of being more cost-effective and provides the opportunity for many people to hear directly from an expert.

Small synchronous groups have a great deal in common with face-to-face ones. Arranging times when everyone can meet is a major limitation in face-to-face group work and the added factor of access to specialist video conferencing equipment in synchronous e-learning contributes to this issue. Video meetings are often limited to a fixed time so it is essential that each participant is able to prepare for the meeting to maximise the contact time. This normally means that the meetings need to be led by one of the group and that essentially an agenda is followed. Although this reduces spontaneity and serendipity during the meetings, considerable progress can usually be made on the task.

There is clearly a low-cost approach to video conferencing, with individual participants using their own cameras over the world wide web. This is perfectly feasible and is more flexible but still requires fixed-time meetings. It is often used in combination with e-mail to maximise its effectiveness.

### Asynchronous learning

A major asynchronous learning method is the mailgroup. While these are normally focused on a particular issue, many e-learning courses have an overall group for the course so that students can discuss any aspect of it. There are then smaller, more specialist mailgroups covering key aspects of the course. You will often be made a member of this type of group as part of enrolling on the programme.

Simply placing learners into the same mailgroup does not guarantee that they will take part. In most cases very little happens unless it is encouraged and in many courses a tutor or tutors are appointed to moderate the group. Their role is to help break down barriers and encourage participation.

Often you will be asked to introduce yourself during the early stages of the course and this often takes the form of:

- who you are;
- what you would like to discuss;
- why you are doing the course;
- anything interesting about yourself.

In a face-to-face group, the most difficult step to take is starting to speak. The same is true in a mailgroup because everyone fears making a fool of themselves. The introduction helps to get the discussion going and will often generate questions, perhaps simply about the course structure, so starting the communication process.

Sometimes the moderators will seek to initiate a debate about an issue by introducing ideas, concepts or issues, either directly or through a student who has been asked to help. These methods have a mixed rate of success. In most mailgroups, a majority of members rarely participate but, just read others' messages. This is sometimes called lurking and is often seen as negative behaviour, but reading the messages and learning from the debate is very similar to listening to questions and answers in a conventional class-room. Although you will benefit from it, you will gain more if you participate by sending messages, asking questions and offering contributions. The more you give, the more you will receive.

At an early stage the group moderator will explain the netiquette govern-ing the communication process or ask members of the mailgroup itself to suggest conditions. This has the advantage of encouraging communication and allowing yourselves to agree the rules. Most people are more likely to obey rules that they have had some say in agreeing.

## Activity
## Introduction to a mailgroup

You have been asked to introduce yourself to a mailgroup explaining:

1. who you are;
2. what you would like to discuss;
3. why you are doing the course;
4. anything interesting about yourself.

You are starting a course to study e-learning methods. What would you say?

**Discussion**
This is my simple introduction. It is fairly short so people will be encouraged to read it, yet it also includes a question that is bothering me.

My name is Alan Clarke.

I am interested in most of the course topics but at the moment I am not entirely sure how much flexibility I have in studying. Can I decide when I do assignments or are there fixed deadlines?

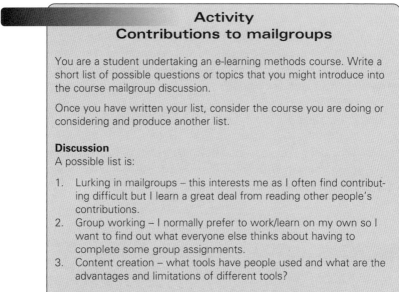

I am doing the course as part of my employer's continuous professional development programme. We are considering using e-learning
methods within the organisation.

In contrast to e-learning, I collect postcards and keep guinea pigs.

What would you say?

## Activity
## Contributions to mailgroups

You are a student undertaking an e-learning methods course. Write a
short list of possible questions or topics that you might introduce into
the course mailgroup discussion.

Once you have written your list, consider the course you are doing or
considering and produce another list.

**Discussion**
A possible list is:

1.  Lurking in mailgroups – this interests me as I often find contribut-
    ing difficult but I learn a great deal from reading other people's
    contributions.
2.  Group working – I normally prefer to work/learn on my own so I
    want to find out what everyone else thinks about having to
    complete some group assignments.
3.  Content creation – what tools have people used and what are the
    advantages and limitations of different tools?

What did you list?

### Individual versus group outcomes

The outcome of e-learning group activities is often specified as an individual
piece of work – that is, you are asked to work with some of your fellow
students but produce your own result rather than submit a joint effort. It is
important before you start a group activity to check what is expected from
you. You may find that:

- an individual outcome (e.g. a personal report or essay) is expected;
- you will be assessed on your contribution to the group – this may
  take the form of assessment by either your tutor/moderator or by

the other group members (e.g. you mark their individual
contributions and they mark yours);

- a group outcome is expected;
- a combination of group or individual outcome in addition to your
contribution forms the assessment;
- the group work is not assessed.

## Co-operative learning

Co-operative learning is essentially two or more learners working together in
a co-operative way that promotes their individual learning. Co-operative
learning activity, especially if the participants are at a distance and initially
know little about each other, requires consideration, care and understanding
of each other. Some aspects for co-operating with others in e-learning are
shown below:

- Do not reply in anger no matter how provoked you feel by an e-
mail.
- Support everyone in the group to play a part.
- Consider all contributions carefully.
- Do not dismiss an idea because you do not understand it – ask for
more details.
- Never send a hostile message.
- Find out about the other members of the group.
- Accept your share of the responsibility for the task.
- Do not let the other participants down by missing a deadline or not
fulfilling your share of the tasks without explanation.
- Keep everyone informed of your progress.
- Ask for help if you need it.
- Explore the proposed concepts and ideas.
- Encourage a team spirit.

There are probably many others but the concept should be clear that co-
operative learning requires more than simply fulfilling a task, it is also about
developing the members of group. One benefit that is especially important in
the context of this book is that it should help extend everyone's e-learning
skills.

## Activity
## Co-operative behaviour

Consider the statements above and how you would implement them. Write down some principles that would help you participate success-fully in a co-operative learning group.

**Discussion**
There are many different ways of achieving successful co-operation and some of these are shown below:

1. It is easy to send an e-mail message so there is a real danger of overreacting or reacting too quickly to what seems to be a provocation. A good principle is never to send a critical message without sleeping on it. You will more often regret sending an e-mail than you will not regret sending one. Reflect on your peer's ideas and views. It is rare that a viewpoint is completely without merit.
2. Don't dismiss any idea without reflecting carefully on it. Just because an idea is from a different perspective does not mean it is poor. Your perspective may be the incorrect one.
3. Don't monopolise the discussion by sending too many e-mails. It is important to allow everyone a chance to speak. e-Learning gives considerable freedom to choose when you take part and some of your peers may be combining studying with a full-time job or family responsibilities which makes answering messages immediately difficult.
4. Always ask for feedback from your peers. This may help them participate.
5. Mailgroups enable you to send e-mail to all members of the group with a single posting but you are also free to send an e-mail directly to one member. This is quite useful if you are seeking help or additional information from another member of the group.

What principles did you identify?

Co-operative and collaborative learning methods have been used extensively in traditional courses. In e-learning many of the ideas have been adopted, extended and adapted to fit within the new environment. Co-operative learning can simply be two learners working together which in a conventional setting probably means their sitting next to each other and sharing ideas and comments. It is immediate, whereas a similar e-learning pairing may depend on e-mail – it is asynchronous and is likely to be spread over a longer time.

Some suggestions for launching a co-operative e-learning group are shown below:

- Spend time introducing yourselves – it is important that you understand each other as much as possible. When you are working at a distance, the possibilities for misunderstandings are great, so minimise them.
- e-Learning gives everyone more freedom to choose when and where and at what pace to take part, so it is useful to start with the agreement of work methods that are as inclusive as possible.
- Agree on how to undertake the task and what each member would like personally to achieve. This may involve dividing the work into sub-tasks or asking someone to act as the secretary or leader of the group. Be willing to take on responsibilities.
- Be realistic about time – it will almost certainly take longer than you think. Consider the deadline (if you have one) and work backwards so that it is achieved. Consider how long each step will take to arrive at. Sometimes it shows that you are already late and so need to change your plans. An example (working backwards) is shown below:

| Deadline | Final report – 11 August |
| Writing report | Four weeks – must begin by 14 July |
| Evidence location and analysis | Six weeks – must begin by 2 June |
| Today's date | 1 June |

Analysis shows you that you must start at once, or reduce the time for some tasks

## e-Learning co-operative methods

Of those approaches and methods used in group and co-operative learning, many are available in both traditional and e-learning. The ones used in e-learning have been adapted to suit the e-learning environment (e.g. learners communicating through e-mail rather than face-to-face). Although e-mail is normally asynchronous, it is possible to mimic a synchronous conversation by asking everyone to take part at a set time. In this way, it is possible for a live event to take place. In some cases a telephone conference can be operated in parallel. If you are taking part in a synchronous event it is good practice to have a notebook ready to record your thoughts so that you are ready to contribute when your opportunity comes.

| Method | Face-to-face | e-Learning |
|---|---|---|
| Brainstorming sessions | Brainstorming sessions are intended to have a large degree of spontaneity, with individual contributions sparking ideas from other participants. The initial round of thoughts is usually not assessed, the subject or issue being thoroughly explored before you start to consider practical issues. | An e-learning equivalent tries to achieve the same results but is likely to last a few days rather than the few hours that a face-to-face event would require. It needs a moderator to maintain time limits and to gather all the ideas together so that assessment can be systematically undertaken. |
| Buzz Groups | Buzz groups are often used in the classroom or conference hall to generate questions or to discuss the speakers' ideas. They normally last only a few minutes and are informal with a small group of participants (i.e. 3 or 4 people) being asked to d iscuss a concept quickly. One member is asked to provide feedback. | They are used for similar purposes in synchronous e-learning (e.g. video and audio conferencing). In asynchronous groups it is difficult to achieve the speed of natural conversation so they are rarely used. |
| Competitions/ role play | Competitions which allow individuals to explore complex situations are an effective way of motivating groups and individuals. Different groups are asked to compete with each other. This can take the form of each group member role-playing a particular situation (e.g. each group acting as a business in competition with others for a contract). | Online competitions are very effective and can involve consideration of complex and involved situations. A face-to-face role-play competition may only last a few hours while an e-learning one may need several weeks. However, the longer period allows for detailed analysis of information to make decisions, so providing more opportunities for in-depth study |
| Informal discussion | Learning often takes place in informal settings away from the classroom or laboratory such as in the corridor after a lecture, over a cup of coffee or while walking between locations. Anywhere that learners can meet and talk is a potential place for learning. | In e-learning you are often separated from other learners so virtual informal locations need to be created such as cybercafés where you can discuss the course or anything else with your peers. |

| | | |
|---|---|---|
| Debates/ discussion circles | Face-to-face debates and discussions are a useful means of exploring issues. Often the topic is polarised into two opposing views in order to test its extremes. | In e-learning, a paper is often presented to provide a foundation for the debate or discussion. Participants are allowed to contribute their views on the paper – extending its argument or criticising it. Often a series of parallel discussions on different issues develops. The debates can last for weeks or a few days and are moderated to ensure that they remain focused. A summary of the discussion is often provided at the end. |
| Interviews | Conventional interviews allow the views of an expert to be presented to an audience and offer the opportunity for audience members to ask supplementary questions, although in practice in a large group few will be able to speak. | An expert and an interviewer undertake a normal question-and-answer session, the difference being that it is sent to the whole group as a series of e-mails. The group can join in by commenting on the answers and asking supplementary questions. |
| Investigations | In small groups, you are asked to carry out an investigation of a particular topic. Normally you will be provided with a starting point (e.g. a document) but you have to decide how to proceed and to produce a report of your results. | The main differences between traditional and e-learning investigations is immediacy and that starting point is often a website or a group of sites. e-Learning investigations last longer. |
| Pairs | Two learners, helping each other to learn, will share views, assist with problems, review material and discuss the course content. It may be a formal or informal arrangement where the learners themselves have decided to study together. | Again, the main differences are distance and time. The pair may never meet face-to-face but develop their relationship through e-mail or other communication methods. |
| Panels | Panels of experts are often used in seminars and conferences to facilitate the scrutiny of a subject. | In a similar way to face-to-face, e-panels allow you to question a group of specialists in order to reveal the issues, the key difference being that the interaction takes place at a distance. |

**Table 9.2** e-Learning co-operative methods – *continued overleaf*

| Method | Face-to-face | e-Learning |
|---|---|---|
| Projects | You need to decide on a division of the tasks, the time-scales and the form of reporting back to the group. | e-Projects are very similar to face-to-face ones, the significant difference being that you do not meet your partners. You need to decide on a division of the tasks, the time-scales and the form of reporting back to the group. Groupware applications can aid project teams to co-operate. |
| Quests | There is no direct equivalent to a WebQuest but some aspects are similar, such as role play. | A special form of online investigation but normally you are provided with a list of websites so that you are not searching for information but analysing it. In some cases each member of the group is given a role to play during the quest. |
| Stories | This is not often employed in a face-to-face setting. | A creative use of the online communication is to write a story jointly with a number of colleagues. An initial paragraph is provided and everyone is allowed to add the next paragraph of the story. This can be an interesting and fun experience. |

**Table 9.2**   *continued*

## Activity
## Co-operative methods

From your own experience, select one of the above approaches and consider it from a co-operative learning perspective. How would you ensure that the extra dimension of personal development is included in the experience?

**Discussion**
I selected the competitions/role play method since it is an approach which I normally avoid but which perhaps I need to understand better. I would:

1.  take on roles that were more demanding than I normally do so that I was able to experience more;
2.  keep a personal diary of the whole activity so I could reflect on what had happened and try to improve my contribution;
3.  ask someone in the group to give me feedback on my contribution.

You may have decided on quite different methods and actions.

## Activity
## Co-operative methods – supporting
## other people

Assisting other learners can be a useful way to help your own learning and is an important part of co-operative learning. From your own experience, select one of the above approaches (different from the previous activity) and consider it from a co-operative learning perspective. How would you ensure that you support your peers?

**Discussion**
I selected the debates/discussion circles method because it is an interesting approach and I have taken part in a wide variety of them. I would:

1.  try to express my own ideas in a straightforward way;
2.  always try to be polite and constructive in my comments;
3.  be willing to give feedback if requested;
4.  encourage participation;
5.  consider carefully all messages and be willing to admit when more relevant ideas than my own are suggested.

This all sounds a little self-righteous but the key point is to respect your peers and be open to new concepts.

## Activity
## Online learning group and co-operative skills assessment

Table 9.3 provides a structure for you to assess your current level of skill, what future level you would like to achieve and what opportunities you aim to take in order to develop your skills.

**Table 9.3** Online learning group and co-operative skills assessment

| Skill | Current skill level | Opportunities to develop skill |
|---|---|---|
| Using communication technology Interpersonal skills Group formation Co-operation | | |

### Discussion
Table 9.4 is intended to show some possible areas you may wish to consider.

**Table 9.4** Personalised online learning group and co-operative skills assessment

| Skill | Current skill level | Opportunities to develop skill |
|---|---|---|
| Using communication technology | Experienced user of e-mail. Occasional participant in video and audio conferencing. Rarely use chat. | Join a chat room discussing a topic that interests me to develop a more informal synchronous communication style. |
| Interpersonal skills | Good face-to-face skills but have less experience in working with others through communication technology. | I will seek to join the voluntary self-help group that some of my fellow students are establishing. I will attempt to transfer my face-to-face skills to the new environment. |
| Group formation | Experienced participant in face-to-face groups but rarely feel comfortable as the leader. Occasionally joined online groups but rarely contribute. | I need to be more than a lurker. I should volunteer to take responsibility for a task and make an effort to participate fully. I will keep a record of my contributions and monitor myself. |

| Co-operation | Reliable member of a group but only occasionally have I reached out to help others take part or considered if I or the others have grown through the experience. | The course includes completion of a group project. I will use this as an opportunity to see if I can actively co-operate with other students. I will reflect on what happens and seek to identify how I can improve my skills. |
|---|---|---|

What did you identify?

## Online seminars and conferences

There is a role for more large-scale e-learning events such as an online seminar or conference. Table 9.5 compares a traditional conference with an online or virtual one. At traditional conferences you are limited to a single theme at any one time, but online conferences allow you to take part in several different themes while continuing with your normal work or studies since you are working asynchronously.

If you consider the comparison table, you will see that an online event offers certain advantages over a conventional conference, such as:

- you can participate in almost everything;
- you can combine the event with your normal activities;
- there are no travel and subsistence costs.

However, the conference does take place over a long period and in order to gain the maximum benefit from the event, you must organise yourself. It is good practice to:

- plan to take part regularly (e.g. every evening). It is difficult to catch up if you fall behind with the debate;
- keep records of issues and ideas so you can reflect on them later;
- not overextend yourself by trying to take part in too many parallel discussions (it is easy to deceive yourself that you can cope with multiple themes only to find yourself falling behind in them all; it is better practice to focus on what interests you most);
- contact individual participants directly if they raise issues that you are especially interested in; this is the equivalent of

| Conference feature | Traditional | Online |
|---|---|---|
| Keynote speaker | Everyone assembles and listens to an expert. | An expert produces a paper and/or presentation using PowerPoint® presentation graphics program which is sent to everyone enrolled in the conference. Alternatively, the paper and/or presentation are available to be downloaded from a conference website. |
| Parallel themes | A series of rooms are prepared where individual speakers present their work and answer questions. | A series of mailgroups are established for each theme and the paper is sent to each registered delegate. They are then free to ask questions of the speaker. |
| Workshops | A series of rooms is prepared and facilitators attempt to focus participants to address the issues of the workshop. | A series of mailgroups are established for each workshop and the facilitator acts as the moderator of the group. |
| Posters | An area is set aside and each participant is given a space to illustrate their work. This normally consists of a wall poster display and supporting papers. At designated times the participants are available to discuss their work with conference delegates. | Each poster is shown on a webpage with e-mail connection to the participants so that their work can be discussed. |

| | |
|---|---|
| Exhibition | An area is provided in which stands showing the products from the different exhibitors are set up. Delegates are able to walk around, look at each stand and discuss the products with company representatives. | Exhibitors provide links to their own websites with e-mail connection so delegates can make enquiries. |
| Informal discussion | An important aspect of any conference is chance meetings with people who share similar interests. | Informal contact is often provided through a conference chat room. |
| Time | Traditional conferences are time-limited. They can range from one day to a week. | Online conferences often last several weeks since delegates are often involved part-time while carrying on with a full-time job or course. |

**Table 9.5**  Comparing traditional and online conferences

talking to presenters at the end of their session or introducing yourself to another conference delegate so you can discuss their work.

## Wikis

Wikis are collaborative writing tools but like any device their success depends on how they are used. In simple terms, a wiki consists of several pages that participants link together. Each participant can edit the content, link pages together and start new pages. Figure 9.1 shows the opening page of a new wiki that I created as an illustration. The application keeps a record of the editing history so that changes can be removed and original versions reinstated. This raises the key question of when a collaborative document is completed. Completion is when the participants agree on the text. There is a need in any collaborative writing exercise to agree:

- an editorial process;
- how to negotiate content;

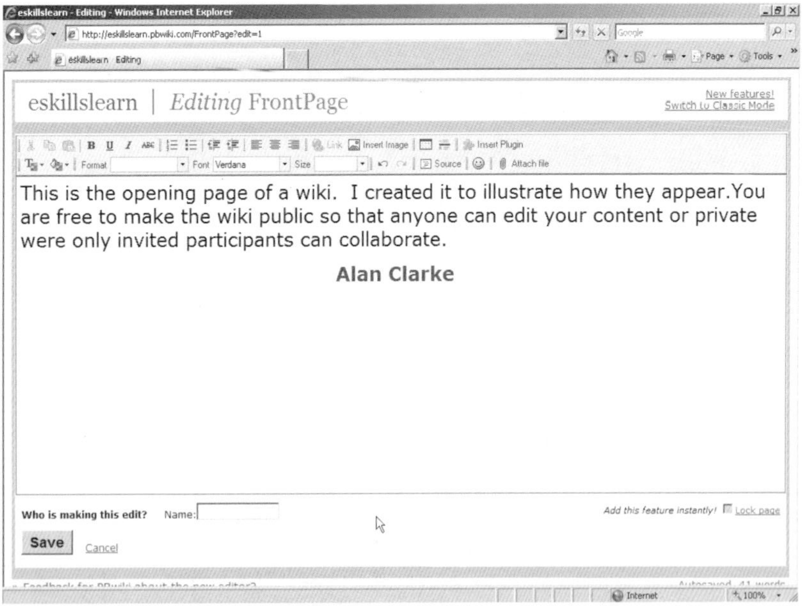

**Figure 9.1**   Wiki (PeanutButterWiki at pbwiki.com)

- the scope of the document;
- participant roles.

A collaborative and co-operative writing process can help a group learn to work together and gain a fresh insight into the topic from the process. Writing for most people is an individual experience or a process of one person writing and others giving feedback. A wiki is a collaborative process and can help overcome many of the barriers we have all developed with writing on our own. It provides an interactive process of review from a group of people who are also sharing in the review as authors.

Writing a collaborative document is a dynamic interactive process and wikis let you make changes easily and quickly. They allow you to correct mistakes in a similar way so the focus should be contributing, since errors can be corrected later. It is often difficult to start to collaborate and many groups will begin by each person writing a separate piece so that you have a long linear document without any joint editing. The way to move forward is to discuss the writing process before you begin and start immediately to negotiate the content of the document.

Blogs and wikis have many things in common but while a blog allows writers to publish their work and their peers to comment on it, a wiki enables the whole group to create the content. Already applications that combine blogs and wikis are being used.

## Activity
## Creating a wiki

With a few friends or colleagues create a wiki either to write a document jointly that explains what the main benefits of ICT to an individual are or to select an alternative project. Use http://pbwiki.com/ or an alternative site to create your wiki.

**Discussion**
The creation of an opening page should be straightforward. However, the main challenge is normally editing someone else's contribution. It is usually easier to add extra text than to delete or change comments. Often a new group working on a joint document will simply keep adding sections so that it becomes longer, since no one wants to be the first to start editing. However, the main benefits of a wiki are in editing and joint collaboration.

What was your experience of writing in a wiki?

### ● Peer assessment

A feature of many group, collaborative or co-operative activities is that your contribution is assessed by your peers as well as your tutors. You will often be asked to assess your colleagues and in some cases provide feedback. The assessment can take many forms but it does place a responsibility on you to make objective judgements. You may also be asked to judge your own performance.

It is useful during the group work to consider:

- the aims and objectives of the group activity;
- your own performance – how you would improve your contribution;
- what the group agreed to do, what roles were allocated and what the timetable was;
- who made the most valuable contribution and why;
- whether anyone caused any problems (e.g. failing to contribute on time);
- who made the least contribution and why.

It is vital to be objective and fair in your assessment. If you are asked to provide feedback, then:

- begin with the best aspects of the person's performance;
- be clear and concise;
- be straightforward;
- move from best aspects to weak points;
- be constructive in your feedback and give suggestions;
- give examples of weaknesses with constructive comments;
- be fair and friendly;
- conclude on a positive point.

## Activity
## Peer assessment

For a course you are undertaking ask a fellow student if you can practise peer assessment. It is probably best to ask them to assess your work while you assess their efforts – that is, undertake a mutual assessment.

**Discussion**
It is useful to compare your efforts with the assessment that you receive from your partner. Ask them to do the same and give you feedback:

1.    Did they feel it was fair, constructive and objective?
2.    Was the assessment clear and straightforward?
3.    What did you learn about your performance?

Provide them with similar feedback if they want it.

Reflect on your experience – how did you feel undertaking the task (often people are reluctant to assess peers), what do you think your colleague thought about the process?

# Summary

## 1.    Group working online
Although e-learning often involves individual learning groups, collaborative learning also plays a major role. Group activities encourage you to compare yourself with other learners, provides peer support and motivation to develop new skills. Although there are many similarities between face-to-face and e-learning groups, a significant difference is often immediacy. e-Mail exchanges can be spread over days, with delays, reflecting the different members' behaviour in using the technology.

*Group formation*
Groups of all types take time to form. They require active participants which can sometimes mean that disagreement is part of the formation process. e-Learning groups will often take longer to form than their face-to-face equivalents.

*Comparing face-to-face with e-learning groups*
There are both similarities and differences between face-to-face and e-learning groups. Some of the main differences are related to:

- time – e-learning groups will normally need more time to complete a task;

- delays – responses from participants and tutors will always experience a time delay due to using e-mail;
- writing – normally e-learning groups will communicate by writing;
- multiple topics – e-learning groups can discuss several topics in parallel;
- participants – e-learning groups can be larger than face-to-face groups and can co-operate with other groups;
- equality – e-mail allows everyone to participate although many people choose to take a passive role;
- records – a full record of all e-mail discussions can automatically be kept.

## 2.   Co-operative learning

Co-operative learning is about a group of learners working together. It is not limited to undertaking a task, but is concerned with developing participants (e.g. improving an individual's learning skills). Over time, a co-operative group may well develop into a community of practice. Some suggestions for launching a co-operative e-learning group are shown below:

- Spend time introducing yourselves.
- Agree working methods that are inclusive.
- Agree how to undertake the task and what each member would like to achieve.
- Be realistic about time.

*e-Learning co-operative methods*

There are many learning approaches and methods used in group and co-operative learning, both in traditional and e-learning. Those used in e-learning have been adapted to suit the e-learning environment (e.g. learners communicating through e-mail rather than face-to-face). Methods include brainstorming sessions, buzz groups, competitions/role plays, informal settings, debates/discussion circles, interviews, investigations, pairs, panels, projects, quests and stories.

### 3. Online seminars and conferences

There is a role for more large-scale e-learning events, such as an online seminar or conference, with a variety of ways of organising these. Some potential advantages of online events are:

- You can participate in almost everything;
- You can combine the event with your normal activities.
- There are no travel and subsistence costs.

However, the conference can take place over several weeks or months and in order to gain the maximum benefit from the event, you do require self-organisation.

### 4. Wikis

Wikis are collaborative writing tools. Each participant can edit the content, link pages together and start new pages. The application keeps a record of the editing history, so changes can be removed and original versions reinstated. There is a need in any collaborative writing exercise to agree on the editorial process, the content, and the scope of the document and on each person's role.

### 5. Peer assessment

In group activities your contribution may be assessed by your peers. This can take a variety of forms, including also assessing your own performance. If you are asked to give feedback, then be objective and fair. It is important to start with strengths before discussing weaknesses and always to be constructive.

# 10 Further Information and Resources

A wide range of additional information and resources will be provided with annotations. This will assist readers to develop further their skills and understanding of e-learning. Websites are dynamic and although all these sites were available at the time of writing, they are likely to change.

## ● Acceptable use policies

www.becta.org.uk – British Educational Communication Technology Agency provides support and assistance to education in the United Kingdom. The website contains many useful resources including acceptable use policies.

## ● Adult learning

www.bbc.co.uk/ – BBC Online provides access to online learning resources
www.careers-scotland.org.uk/ – information about adult learning in Scotland
www.careerswales.com – careers information for children and adults
www.niace.org.uk – National Institute for Adult Continuing Education in England and Wales
www.waytolearn.co.uk/ – information about adult learning opportunities in England

## ● Assessing quality of online resources

www.vts.intute.ac.uk/ – Intute: Social Sciences virtual training suite to help you use the internet as an educational resource

## ● Biography

www.anb.org/ – American National Biography
www.biography.com/ – many thousands of biographies
www.s9.com/biography/ – biographical dictionary

## ● Blogging

http://flux.futurelab.org.uk/index.php/2006/11/28/hello-world/ – Future Lab's Educational Blog
http://oedb.org/library/features/top-100-education-blogs – 100 best educational blogs
www.blogger.com/ – create your own blog
www.open.ac.uk/openlearn/home.php – Open University website providing access to free learning materials and allowing you to develop an online learning diary

## ● Bookmarks

http://del.icio.us/ – online bookmarking service

## ● Books

www.abebooks.co.uk – worldwide used and out-of-print books
www.amazon.com – probably the best known online bookshop in the world
www.bookbrain.co.uk – this search engine will help you to locate a book in a range of online bookshops. It compares prices and the cost of postage and packing.
www.booksinprint.com/ – how to locate any book which is currently available
www.thebookplace.co.uk/ – The Book Pl@ce

## ● Buying online

www.consumerdirect.gov.uk/ – advice to consumers on buying goods and services

## Chat

http://messenger.yahoo.com/chat.php – Yahoo chat/messenger

## Creative commons

http://creativecommons.org/ – copyright licences

## Databases

www.bl.uk/ – British Library
www.eric.ed.gov/ – Educational Resource Information Centre – major educational resource – databases, journals and publications

## Dictionaries

http://dictionary.reference.com/ – online dictionary
www.askoxford.com/ – online dictionary
www.m-w.com/ – Merriam Webster online dictionary
www.oed.com/ – Oxford English Dictionary – subscription service
www.yourdictionary.com/ – free online dictionary with many links for specialist subjects

## Disabilities

http://webxact.watchfire.com/ – provides a service to allow you to test a webpage for accessibility
www.abilityhub.com/ – Abilityhub – information about assistive technology
www.abilitynet.org.uk – Abilitynet – a charity which provides help, advice and support in using ICT for disabled people
www.abledata.com/ – Abledata – information about assistive technology
www.closingthegap.com/ – Closing The Gap Inc – an organisation which provides help with technology for people with special needs – 526 Main Street, PO Box 68, Henderson, Minnesota 56044, USA
www.drc-gb.org/ – Disability Rights Commission
www.dyslexic.com/ – help with dyslexia
www.rnib.org.uk – Royal National Institute of Blind People (RNIB)
www.rnid.org.uk – Royal National Institute for Deaf and Hard of Hearing People (RNID)

www.skill.org.uk – Skill: National Bureau for Disabled Students in the United Kingdom

www.techdis.ac.uk/ – help for disabled students and staff in higher and further education

www.trace.wisc.edu – the Trace Research and Development Center (University of Wisconsin-Madison) concentrates on making ICT more available and useful to disabled people

## Document format

www.adobe.com – portable document format for creating and reading publications

www.mslit.com/default.asp?mjr=FRE – electronic document/book creation and reading software

## Educational resources

http://aclearn.qia.org.uk/ – resources for adult learning

http://excellence.qia.org.uk/ – Excellence Gateway – resources for further education

http://ferl.qia.org.uk/ – Further Education Resources for Learning website

www.aace.org/ – Association for the Advancement of Computing in Education

www.alt.ac.uk/ – Association for Learning Technology

www.csu.edu.au/education/library.html – Education Virtual Library

www.educationindex.com/education_resources.html – lists of educational sites on the internet

www.free.ed.gov/ – US Federal Government educational resources

www.hw.ac.uk/libwww/irn/irn154/irn154.html – Internet Resources

## e-Mail addresses

www.theultimates.com/email/ – large list of individual addresses

## e-Portfolio

http://electronicportfolios.org/blog/ – Dr Helen Barrett's blog discussing e-portfolios

http://electronicportfolios.com/ALI/samples.html – examples provided by
  Dr Helen Barrett
http://eportfolio.psu.edu/ – Penn State gallery of e-portfolio examples
www.eife-l.org/publications/eportfolio/ – European Institute for e-Learning
www.elearnspace.org/Articles/eportfolios.htm – information about e-portfolios
www.jisc.ac.uk/assessment.html – e-assessment
www.mahara.org/ – open source e-portfolio with demo to try
www.nottingham.ac.uk/e-portfolio/ – Nottingham University centre for e-
  portfolio development

### Emoticons

Definitions of a wide range of emoticons:
www.computeruser.com/resources/dictionary/emoticons.html
www.smileydictionary.com/
www.windweaver.com/emoticon.htm

### English

www.bbc.co.uk/worldservice/learningenglish/ – help with learning the
  English language

### Glossary

www.sharpened.net/glossary/index.php – computer and internet terms
  glossary

### Health and safety

http://europe.osha.eu.int/ – European Agency for Safety and Health at Work
www.hhs.gov/ – US Department of Health and Human Services
www.hse.gov.uk/ – UK Health and Safety Executive

### ICT

www.e-skills.com – sector skills council for ICT user skills
www.learndirect.co.uk – learndirect provides many e-learning courses

# Information

http://europa.eu.int/ – European Union
www.nhsdirect.nhs.uk/ – National Health Service
www.number-10.gov.uk – office of the British Prime Minister – 10 Downing Street
www.un.org/ – United Nations
www.vts.intute.ac.uk/ – virtual training suite – free tutorials to develop your information skills
www.whitehouse.gov/ – US President's White House

# Internet resources

www.bbc.co.uk/learning/ – BBC Television learning resources
www.channel4.com/ – Channel 4 Television – offers learning materials
www.intute.ac.uk/ – Resource Discovery Network assessed web resources
www.vlib.org.uk – WWW Virtual Library – an essential catalogue of internet resources

# Internet telephony

www.skype.com/intl/en-gb/ – a means of making telephone calls through the internet

# Journals

Many journals are only available on subscription. Your college or employer may be able to provide you with access to them.
www.e-journals.org/ – list of e-journals across many subjects
http://ejournals.ebsco.com/ – e-journal service
http://scholar.lib.vt.edu/ejournals/JTE/ – Journal of Technology Education.
www.lib.washington.edu/types/ejournals/ – a list of electronic journals compiled by the University of Washington
www.scre.ac.uk/is/webjournals.html – SCRE Centre, University of Glasgow list of e-journals
www.usdla.org/html/journal/ – Journal of the US Distance Learning Association

## ● Learning centres (ICT)

http://cybercaptive.com/ – this is a search engine to help you locate a cyber-cafe near to you

www.helpisathand.gov.uk/ – Help is at Hand is a website to support the staff of UK Online Centres

www.learndirect.co.uk/ – learndirect organises a network of centres in the UK providing access to a wide range of online training courses including many related to developing ICT skills

www.peoplesnetwork.gov.uk/ – People's Network is a government initiative to provide ICT facilities at all public libraries in Great Britain

www.ufi.com/ukol/ – UK Online Centres are a government initiative to provide public access to ICT

## ● Learning materials

http://ocw.mit.edu/index.html – free access to course materials supporting over a thousand courses offered by the Massachusetts Institute for Technology

http://ocwconsortium.org/ – open courseware consortium – offers free access to materials

http://openlearn.open.ac.uk/ – free access to thousands of hours of Open University learning materials

www.hewlett.org/Programs/Education/OER/openEdResources.htm – Open Education Resources Program

## ● Learning styles

www.engr.ncsu.edu/learningstyles/ilsweb.html – learning style questionnaires

## ● Libraries

http://blpc.bl.uk/ – the British Library public catalogue

http://portico.bl.uk/gabriel/index.html – European Library

www.ifla.org/VI/2/p2/natlibs.htm#U – list of addresses of world libraries

www.ipl.org/ – Internet Public Library

www.lii.org – Librarian's Index to the internet

www.loc.gov/ – the Library of Congress – search the catalogue

www.nla.gov.au – National Library of Australia

www.nlb-online.org/ – National Library for the Blind
www.questia.com/ – Online Library

## Mailgroups

www.jiscmail.ac.uk – list of mailgroups for higher and further education in
  Great Britain provided by Joint Information Systems Committee
www.lsoft.com/lists/listref.html – list of listserv mailgroups

## Managed Learning Environments

http://ferl.qia.org.uk/index.cfm – FERL site is part of the Quality
  Improvement Agency's Excellence Gateway and contains information
  about Managed and Virtual Learning Environments
http://moodle.org/ – Moodle is an open source course management system
www.jisc.ac.uk/whatwedo/programmes/programme_buildmle_hefe/project
  _mle_activity.aspx – Joint Information Systems Committee is a UK educational advisory body which provides help on the use of technology in
  learning

## Netiquette

http://en.wikipedia.org/wiki/Netiquette
www.albion.com/netiquette/
www.learnthenet.com/english/html/09netiqt.htm

## Newsletter

www.intute.ac.uk/ – web resources
www.ltscotland.com/ – Learning and Teaching Scotland
www.moneymatterstome – online resources for financial capability
www.open.ac.uk/openlearn/home.php – Open University Learning Materials

## Open source and free applications

http://audacity.sourceforge.net/ – Audacity is a sound-editing application
http://ganttproject.biz/ – Gantt Project is an application to manage projects

http://lame.sourceforge.net/index.php – Lame is a sound file converter
www.bbc.co.uk/opensource/ – BBC open source project site
www.freewarehome.com/ – freeware website
www.gimp.org/ – GIMP is a photograph manipulation application
www.google.co.uk – Google Calendar, Google Docs and spreadsheets, Google Pack and Google Mail
www.google.co.uk – Picasa is a picture organisation application
www.mozilla-europe.org/en/products/firefox/ – Firefox is a web browser
www.openoffice.org/ – openoffice is an open source office suite of applications that you can download

### Plagiarism

www.jiscpas.ac.uk/ – plagiarism advisory service
www.mydropbox.com/ – site aimed at stopping plagiarism in higher education
www.plagiarism.org/ – learning centre

### Podcasts

http://audacity.sourceforge.net/ – open source audio recorder and editor
http://epnweb.org/ – Education Podcast Network – this is aimed mainly at children's education but includes many useful items
www.how-to-podcast-tutorial.com/index.htm – explains how to develop a podcast
http://itunes.stanford.edu/ – podcasts of lectures from Stanford University
http://lame.sourceforge.net/index.php – MP3 encoder
www.switchpod.com/ – podcast host
www.bloglines.com/ – newsreader aggregator

### Search engines

| | |
|---|---|
| AllThe Web.com | www.alltheweb.com |
| AltaVista | http://altavista.com/ |
| | www.uk.altavista.com/ |
| Ask | http://uk.ask.com/?o=312 |
| Excite | www.excite.com/ |
| Fast | www.alltheweb.com |
| Google | www.google.co.uk |

| | |
|---|---|
| HotBot | www.hotbot.com/ |
| Looksmart | www.looksmart.com/ |
| Lycos | www-uk.lycos.com/ |
| MSN Search | www.msn.com/ |
| Northern Lights | www.nlsearch.com/ |
| Webcrawler | www.webcrawler.com/ |
| Yahoo | http://uk.yahoo.com/ |

### Shareware

www.shareware.com – search for shareware

### Study

www.mantex.co.uk/homepage.htm – books, reviews and other help with studying

### Tools

www.winzip.com/ – compression tool

### Virtual experiments

www.chem.ox.ac.uk/vrchemistry/labintro/newdefault.html – University of Oxford examples of chemical virtual experiments
www.explorescience.com/ – scientific experiments for children
www.seed.slb.com/en/scictr/lab/index_virtual.htm – a range of experiments

### Virtual Learning Environments (see also Managed Learning Environments)

http://moodle.org/ – open source environment

### WebQuest

http://webquest.org/index.php – San Diego State University WebQuest resources

### Wikis

http://en.citizendium.org/wiki/Main_Page – Citizens' Compendium
http://en.wikipedia.org/wiki/Wiki – wiki encyclopedia
www.pbwiki.com – PeanutButterWiki
www.wiki.com/ – wiki search engine

### Yellow Pages

www.wayp.com/ – this is a site which provides access to international addresses and telephone numbers

# Appendix A
# Assessing Your Learning Skills

e-Learning requires a mixture of many different skills. Some of them should be familiar to you from other learning experiences but many have been changed or modified to fit within the online environment. Table A.1 on page 292 contains many of the key skills for e-learning. Before studying this book, it is worthwhile assessing your current skills and then, as you undertake the various activities within the book, returning to the assessment and considering your progress.

The table is cross-referenced to the different parts of the book, providing you with a study map if you are seeking to improve a particular aspect of your skills. Appendix C provides a checklist of your ICT skills.

| e-Learning skills | Comments | Suggestions for improvement | Assessment |
|---|---|---|---|
| Reading | Browsing or being able to scan a text for the key points is an important skill when reading online content. | Chapter 2 – traditional learning skills<br>Chapter 4 – e-journals, online databases and libraries<br>Chapter 8 – communication | |
| Writing | 1. Keyboard – this is one of the main ways of communicating through a computer so it is a core skill.<br>2. Assignments – this is essentially the same skill that you need for traditional studies.<br>3. Notes – taking notes is essential in many forms of learning.<br>4. e-Mail and other communication messages – this is the skill of being able to write concise but clear messages that convey your ideas, views and concerns.<br>5. Blogs – this calls for you to write reflectively and add | Chapter 2 – traditional learning skills<br>Chapter 3 – blogs<br>Chapter 4 – communication technology and learning environments<br>Chapter 8 – communication and blogs<br>Chapter 9 – wikis | |

| | constructive comments to your peers' blogs.<br>6. Wikis – this is concerned with collaborative writing. | |
|---|---|---|
| Collaboration and co-operation with other learners | Many forms of e-learning require you to collaborate or co-operate with other learners. | Chapter 9 – collaborative and co-operative learning |
| Reflection | Learning about your experiences is a part of all forms of learning. | Chapter 3 and 4 – blogs<br>Chapter 5 – e-learning reflection<br>Chapter 6 – more practice |
| Time management | Being able to manage your studies is particularly important if you are an e-learning student because you are relying on yourself. | Chapter 5 – e-learning time management<br>Chapter 6 – more practice |
| Acceptance of responsibility | When you are an e-learner you are mainly responsible for your own learning. In many cases no one else will remind you about deadlines etc. | Chapter 2 – traditional learning skills<br>Chapter 5 – e-learning acceptance of responsibility |

**Table A.1**  Assessing e-learning skills – *continued overleaf*

| e-Learning skills | Comments | Suggestions for improvement | Assessment |
|---|---|---|---|
| Planning | e-Learners often need to be able to plan their studies efficiently so they fit into their wider responsibilities. | Chapter 5 – e-learning planning<br>Chapter 6 – more practice | |
| Searching skills – world wide web | This is a complex set of knowledge and skills, involving the understanding of different types of search engines and search techniques (e.g. Boolean). | Chapter 3 – searching the web | |
| Navigation | To move around the world wide web's structure you need to understand hypertext links and the navigation features of browsers. | Many of the activities within the book require you to practice your navigation skills | |
| Assessing quality – world wide web | Locating sites is one important skill but being able to judge the quality of the information is another related skill. | Chapter 3 – judging the quality of websites<br>Many activities throughout the book require you to judge quality of online content | |

| | | |
|---|---|---|
| Self-assessment | This involves a combination of skills such as considering feedback, asking questions and being well informed about required standards. | Chapter 5 – e-learning self-assessment<br>Chapter 6 – more practice<br>Chapter 7 – e-portfolios |
| Peer assessment | In some e-learning courses learners are asked to assess each other's contribution and in some cases provide feedback. | Chapter 9 – peer assessment and feedback |
| Problem solving | 1. Individually.<br>2. Within a group. | Chapter 5 – e-learning problem solving<br>Chapter 6 – more practice |
| Coping with stress | All forms of learning can be stressful but studying on your own is often particularly prone to creating stress. | Chapter 2 – traditional learning skills<br>Chapter 5 – e-learning to cope with stress<br>Chapter 6 – more practice |
| Motivating yourself | Motivation is key to successful learning and being able to motivate yourself is particularly important in e-learning. | Chapter 5 – e-learning motivation<br>Chapter 6 – more practice |

**Table A.1** *continued*

| e-Learning skills | Comments | Suggestions for improvement | Assessment |
|---|---|---|---|
| Research | Investigating a topic is part of many forms of learning. | Chapter 2 – traditional learning skills<br>Chapter 3 – Searching the web and judging the quality of websites<br>Chapter 4 – e-journals, online databases and libraries<br>Chapter 5 – e-learning research skills<br>Chapter 6 – more practice | |

**Table A.1** *continued*

# Appendix B
# Tips for the Successful
# e-Learning Student

1. **Collaboration** – the online environment provides you with lots of opportunities to co-operate with your peers – to share and reflect on your experience of e-learning. If you participate fully in the experience, you will benefit both through your personal experience and also from your peers.

2. **Writing skills** – the key to online communication. You need to be able to write short, clear messages to communicate your needs, ideas and views by e-mail. However, remember netiquette to ensure you are not offensive.

3. **Reading skills** – these are important because a large amount of the e-learning content is written.

4. **Motivation** – you are in control of when, where and at what pace you learn but you must be able to motivate yourself to take advantage of the opportunities that this provides.

5. **Confidence** – e-learning provides many opportunities but you must have the confidence to take advantage of them (e.g. to take the initiative and contact your peers).

6. **Commitment** – the freedom to choose when you learn must be accompanied by a regular commitment to the course. It is better in most cases to give a small regular commitment of time to the course rather than an occasional large effort.

7. **Using your tutor** – e-learning can often feel lonely and isolating but you have a tutor so use him or her. When you have a question, some doubt or you simply want to check something, contact your tutor who is there to help you.

8. **Miscellaneous** – there are some small tips that will make your more successful. They include:

   - checking your e-mail regularly (e.g. daily);
   - visiting your conference forums regularly;

- allowing people time to respond to your messages – remember that everyone else may not have the same freedom as you to learn when they want to;
- telling everyone if your e-mail address changes;
- keeping a record of your passwords and user ID in a safe place;
- backing up your records regularly.

9. **Managing your time** – you need to plan your studying and assignments. It is important to be realistic about how much you can achieve in a given time period.

10. **Managing your own environment** – it is vital to organise yourself to make your environment suitable for learning. This includes:

- taking regular breaks;
- giving yourself time for reflection;
- creating space for your books, files and computer – everything should be close to you when you are studying so your concentration is not broken.

11. **Exploring/investigating** – the online environment has been designed to help you learn. It is useful to explore this new world to understand how best it can help you with your studies.

12. **Feedback** – take advantage of any opportunities to receive feedback from peers and tutors and consider all of it carefully. Remember to be constructive when giving feedback.

13. **Computer skills** – it is vital to start your e-learning with a basic foundation of computer skills but you will need to develop these by using every problem as an opportunity to learn new skills.

14. **Employing the resources provided** – e-learning courses offer many different resources for you, so make sure you are aware of them, for example:

- online conferences;
- blogs;
- interactive learning materials;
- self-assessment tests;
- wikis.

15. **Learning style** – it is useful to be aware of your own learning preferences in order to make informed decisions about the course.

# Appendix C
# Assessing Your ICT Skills

In order to be a successful e-learner, you must have good ICT skills. Chapter 3 provides an introduction to some aspects of the necessary knowledge and skills but this checklist provides a more comprehensive means of assessing your competence. If you need to develop your technical skills, then many colleges provide short courses for students or if you are studying in the United Kingdom then learndirect offers a range of ICT e-learning courses (www.learndirect.co.uk). You should also visit the e-skills website for information about ICT user skills (www.e-skills.com).

| Task | Sub-task | Assessment |
|---|---|---|
| Switch equipment on and off | | |
| Open applications (e.g. word-processing, spreadsheets and databases) | | |
| Close applications | | |
| Use Windows® operating system or other operating system | 1. Resize windows<br>2. Select icons<br>3. Choose menus options<br>4. Use scroll bars<br>5. Use toolbars<br>6. Use help | |
| Adjust accessibility options on Windows® operating system | 1. Change the contrast<br>2. StickyKeys<br>3. FilterKeys<br>4. ToggleKeys | |

**Table C.1**   Assessing ICT skills – *continued overleaf*

| Task | Sub-task | Assessment |
|---|---|---|
| | 5. SoundSentry<br>6. ShowSounds<br>7. Cursor blink rates and width<br>8. Controlling the mouse pointer with the keyboard number pad | |
| Use a keyboard | 1. Enter text and numbers<br>2. Special function keys (e.g. insert, ctrl and alt)<br>3. Function keys<br>4. Num and Caps lock | |
| Use a mouse | 1. Click left and right buttons<br>2. Drag and drop<br>3. Highlight | |
| Save and transport information | 1. On to floppy disks<br>2. On to USB memory sticks<br>3. On to CD-Read Write disks | |
| Use a digital camera | 1. Take pictures<br>2. Store on a computer<br>3. Edit images | |
| e-Portfolio | 1. Add evidence to an e-portfolio<br>2. Select and present evidence<br>3. Add comments | |
| Use a sound recorder | 1. Record speech<br>2. Store sound files on a computer<br>3. Edit speech files | |
| Use a scanner | 1. Pictures<br>2. Text | |
| Word-processing | 1. Enter<br>2. Insert text | |

**Table C.1** *continued*

| Task | Sub-task | Assessment |
|------|----------|------------|
| | 3. Insert pictures<br>4. Insert tables<br>5. Delete<br>6. Copy<br>7. Cut<br>8. Paste<br>9. Drag and drop<br>10. Find and replace<br>11. Undo and redo<br>12. Save<br>13. Save as<br>14. Print<br>15. Track changes | |
| Spreadsheets | 1. Enter<br>2. Insert text and numbers<br>3. Delete<br>4. Copy<br>5. Cut<br>6. Paste<br>7. Drag and drop<br>8. Find and replace<br>9. Undo and redo<br>10. Save<br>11. Save as<br>12. Print<br>13. Formula<br>14. Charts and graphs | |
| Databases | 1. Search for information<br>2. Add information to a database<br>3. Print information | |
| Managed files and folders | 1. Open<br>2. Close<br>3. Save<br>4. Save as<br>5. Print<br>6. Rename<br>7. Identify different formats | |

**Table C.1**   *continued*

| Task | Sub-task | Assessment |
|------|----------|------------|
| | 8. Compress files<br>9. Create folders | |
| Use the internet | 1. Connect to the internet<br>2. Enter website addresses (URLs)<br>3. Navigate websites<br>4. Use search engines:<br>  • use directories<br>  • use meta-engines<br>  • use multiple search criteria<br>  • relational operators e.g. =, >, <=, logical operators AND and OR<br>5. Navigate websites:<br>  • hyperlinks<br>  • forward and back<br>  • save and use favorites<br>6. Download files<br>7. Upload files | |
| Use e-mail | 1. Open an e-mail application<br>2. Open e-mails inbox<br>3. Use e-mails:<br>  • delete<br>  • produce new messages<br>  • send<br>  • forward<br>  • insert attachments<br>  • use an address book<br>  • employ Netiquette<br>  • use distribution lists | |
| Blogs | 1. Access application<br>2. Enter information<br>3. Save entries<br>4. Add comment<br>5. Edit entries | |

**Table C.1**   *continued*

| Task | Sub-task | Assessment |
|------|----------|------------|
| Wikis | 1. Access application<br>2. Enter information<br>3. Edit information<br>4. Save information | |
| Viruses | Configure virus protection software to protect your system | |
| Spyware | Configure spyware software to protect your software | |

**Table C.1**   *continued*

# Appendix D
# Referencing Electronic Sources

The world wide web and other electronic sources of information (e.g. CD-ROM) are now major resources for research and other academic information. This poses the question of how to reference electronic sources. This is not a single question since there are several types of electronic information. A referencing system needs to cope with these different types and the problem is compounded by the nature of electronic information which is dynamic, with websites continuously changing and developing, whereas a reference is essentially a static image of the information at a particular point in time. The Harvard citation system is widely used for the conventional referencing of books and journals and provides the basis for referencing electronic information.

The main types of electronic reference that you may encounter are:

- web page with an author;
- web page without an author;
- web article/paper only published online;
- web article based on a paper source;
- online publication (e.g. journal or e-book);
- CD-ROM or DVD source.

The examples below show the references for a variety of types of electronic sources with and without dates of publication.

1.  Information published on a webpage with an identified author but without a date of publication.
    *Example*:
    Clarke, A. Why ICT is a Skill for Life – A Personal View (online), NIACE. Available from ww.niace.org.uk/Research/ICT/ICT-skillforlife-view.htm (accessed on 20 April 2007).

The general form for this example is:

Author. Title (online). Publisher. Available from URL (accessed on date).

2. Information published on a webpage with no identified author or publication date

   *Example*:

   ITQ Unit Qualification Structure (online), E-skills. Available from http://itq.e-skills.com/Resource-Library/Qualifications-and-Assessment/ 1366 (accessed on 3 May 2007).

   The general form for this example is:

   Title (online), publisher. Available from URL (accessed on date).

3. Journal only published online

   *Example*:

   e-skills bulletin, 2006 (online). Available from www.e-skills.com/cgi-bin/orad.pl/414/e-skills_bulletin_q4_06_final1.pdf?. issue 19 Q4 (accessed on 3 May 2007).

   The general form for this example is:

   Title (online), date. Available from URL. Issue number (accessed on date).

4. e-Mail message as part of a discussion group

   *Example*:

   Clarke, A, 3 May 2007, Re-Study Skills (online). Available from study-skills@studymail.ac.uk (accessed on 3 May 2007).

   The general form for this example is:

   Author, date Title (online). Available from URL (accessed on date).

   If the e-mail message was part of a private communication, it would take the form of:

   Author (e-mail address), date sent. Title. e-Mail to recipient's name (Recipient's e-mail address).

5. CD-ROM or DVD information

   *Example*:

   Clarke, A, 2006 (CD-ROM), CLAIT 2006 Tutor's Pack. London. Hodder Arnold

   The general form for this example is:

   Author, Publication Date (Medium), title. Place of Publication. Publisher Referencing guidelines change regularly so you should always check your own college's rules for referencing.

# Glossary

Explanation of the Technical and Specialist Terms used in e-Learning

**Adobe Acrobat** a document file format which is widely used on the internet for disseminating publications. The file can be identified by its extension .pdf – portable document format. The files need the Adobe Acrobat reader to open them and this is available for free

**ADSL (Asymmetric Digital Subscriber Line)** a high-speed telephone line designed for exchanging electronic data (ADSL is replacing ISDN lines)

**Adware** software that is added to your computer without your permission to monitor your use and perhaps to steal your information

**applets** small programmes which often provide interactive features on websites and online learning materials

**assistive technology** adaptive equipment and alternative methods for helping disabled people to use ICT

**asynchronous** a communication method that does not require the learners or tutors to be online at the same time

**authoring** the process of creating computer-based learning materials

**authoring system** software tool or application that assists you to create e-learning materials

**backing up** making a copy of your files to prevent the loss of your work. It applies to copying either a single electronic document or all your files. There are many ways of backing up your information, such as writing the data to a CD-RW or DVD-RW disk

**bandwidth** this is the size of the connection you have with the internet. The larger the bandwidth, the faster and more effective the service you will be able to get

**BBS** Bulletin Board Systems

**blended learning** a mix of several different learning approaches (e.g. traditional classrooms methods combined with e-learning)

**blogging** a public but personal online diary or journal based on a website

**bookmark** the way that browsers allow you to mark a webpage so that you can quickly locate it again. It is sometimes called a 'favorite'.

**browser** an application which allows you to view, save and print websites

**bulletin board** an online location where you can post and collect messages

**button** a small area which, if you click on it, will move you to a new area of the package or open a feature

**CAI (Computer assisted instruction)** a name for some forms of e-learning material (*see also* **CAL, CBT** and **TBT**)

**CAL (Computer assisted learning)** a name for some forms of e-learning materials (*see also* **CAI, CBT** and **TBT**)

**CBT (Computer-based training)** a name for some forms of e-learning materials (*see also* **CAI, CBT** and **TBT**)

**CGI** Common Gateway Interface

**chat** online synchronous text communication

**citation** if you have used the contents of a book, journal article or other resource in an essay or other form of work, then you must cite the author in your text and give the full reference so that readers can locate your source. This is called a citation

**collaborative learning** learning in and with a group of other learners

**compression** a method of making a large file smaller so that it can be more easily transported (*see* **zip**)

**computer-based learning** learning material delivered and supported through the use of a computer

**Computer mediated communication (CMC)** the use of communication technologies to allow people to communicate while living or working at a distance from each other

**conferencing** there are many forms of online conferencing but essentially it is a platform in which group of people can meet virtually in a variety of ways. Many conferences will combine mailgroups, bulletin boards and chat rooms

**cookies** these are small pieces of information that websites place on your computer to allow them to recognise the patterns of your visits to their site so that they can customise their service to you

**courseware** these are chunks of e-learning materials. They can vary in size from a single chunk covering a small piece of learning to an entire learning or training course

**creative commons** a type of copyright licence when the author wants to provide freedom to use his/her work but with some controls

**dial-up** this is the most straightforward way of connecting to the internet through a telephone line which is also used for normal calls

**downloading** when you move a file of electronic information (e.g. a picture, acrobat file, etc.) from a website to your own computer the process is called downloading

**encryption** protecting information by encoding it (i.e. turning it into code using a special application)

**e-learning** learning which is supported and delivered through the use of ICT

**e-portfolio** an electronic collection of evidence to demonstrate your knowledge, understanding and competence in your subject

**Extranet** a single organisation intranet which has some aspects open to external users, although these are often password-protected

**FAQ** Frequently Asked Questions – lists of questions which users of websites and other online resources have asked in the past. They are displayed on the website and online resource to help new users

**firewall** a security system which protects a computer from unauthorised access

**flame** an angry or offensive e-mail message

**forum** online discussion area where you can read and post messages to your colleagues

**freeware (open source applications)** free software which often does not limit your use of it

**FTP (File Transfer Protocol)** a method of transferring a file over the internet

**GIF** an image file format

**GPS** Global Positioning System

**groupware** applications that allow people linked through a network (e.g. internet) to share information and work co-operatively and collaboratively

**GUI** Graphic User Interface

**help desk** technical support service often accessed by telephone

**home page** this is the first page of a website and often serves the purpose of explaining the nature of the website

**HTML** Hypertext Markup Language

**Hypertext Markup Language (HTML)** the language in which websites are constructed so that a browser can view them

**icon** small picture symbol which links you to other areas of a website or system or opens an application

**ICT** Information and Communication Technology

**ILT (Information and Learning Technology)** another way of saying e-learning (ILT is also the Institute for Learning and Teaching)

**information and communication technology (ICT)** the combination of computer and telecommunication technology

**Integrated Service Digital Network (ISDN)** a high-speed telephone line designed for the transfer of computer data (ISDN is being replaced by ADSL lines)

**Internet Service Provider (ISP)** an organisation that will link you to the internet some offer other services

**intranet** an internet that is limited to a single organisation (e.g. a college)

**IRC** Internet Relay Chat

**ISDN** Integrated Service Digital Network

**ISP** Internet Service Provider

**Java** a popular programming language often associated with websites

**JPEG** an image file format

**LAN** Local Area Network of computers

**learning objects** a distinct piece of e-learning material that you can combine with other objects to form a programme

**LMS (Learning Management System)** essentially an alternative expression for a Managed Learning Environment or Virtual Learning Environment

**lurking** taking a passive part in an online discussion group or conference (i.e. receiving the messages without responding to them)

**mailgroups** a group of participants linked through e-mail so that by sending a single e-mail to the group address, everyone receives the message

**metadata** data about the content of the learning material

**m-learning** mobile learning or delivering e-learning through portable communication systems such as a mobile telephone, laptop computer, etc.

**modem** a piece of equipment that allows you to link your computer to the internet

**moderator** the person who takes responsibility for mailgroups and other forms of online communication and facilitates and encourages discussion

**MPEG** a video file format

**multicasting** e-mail, video, audio or other form of broadcast across the world wide web

**multimedia** the presentation of materials using a mixture of media such as video, sound, animation, text and graphics

**netiquette** a set of rules, often mutually agreed, that govern the content of e-mails and how they are used

**newsgroup** a service which allows you to access information on a particular topic

**offline** using a computer when it is not linked to the internet

**online learning** learning that is delivered and supported through the internet

**patch** a software package intended to correct a problem with an existing application

**PDA (Personal Digital Assistant)** a hand-held computer device

**plug-ins** these are additional pieces of software that allow your browser to view extra file formats (e.g. multimedia)

**podcast** a sound programme (e.g. interview or lecture) that can be down-loaded or listened to online

**Point of Presence** a local telephone point which your modem calls to make a telecommunication link to the internet

**POP** Point of Presence

**portal** a special type of website giving access to a wide range of other related sites and online resources

**portfolio** see e-portfolio

**real time** synchronous (at the same time) communication when everyone has to be online to take part

**RSS (Real Simple Syndication)** the means to access a range of content (e.g. podcasts and blogs) without the need to visit each site. The new content is sent to you

**screen reader** an application which reads the text displayed on a computer screen out loud so that visually impaired users can access the system

**search engine** an application which searches the world wide web to locate webpages that match your search words

**shareware applications** applications that you can use in order to evaluate them before you buy

**spam** unrequested e-mails, in some cases advertising products or services; essentially the electronic equivalent of junk mail

**spyware** software that is installed on your computer without your permission to monitor your behaviour and potentially steal your information

**streaming** a technique that allows video and audio to be transmitted so that you can begin watching the video or listening to the audio before the whole content has arrived at your computer. It avoids the long delays caused by sending large video or audio files

**synchronous** a communication method that requires the learners or tutors to use it at the same time

**TBT (technology-based training)** a name for some forms of e-learning materials (*see also* **CAI**, **CBT** and **CBL**)

**TCP/IP** Transmission Control Protocol/Internet Protocol

**thread** a series of e-mail messages that are linked to a particular issue, topic or theme

**Transmission Control Protocol/Internet Protocol (TCP/IP)** the standards that underpin the internet

**Uniform Resource Locator (URL)** the address of a webpage (e.g. www.bbc.co.uk)

**upload** moving an electronic file from your computer to a website

**URL** Uniform Resource Locator

**USB (Universal Serial Bus)** a device to connect peripherals to a computer

**virus** a programme designed secretly to replicate itself without the user's permission or knowledge. Often these programmes are designed to harm your system by deleting critical files or data.

**vodcast** a video sequence (e.g. demonstration of a science experiment) that is available for downloading or viewing online

**W3C** the organisation which sets standards for the world wide web

**web 2.0** a group of technologies that assist users of the world wide web to create content such as blogs, wikis and podcasts

**weblog** the product created by blogging

**webmaster** the person who administers a website

**WebQuest** an online investigation utilising the information available on the world wide web

**wiki** an online application that allows people to work together collaboratively to create a joint document

**WYSIWYG** ('What you see is what you get') this refers to the appearance of a document or image on the screen compared to its printed appearance (i.e. it is identical)

**XML (eXtensible Markup Language)** a new development in languages used to develop websites

**zip/unzip** a compressed file format that allows you to send large files over the internet

# References and Further Reading

Bartlett-Bragg, A. (2003), Blogging to Learn, Knowledge Tree e-journal.

Blood, R. (2002), *The Weblog Handbook: Practical Advice on Creating and Maintaining Your Blog* (Cambridge, MA: Perseus).

Clarke, A. (1998), *IT Awareness Raising for Adults* (Department of Education and Employment, Sheffield, OL 254).

Clarke, A. (2001a), *Designing Computer Based Learning Materials* (Aldershot: Gower).

Clarke, A. (2001b), *Assessing the Quality of Open and Distance Learning Materials* (Leicester: NIACE).

Clarke, A. (2002a), *Online learning and Social Exclusion* (Leicester: NIACE).

Clarke, A. (2002b), *New CLAIT Student Workbook* (Abingdon: Hodder and Stoughton).

Clark, A. and Hussain-Ahmed, S. (2006), *Signalling Success: Paper-free Approaches to Recognising and Recording Learner Progress and Achievement* (Leicester: NIACE).

Coombies, H. (2001), *Research Using IT* (Basingstoke: Palgrave Macmillan).

Cottrell, S. (2008), *The Study Skills Handbook*, 3rd edn (Basingstoke: Palgrave Macmillan).

Cox, R., Dineen, F., Mayes, T., McKendree, J. and Stenning, K. (1999), *Vicarious Learning from Educational Dialogue: Proceedings of the Computer Support for Collaborative Learning (CSCL)*, 1999 Conference, eds C. Haodley and J. Roschelle (Palo Alto, CA: Stanford University Press and Lawrence Erlbaum Associates.

Dawson, Di (2007), *Handheld Technologies for Mobile Learning: e-guidelines 12*, NIACE.

Dewey, J. (1933), *How We Think* (Boston, MA: D. C. Heath and Co.).

Dodge, B. and March, T. (1995), Some thoughts About WebQuests, http://edweb.sdsu.edu/courses/edtec596/about_webquests.html

Dolowitz, D., Buckler, S. and Sweeney, F. (2008), *Researching Online* (Basingstoke: Palgrave Macmillan).

Downes, S. (2005), *Educational Blogging*, Educase Review, September 2004.

Falchikov, N. (2005), *Improving Assessment through Student Involvement* (New York: Routledge Falmer).

Fraser, J. (2005), 'Blogging essentials for teachers and learners', *Computer Educational Journal*, Autumn 2005, Issue 111, pp. 8–11.

Hara, N. and Koling, R. (2000), Students' distress in a web-based distance education course, www.slis.indiana.edu/SCI/wp00-01.html

Health and Safety Executive (2000), *Working with VDUs* (Bootle: HSE Books).

Health and Safety Executive (2003), *Aching Arms (or RSI) in Small Businesses* (Bootle: HSE Books).

Honey, P. and Munford, A. (1986), *A Manual of Learning Styles* (Maidenhead: Peter Honey).

Kolb, D. A. (1984), *Experiential Learning: Experience as the Sources of Learning and Development* (Englewood Cliffs, NJ: Prentice Hall).

Lave, J. and Wenger, E. (1991), *Situated Learning: Legitimate Peripheral Participation* (Cambridge: Cambridge University Press).

Moon, J. (1999), *Reflections in Learning and Professional Development* (London: Kogan Page).

Nipper, S. (1989), *Third Generation Distance Learning and Computer Conferencing* (London: Mindweave).

Nonnecke, B. and Preece, J. (2001), *Why Lurkers Lurk*, American Conference on Information Systems.

Palloff, R. M. and Pratt, K. (1999), *Building Learning Communities in Cyberspace: Effective Strategies for the Online Classroom* (San Francisco, CA: Jossey-Bass).

Race, P. (1994), *The Open Learning Handbook* (London: Kogan Page).

Stefani, L., Mason, R. and Pegler, C. (2007), *The Educational Potential of e-Portfolios – Supporting Personal Development and Reflective Learning* (London: Routledge).

*Terena* and Netskills (2002), *Internet Users' Reference* (Harlow: Addison Wesley).

Wenger, E. (1999), *Communities of Practice: Learning, Meaning, and Identity (Learning in Doing: Social, Cognitive and Computational Perspectives)* (Cambridge: Cambridge University Press).

Electronic Portfolios (online), available at http://en.wikipedia.org/wiki/Electronic_portfolio, accessed on 7 May 2007.

# Index